CW00351415

A Special Issue of
Memory

Memory for Proper Names

Edited by

Gillian Cohen

The Open University, Milton Keynes, UK

Deborah M. Burke

Pomona College, California, USA

LEA LAWRENCE ERLBAUM ASSOCIATES, PUBLISHERS LEA
Hove (UK)   Hillsdale (USA)

Lawrence Erlbaum Associates Ltd., Publishers
27 Palmeira Mansions
Church Road
Hove
East Sussex, BN3 2FA
UK

British Library Cataloguing in Publication Data

Memory for Proper Names. - (Memory series, ISSN 0965-8211)
    I. Cohen, Gillian II. Burke, Deborah M.
    Series
    153.1

    ISBN 0-86377-918-2

Subject Index compiled by Jackie McDermott
Cover design by SB Graphics, Hove
Typeset by DP Photosetting, Aylesbury
Printed and bound in the United Kingdom by BPCC Wheatons Ltd., Exeter

Contents

* This book is also a special issue of the journal *Memory* which forms Issue 4 of Volume 1 (1993).
The page numbers used here are taken from the journal and so begin with p.249

MEMORY, 1993, *1* (4), 249–263

Memory for Proper Names: A Review

Gillian Cohen

The Open University, Milton Keynes, UK

Deborah M. Burke

Pomona College, California, USA

INTRODUCTION

Proper names have a frustrating propensity to be forgotten. A considerable amount of laboratory and naturalistic data has demonstrated this vulnerability of proper names to memory errors both in learning new names and in retrieving familiar names. Moreover, retrieval of familiar proper names is especially affected in old age and in some cases of aphasia. This pattern of vulnerability offers an important opportunity for gaining insight into basic memory processes and architecture by identifying the characteristics of proper names that disrupt memory.

In this special issue of *Memory*, we present studies of proper names that offer new empirical findings and theoretical developments. Research on proper names has encompassed a range of methodologies, and this issue includes experimental, developmental, neuropsychological, philosophical, and computational approaches. The various phenomena yielded by these approaches increase our understanding of critical differences between proper names and other words in their memory representation and processing. In this introductory review, we begin with a summary of four classes of findings on memory for proper names that make the case that proper names show distinct memory properties, followed by a description of the models that have been put forward to account for these findings. We then consider the development of some of the models presented in this volume and their ability to account for the new findings reported here.

Requests for reprints should be sent to Gillian Cohen, Human Cognition Research Laboratory, The Open University, Walton Hall, Milton Keynes, MK7 6AA, UK. E-mail: G.M.Cohen@open.ac.uk; *or* to Deborah Burke, Department of Psychology, Pomona College, Claremont, CA 91711, USA. E-mail: DBURKE@POMONA. CLAREMONT. EDU

Preparation of this paper was supported in part by Grant AG08835 from the National Institutes of Health to Deborah Burke.

PREVIOUS FINDINGS ON MEMORY FOR PROPER NAMES

New Learning

Proper names are more difficult to learn than other biographical information about a person who is encountered for the first time. Cohen and Faulkner (1986) presented subjects with short biographical sketches about fictitious characters and compared recall of person names, place names, occupations, and hobbies. Recall of person names was poorer than recall of any other type of information (see also Stanhope & Cohen, 1993). Although proper names are, on average, lower in frequency of occurrence in the language than other classes of words, this does not seem to be the source of the learning deficit. Using name-occupation homophones such as *Baker-baker* and *Potter-potter*, McWeeny, Young, Hay, and Ellis (1987) tested recall of names and occupations paired with pictures of unfamiliar men. Recall of occupations was superior to recall of names, even though the same words were used in each category across subjects (see also Cohen, 1990a). Thus, the name *Baker* is more difficult to recall than the occupation *baker*, an effect that cannot be attributed to differences in the phonological form or frequency of occurrence of occupations *vs* proper names. Indeed, under some conditions, uncommon, unusual names (e.g. *Felix*) are learned faster than common, familiar names (e.g. *John*) (Stanhope & Cohen, 1993).

Cohen (1990a) has argued that the relative meaninglessness of proper names compared to other words is a source of vulnerability in memory because names such as *Baker* cannot be encoded in such a rich semantic network as words like *baker*. That is, we know many more semantic propositions about the occupation *baker* than the name *Baker*. Consistent with this, Cohen demonstrated that, with a face as cue, meaningless names (e.g. *Mr Ryman*) are harder to recall than meaningful occupations (e.g. he is a *baker*), but this result reversed when the names were meaningful (e.g. *Mr Baker*) but the occupation was meaningless (e.g. he is a *ryman*).

Retrieval of Familiar Names

Proper names of familiar people are more difficult to remember than other types of biographical information. Using diaries to record naturally occurring errors in person identification during everyday interactions, subjects often remembered a known person's occupation without being able to retrieve his or her name. They did not, however, remember a person's name without remembering his or her occupation (Young, Hay, & Ellis, 1985). Parallel findings in the laboratory demonstrated that subjects often judged a picture of a famous person as familiar, and knew the person's occupation without being able to retrieve the person's name. There were only a very few instances where a name was remembered but not the occupation (Hanley & Cowell, 1988). These findings have been described by a sequential stage model of face recognition in which information about the visual appearance of a face, the identity of the person, and the name are each stored separately and hierarchically in memory. Retrieval occurs sequentially with name information only accessed after information about person identity has been retrieved (e.g. Bruce & Young, 1986).

The vulnerability of the retrieval process for proper names is also seen in the tip-of-the-tongue (TOT) phenomenon, one of the most dramatic instances of word retrieval failure. In the TOT state, a person is unable to produce a word although they are certain that it is known; its representation in memory can be verified by correct recognition or spontaneous retrieval of the target at a later time. A number of studies have demonstrated that TOTs for names can easily be elicited in the laboratory with pictures or verbal descriptions of famous people (Brennen, Baguley, Bright & Bruce, 1990; Hanley & Cowell, 1988; Maylor, 1990; Yarmey, 1973). Cohen and Faulkner (1986) established that spontaneous TOTs for proper names occurred frequently in everyday life, and that TOTs were more common for acquaintance names than for any other type of proper name.

The TOT state represents a selective impairment of phonological information in a name, not semantic information associated with the name. Thus, subjects in a TOT state can report information about the person such as their profession or appearance, even though the name is not accessible (e.g. Brennen et al., 1990; Cohen & Faulkner, 1986; Yarmey, 1973). Moreover, when TOTs for proper names were induced with biographical descriptions, presenting photographs of the person did not aid resolution whereas cueing with the person's initials did (Brennen et al. 1990; Hanley & Cowell, 1988). The impairment therefore is at the stage of access to phonological information.

An important question is whether proper names are any more susceptible to TOT states than other classes of words. Gruneberg, Smith, and Winfrow (1973) asked subjects to self-induce TOT states and found that blocks for acquaintance names were more common than for any other type of word. Burke, Mackay, Worthley, & Wade (1991) analysed TOT experiences recorded by subjects in a diary during everyday life and found more TOTs for proper names than any other word types (e.g. object names, abstract words); within proper names more TOTs were reported for acquaintance names than for any other type of proper name.

The prevalence of people's names in naturally occurring TOTs may reflect differences between proper names and other words, not so much in ease of retrieval, but rather in how they are used (see Brown, 1991). For example, TOTs for proper names may be more noticeable, and thus more likely to be reported, because names are required in situations such as introducing or greeting someone, when alternative words are not acceptable. This problem disappears when TOTs are induced by an experimenter in the laboratory because the opportunity for TOTs can be equated across different types of word. However, there have been relatively few studies comparing the number of experimenter-induced TOTs for different types of words. The extant findings are that older adults, aged 65 years or more, experience more TOTs for proper names than for other word types such as object names, but this effect is not consistently found for young adults (Burke, Mackay, Worthley, & Wade 1991; Burke, Rastle, & Mariner, 1991). The deficit for proper names may be underestimated for both age groups because acquaintance names have not been used in laboratory research and they are the most frequent target in spontaneous TOTs.

Thus, retrieval failures are more frequent for proper names than for other words, although this difference does not emerge in every situation. However, in terms of the characteristics of retrieval failures, proper names seem very similar to other words. TOTs for all types of words, not just proper names, are characterised by access to semantic information but impaired access to phonology (e.g. May & Clayton, 1973). We know of no cases in normal adults of *reverse TOTs*, where a person, object, or concept can be named, but semantic knowledge is temporarily inaccessible. Thus Young et al.'s (1985) report that no errors in person identification occurred in which a person was named but not otherwise identified may reflect a general principle that semantic information is more accessible than phonological information for concepts of people as well as for objects and abstract concepts.

Moreover, there is other evidence that the asymmetry in accessibility of names and semantic information is strikingly similar in processing both faces and objects. Faces can be categorised (e.g. as famous *vs* non-famous) more rapidly than named (Johnston & Bruce, 1990; Young, Ellis, & Flude, 1988; Young, McWeeny, Ellis, & Hay, 1986) just as object pictures can be categorised (e.g. as food *vs* not food) more rapidly than named (e.g. Potter & Faulconer, 1975). Similarly, printed words can be named more rapidly than categorised for both proper names (Young, McWeeny, Ellis, & Hay, 1986) and object names (Potter & Faulconer, 1975; see also Young, Ellis, Flude, McWeeny, & Hay, 1986, for further evidence of parallel effects for faces and objects in the accessibility of semantic and phonological information). These parallel findings for object names and proper names suggest general and fundamental properties of the architecture of semantic and phonological representation, not just an architecture specific to proper names. This is an important constraint for models of proper names: they must explain commonalities between people's names and object names in the greater accessibility of semantic than phonological information, while also providing an account of why proper names are more difficult to learn and retrieve than common names.

Adult Aging and Memory for Proper Names

Older adults' problems in remembering names are proverbial (e.g. "I'll never forget whats-her-name") and figure prominently in their self-reports (Cohen &

Faulkner, 1984; Sunderland, Watts, Baddeley, & Harris, 1986). The pattern of age difference, however, appears to differ for learning names for unfamiliar people compared to recalling well known names. Older adults consistently perform more poorly than young adults on tasks requiring recall of newly learned information (see Mackay & Burke, 1990, for a review). However, although older adults have poorer recall of newly learned names than young adults (e.g. Crook & West, 1990), the age deficit in learning names is no larger than the deficit in learning other biographical information such as occupation (Cohen & Faulkner, 1986).

In retrieval of well known words, however, the age decline appears to be greater for proper names than for other types of words. In a study of naturally occurring TOTs, older adults reported relatively more TOTs for proper names and for object names than young adults, whereas this age difference reversed for abstract words (Burke, Mackay, Worthley, & Wade, 1991). In studies of laboratory induced TOTs, the age increase was consistently larger for proper names than for other word types (Burke, Mackay, Worthley, & Wade, 1991; Burke, Rastle, & Mariner, 1991). Thus, the aging pattern is that learning deficits for proper names are comparable to those for other word types, but well known proper names suffer disproportionate retrieval deficits relative to other word types. Age effects in memory for proper names are explicable on two assumptions. The first assumption is that, as in some of the models described here, the architecture of the system is such that proper names receive less activation than other words. The second assumption is that aging is accompanied by a reduced level of activation transmitted to all target items. In older adults, therefore, the combined effect of these two factors produces the observed retrieval deficit for proper names.

Selective Impairment of Retrieval of Proper Names in Aphasia

Naming deficits are a common symptom in all types of aphasia (e.g. Kremin, 1988). In some cases, the naming impairment is limited to specific categories of words, for example, actions or nouns, or even more selectively to specific categories within nouns. One of the more striking cases is a patient described by Hart, Berndt, and Caramazza (1985) who had a naming deficit limited to instances of the categories of fruits and vegetables. It is unsurprising, therefore, that there are several reports of patients with selective deficits for proper names. In some patients the naming deficits applied only to people's names (McKenna & Warrington, 1980; Lucchelli & De Renzi, 1992) and in others they extended to geographical proper names as well, e.g. names of countries and cities (Semenza & Zettin, 1988; 1989).

However, two aspects of the pattern reported for proper names seemed to distinguish them from other classes of words. First, the reverse pattern of selective preservation of proper names has been absent, with the notable exception of the patient described by McKenna and Warrington (1978) who showed selective preservation of naming countries, despite impairment in naming people. Several papers in this volume, however, demonstrate preservation of proper names together with severe naming impairments for other word types. Thus, proper names are no longer distinguished by selective impairment without selective preservation.

There is some evidence, however that the impairment of proper names is distinguished by the selectivity of the deficit. Impairment of naming people has been reported in patients with normal performance on other language tasks. For example, Lucchelli and De Renzi's patient T.L. performed normally on the Token Test and the Boston Naming Test, but was unable to name relatives and close friends, and was impaired in naming famous people, despite being able to supply biographical information. Such a pure deficit is rare in selective naming deficits; further research is needed to determine whether it is unique to proper names.

THEORETICAL FRAMEWORKS FOR MEMORY FOR PROPER NAMES

These findings have led researchers to focus theoretical efforts on constructing models to postulate representational and processing differences between proper names and other words that explain the special difficulty of proper names.

The Sequential Stage Model

The main account until recently has been the sequential stage model (e.g. Bruce & Young, 1986; McWeeny et al., 1987; Young et al., 1985). Figure 1 shows the three basic representational modules that must be accessed within the model for successful naming of a familiar face. Each face recognition unit stores a visual description of a known face and allows perceptual classification of the face as one that is familiar. Activation of a face recognition unit produces access to a person identity node (PIN) associated with that face. The PIN stores biographical information such as the person's occupation or nationality. The name code is only accessed after activation of the PIN.

The sequential nature of stages in this model explains why biographical information about a person may be recalled without name recall, but the name of a person is not recalled without biographical information. Moreover, the representational modules are parallel to those that have been proposed for object identification (see Bruce & Young, 1986) and thus are consistent with the findings reviewed earlier that objects and faces show the same asymmetry in retrieving semantic *vs* name information. However, it is unclear how the model accounts for the findings that proper names are more susceptible to retrieval deficits than object names. Bruce and Young argue that identification of faces involves a more difficult discrimination task than identification of objects

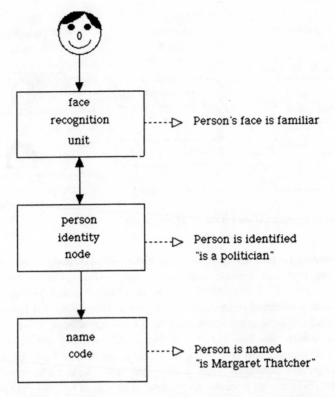

FIG. 1. Basic components of Bruce and Young's (1986) sequential stage model of face naming.

because, for example, face naming involves discrimination of a particular face within the category of faces, whereas object naming merely involves identification of the category of the object. Thus face recognition units may require components not necessary for object recognition. It is unclear how this could be extended to account for name retrieval deficits triggered by verbal descriptions rather than by faces.

Finally, Stanhope and Cohen's (1993) results are incompatible with a strictly sequential model. They found that names could be accessed when no biographical information was presented, and it was harder to recall a name when it was paired with an occupation than when the name was presented alone. Instead of facilitating access to the name, information about the occupation interfered with memory for the name.

Interactive Activation and Competition Model

The sequential model has been reformulated as an interactive activation and competition (IAC) model in which stages are replaced with separate pools of

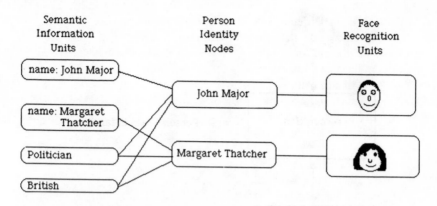

FIG. 2. Basic components of the IAC model of face naming.

units consisting of face recognition units, person identity nodes, and semantic information units that include both names and semantic information stored together (Burton & Bruce, 1992). Units in different pools are linked by excitatory, bi-directional connections. Each person identity node is linked to all its associated semantic information units with some semantic units having more links than others (see Fig. 2). The bi-directional nature of the links causes excitation to spread through the system, with units that have more links receiving greater activation than units with fewer links. The reverbatory activation aids retrieval. Because names tend to be shared by fewer people than other semantic information such as occupation or nationality, names will receive less activation on average than other semantic information units.

Thus, the crucial factor that differentiates proper names like *John Major* from other semantic information such as politician, British, is that the name is (relatively) unique. Information like politician or British is easier to retrieve because it is shared by, and therefore connected to, a number of PINs, and accrues activation from each. The connection to the proper name *John Major* is unique, a one-to-one connection that cannot accrue activation from elsewhere. Thus reduced connectivity of names in the network and the resulting reduction in activation explains the difficulty of name retrieval. This model explains why it is more difficult to retrieve a person's name than semantic information about the person, but it is unclear how it would explain the same asymmetry for objects whose names are not unique.

The Representational Model

Cohen (1990a) suggested that proper names are difficult to recall because they are meaningless and arbitrary. These two factors are logically related. A proper name like *John* is arbitrary because the individual could have been called something different. Different individuals with different characteristics could all be called *John* because there are no attributes, other than gender, that are necessary or sufficient (or even typical) for an individual to be called *John*. It follows from this that proper names are meaningless and almost entirely lacking in semantic attributes. Although people have semantic attributes, names do not. Where names such as *Baker*, do have a meaning, this is misleading in that the individual denoted by the name is usually not a baker. In recall, other words like object names recruit activation from the many semantic associates to which they are linked, but proper names, having fewer links, receive relatively impoverished activation. Hence aging and traumas are more likely to affect proper names than other words.

This model is supported by findings that the level of performance in proper name recall is similar to recall of meaningless nonwords (Cohen, 1990a) or arbitrarily paired associates (Semenza & Zettin, 1988). The use of mnemonic strategies to construct meaningful associations for proper names improves recall (Morris, Jones, & Hampson, 1978) and, when subjects are permitted to generate and assign names to faces they choose names that suit or fit the faces in some way, so that the face-name link is less arbitrary and subsequent recall of the names is improved (Price & Cohen, 1993). In addition, there appears to be a gradient of recall across different types of proper names (Cohen & Faulkner, 1986) such that famous names and geographical names cause fewer problems than acquaintance names. This gradient is predicted by the model because it reflects variations in meaningfulness. Famous names like *Hitler* or geographical names like *Paris* come to take on semantic connotations, as shown by the fact that they can be adjectivised (*Hitlerian, Parisian*) and are easier to recall because they are more meaningful.

According to the Representational model, names are harder to recall when the same names are shared by many different people than when they are highly distinctive names that are shared by few people (Stanhope & Cohen, 1993). Similarly, the names of people who share many of the same attributes (e.g. they are all doctors with beards), but have different names, are also harder to recall (Cohen, 1990b). In both cases multiple links cause interference rather than facilitation because activation diverges and is diffused among competing items rather than converging on the target name.

Node Structure Theory

The Node Structure Theory (NST) is an interactive activation model that provides a detailed account of language perception and production (Mackay, 1987) and has been extended to a range of phenomena, for instance, memory and aging (Mackay & Burke, 1990), and TOT states and memory for proper names (Burke, Mackay, Worthley, & Wade, 1991). Figure 3 illustrates aspects of the NST representation of the proper name *Baker* and the occupation *baker*. These

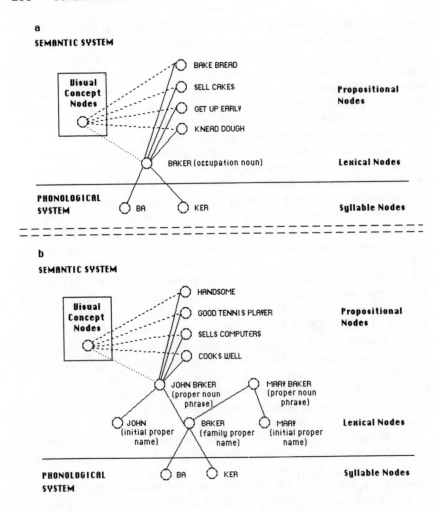

FIG. 3. Basic components of the NST model of proper name retrieval.

nouns are represented by separate propositional nodes and lexical nodes, but common phonological nodes. As in the Representational model, proper names differ from other words in their semantic representation and this contributes to observed differences in memory performance.

As illustrated in Fig. 3a, the lexical node for the occupation *baker* is connected to a number of semantic propositions representing information about bakers, such as "bakes bread", "gets up early", and "kneads dough". With initial input such as "John is a baker", a connection is formed between the lexical node, *baker*, and the visual concept node (VCN) representing John's appearance. This VCN can also be connected to the semantic nodes representing information about bakers, so that a large number of connections link the VCN directly or indirectly to the occupation noun. These connections produce summation of priming that will facilitate retrieval of *baker* and its connected phonological nodes when the person is seen again. Nodes representing common nouns such as *baker* are therefore relatively invulnerable to the deficits in transmission of priming that cause retrieval failures within the NST.

The node for *John Baker* is also connected to a number of semantic propositions representing information about him. However, intervening between this node and the phonological nodes that must be activated for name retrieval are the nodes representing the family name *Baker* and the name *John. Baker* does not receive convergence of priming, even if it is the name of well known acquaintances with many semantic propositions as in Fig. 3b. Only a single connection links the node for *John Baker* to *Baker*. Unlike the occupation *baker*, the family name *Baker* lacks connections to semantic information that can be connected with a VCN representing a person's appearance. Without convergence of priming, nodes for proper names are more vulnerable to retrieval deficits.

The Token Reference Model

Semenza (Semenza & Zettin, 1988) has emphasised the status of proper names as 'pure referring expressions' which, in philosophical terms, have reference but not sense, and thus are relatively meaningless. He has offered a theoretical explanation of the difficulty of recalling proper names in terms of the type/token distinction, which draws attention to structural differences between the representation of proper names and object names. An object name (like *cabbage*) refers to a type, or category, whereas a proper name like *Bill Clinton* refers to a token, or individual. Thus the link between name and referent is one-to-many for type reference (because the name refers to all the members of the category) but one-to-one for token reference. This model makes the assumption that token reference would necessarily be weaker than type reference because of its reliance on a single link. Type reference, and hence retrieval of object names, would benefit from activation converging from the many-to-one links on the target name.

Common Principles Shared by Different Models

Clearly, there are marked similarities and shared assumptions between these models. All the explanations rely, in one way or another, on the concept of connectivity to explain the recall deficit for proper names as compared with object names. According to the Token Reference model, the IAC model, and the NST model, proper name recall is disadvantaged because there is only a single unique connection from the individual to the name. In both the Bruce and Young

Sequential Stage model and the NST model, activation is further diminished because it is indirect: there are no direct connections from face to name in the stage model and no direct connections from the VCN or the propositional nodes to the name in the NST model. The NST model, the IAC model, and Cohen's Representational model share the assumption that particular name-individual links should not be considered in isolation but in the context of other related items. Structural relations between items are a crucial factor because the pattern of connectivity governs the extent to which activation converges on the target and summates, or diverges away from it and dissipates. So there are three aspects of connectivity that have been identified as influencing recall: the number of connections; whether connections are direct or indirect; and the pattern of shared connections.

NEW DEVELOPMENTS IN MEMORY FOR PROPER NAMES

This section is not intended to preview the contents of this issue of *Memory* comprehensively, but to note some of the new findings, to highlight some of the issues that are raised, and to consider the extent to which they entail revision of the existing theoretical models.

The most striking new development is the finding, reported in all four of the clinical case studies in this issue, of cases where proper names are selectively preserved when object names or other words are impaired. This novel finding contrasts with the cases of selective impairment of proper names that have previously been reported. The cases reported here clearly establish the existence of a double dissociation between proper names and other words. The fact that proper names can be selectively preserved entails a radical rethinking of the models described in the previous section, all of which are geared to explaining a deficit in proper name recall. We must now ask what kind of a model could break down in such a way that *either* proper names *or* other words are impaired. At present only some tentative suggestions can be made. Semenza (this issue) has tackled this problem by recasting the Token Reference model and arguing that the single link from name to referent would benefit proper names, because activation would be stronger and more concentrated than in the multiple links that characterise type reference for object names. Of course, it is unclear how this could account for the fact that there are more retrieval failures for proper names than for object names in normals. Another possibility is that selective deficits for proper names or for object names are simply examples of the kind of selective category deficits (e.g. for animals) that have long been recognised.

The double dissociation of proper names and object names appears to entail a separation of representations, processing channels, or both, so that these might be independently damaged. Its existence underlines the fact that any satisfactory model will need to include both person naming and object naming in order to explain the parallels in performance noted earlier, and the observed dissociation.

Valentine and his co-authors have provided an integrated model of word naming and person naming and his repetition priming experiments reported in this issue are a further step towards mapping the relationship between proper names and other words.

Another approach is suggested by the ability of the IAC network to model both activation and competition. Burton & Bruce's account (in this issue) of the performance of the model in different tasks shows that the multiple connectivity of object names and other words is advantageous if it converges and summates at the response output. In some kinds of task, however, a higher degree of connectivity produces competition so that unique or low frequency items like proper names, with fewer connections, fare better. This approach may prove powerful enough to explain the diverse patterns of deficit that are now coming to light.

Other contributions to this issue have revealed additional factors, which contribute to the difficulty of recalling proper names that is normally experienced. Bredart (this issue) has shown that whereas objects usually have several alternative labels (e.g. car, estate car, Volvo, vehicle), most people and places have only a single label so that retrieval of proper names is disadvantaged by the lack of alternatives. Brennen (also in this issue) has suggested that proper names are harder to recall because the set of acceptable phonological representations for proper names is indefinitely large. This unbounded set size means that search is more difficult and it is harder to reconstruct proper names from partially recalled fragments. These ideas can be accommodated by several of the existing models. However, the experiments reported here by Craigie & Hanley, which demonstrate a pattern of conditional probabilities associated with the recall of the facial features, occupation, and name of famous individuals provides striking support for the Sequential Stage model, and the effects of various mnemonic strategies studied by Brooks, Friedman, Gibson, and Yesavage seem to fit most comfortably with the Representational model.

La Palme Reyes, Macnamara, Reyes, and Zolfaghari (this issue) present an analysis of the logic of proper names in which proper names individuate a person in a kind (category). They specify the knowledge of kinds that would seem to be a prerequisite for a young child to be able to learn a proper name. Their analysis presents several points that should influence memory models of proper names, for instance, the logical link between common and proper names, and the distinction between a proper name as a linguistic entity and as a meaningful entity that denotes a particular individual.

It is apparent that no definitive answers to questions about the representation and processing of proper names emerge from this issue of *Memory*, which is more by way of a progress report than a final solution. Until recently, theoretical models have evolved to try to account for the empirical findings as they emerged, but a new phase of research can now be identified in which the models are becoming more precisely specified and are generating more specific and testable predictions. This new approach, together with the increasingly close collaboration between researchers from all the different methodologies represented here, promises to shed more light on memory for proper names in the near future.

REFERENCES

Brennen, T., Baguley, T., Bright, J., & Bruce, V. (1990). Resolving semantically induced tip-of-the-tongue states for proper nouns. *Memory & Cognition, 18*, 339–347.

Brown, A.S. (1991). A review of the tip-of-the-tongue experience. *Psychological Bulletin, 109*, 204–223.

Bruce, V. & Young, A. (1986). Understanding face recognition. *British Journal of Psychology, 77*, 305–327.

Burke, D.M., Mackay, D.G., Worthley, J.S., & Wade, E. (1991). On the tip-of-the-tongue: What causes word finding failures in young and older adults. *Journal of Memory and Language, 30*, 542–579.

Burke, D.M., Rastle, K., & Mariner, C. (1991, November). *The tip-of-the-tongue (TOT) experience: The effects of recency, frequency and aging.* Paper presented at the meeting of the Psychonomic Society, San Francisco.

Burton, A.M., & Bruce, V. (1992). I recognize your face but I can't remember your name: A simple explanation? *British Journal of Psychology, 83*, 45–60.

Cohen, G. (1990a). Why is it difficult to put names to faces? *British Journal of Psychology, 81*, 287–297.

Cohen, G. (1990b). Recognition and retrieval of proper names: Age differences in the fan effect. *European Journal of Cognitive Psychology, 2*, 193–204.

Cohen, G., & Faulkner, D. (1984). Memory in old age: "Good in parts". *New Scientist, 11*, 49–51.

Cohen, G., & Faulkner, D. (1986). Memory for proper names: Age differences in retrieval. *British Journal of Psychology, 4*, 187–197.

Crook, T.H., & West, R.L. (1990). Name recall performance across the adult life-span. *British Journal of Psychology, 81*, 335–349.

Gruneberg, M.M., Smith, R.L., & Winfrow, P. (1973). An investigation into response blockaging. *Acta Psychologica, 37*, 187–196.

Hanley, J.R., & Cowell, E.S. (1988). The effects of different types of retrieval cues on the recall of names of famous faces. *Memory & Cognition, 16*, 545–565.

Hart, J., Berndt, R.S., & Caramazza, A. (1985). Category-specific naming deficit following cerebral infarction. *Nature, 316*, 439–440.

Johnston, R.A., & Bruce, V. (1990). Lost properties? Retrieval differences between name codes and semantic codes for familiar people. *Psychological Research, 52*, 62–67.

Kremin, H. (1988). Naming and its disorders. In F. Boller & J. Grafman (Eds.), *Handbook of neuropsychology.* Amsterdam: Elsevier Science Publishers.

Lucchelli, F., & De Renzi, E. (1992). Proper name anomia. *Cortex, 28*, 221–230.

Mackay, D.G. (1987). *The organization of perception and action: A theory for language and other cognitive skills.* Berlin, Heidelberg, London, Paris, New York, Tokyo: Springer-Verlag.

Mackay, D.G., & Burke, D.M. (1990). Cognition & aging: A theory of new learning and the use of old connections. In T. Hess (Ed.), *Aging and cognition: Knowledge organization and utilization,* pp. 1–51. Amsterdam: North-Holland.

May, J.E., & Clayton, K.N. (1973). Imaginal processes during the attempt to recall names. *Journal of Verbal Learning and Verbal Behavior, 12*, 683–688.

Maylor, E.A. (1990). Recognizing and naming faces: Aging, memory retrieval and the tip of the tongue state. *Journal of Gerontology: Psychological Sciences, 45*, 215–225.

McKenna, P., & Warrington, E.K. (1978). Category specific naming preservation: A single case study. *Journal of Neurology, Neurosurgery and Psychiatry, 41*, 571–574.

McKenna, P., & Warrington, E.K. (1980). Testing for nominal dysphasia. *Journal of Neurology, Neurosurgery and Psychiatry, 43*, 781–788.

McWeeny, K.H., Young, A.W., Hay, D.C., & Ellis, A.W. (1987). Putting names to faces. *British Journal of Psychology, 78*, 143–149.

Morris, P.E., Jones, S., & Hampson, P. (1978). An imagery mnemonic for the learning of people's names. *British Journal of Psychology, 69*, 335–336.

Potter, M.C., & Faulconer, B.A. (1975). Time to understand pictures and words. *Nature, 253*, 437–438.

Price, E., & Cohen, G. (1993). *Memory for proper names: The effects of generation and assignment.* Unpublished manuscript.

Semenza, C, & Zettin, M. (1988). Generating proper names: A case of selective inability. *Cognitive Neuropsychology, 5*, 711–721.

Semenza, C., & Zettin, M. (1989). Evidence from aphasia for the role of proper names as pure referring expressions. *Nature, 342*, 678–679.

Stanhope, N., & Cohen, G. (1993). Retrieval of proper names: Testing the models. *British Journal of Psychology, 84*, 51–65.

Sunderland, A., Watts, K., Baddeley, A.D., & Harris, J.E. (1986). Subjective memory assessment and test performance in the elderly. *Journal of Gerontology, 41*, 376–384.

Yarmey, A.D. (1973). I recognize your face but I can't remember your name: Further evidence on the tip-of-the-tongue phenomenon. *Memory & Cognition, 1*, 287–290.

Young, A.W., Ellis, A.W., & Flude, B.M. (1988). Accessing stored information about people. *Psychological Research, 50*, 111–115.

Young, A.W., Ellis, A.W., Flude, B.M., McWeeny, K.H., & Hay, D.C. (1986). Face-name interference. *Journal of Experimental Psychology: Human Perception and Performance, 12*, 466–475.

Young, A.W., Hay, D.C., & Ellis, A.W. (1985). The faces that launched a thousand slips: Everyday difficulties and errors in recognizing people. *British Journal of Psychology, 76*, 495–523.

Young, A.W., McWeeny, K.H., Ellis, A.W., & Hay, D.C. (1986). Naming and categorizing faces and written names. *Quarterly Journal of Experimental Psychology, 38A*, 297–318.

MEMORY, 1993, *1* (4), 265–280

Production of Proper Names: A Clinical Case Study of the Effects of Phonemic Cueing

Carlo Semenza and Teresa Maria Sgaramella

Dipartimento di Psicologia Generale, Università degli studi di Padova (I), Italy

The production of proper names is a task that in everyday life is particularly prone to temporary failures, especially in elderly subjects. The reason for this is still rather obscure but indications in recent literature suggest an independent status for proper names in comparison with common ones, which may entail differences in processing or in processing demands. The main sources of empirical evidence come, on the one hand, from studies of face and person identity recognition and, on the other, from neuropsychological observations. All the findings appear to concur in supporting theoretical distinctions that have been made for a long time in the field of philosophy of language. These distinctions have directed the endeavours of experimental research.

The present study describes, for the first time, a neuropsychological patient who shows, in certain conditions, a sparing of proper names despite an otherwise deeply troubled linguistic production. This finding may appear to be counterintuitive, considering the fact that proper names are viewed, in general, as more difficult to produce than common ones. However, in consideration also of other emerging neuropsychological and experimental findings, it is proposed that possible differences in lexical access for the two categories of common and proper names may explain the phenomenon and still be consistent with mainstream philosophical theories.

INTRODUCTION

The Philosophical/linguistic Background

A long tradition of philosophical theories about proper names probably started with Mill (1843), who wrote "Proper names are not connotative: they denote

---

Requests for reprints should be sent to Carlo Semenza, Dipartimento di Psicologia Generale, Piazza Capitaniato 3, 35139 Padova (I), Italy.

We are indebted to Gillian Cohen, Karalyn Patterson, and Deborah Burke for helpful comments on earlier versions of this work, and we acknowledge support from MURST and CNR grants to Carlo Semenza.

individuals who are called by them: but they do not indicate or imply any attributes as belonging to those individuals''... "A proper name is but an unmeaning mark".

Along the same line, later philosophers (e.g. Wittgenstein, 1922, and more recently Kripke, 1980) used, more or less explicitly, Frege's (1892) distinction between the two aspects of meaning: 'sense' and 'reference'. They argued that proper names just carry 'reference', that is they denote the individuals or the entities that are called by them, but have no 'sense'—they do not describe any property or imply any attribute. They are the opposite of 'descriptions', which have sense, and which encompass all common nouns. For example, the proper name 'George Bush' refers only to the bearer of this name and does not itself provide any other information. On the other hand, the word 'president' is a description insofar as it implies the definition of a person who is chief of a nation or a club etc., and who may have executive powers or just an honorary role. This difference is reflected in a number of facts. Changing proper names does not alter, as with common names, any property of the bearer: 'Karol Wojtyla' is not a different person from 'John Paul II', but a 'cardinal' has different properties from a 'pope'. Anybody would understand the meaning of the sentence 'There are no popes in Japan', whereas they would not fully understand sentences like 'There are no Wojtylas in Japan' unless they knew that Wojtyla is actually the name of the pope.

This notion of proper names as only conveying reference is not unchallenged. Other philosophers (e.g. Russell, 1905, and more recently Searle, 1969; 1971) prefer to think that they are not completely meaningless labels, but just shorthand descriptions. For the sake of the present study, however, this distinction can be set aside. It will suffice to regard proper names as bearing little, if any, meaning at all; the link with their referent being weaker and more arbitrary than that between a common name and its referent.

A substantially similar argument comes from modern linguistics. An important distinction in conceptual structure is the binary feature type/token (Jackendoff, 1983; Katz, 1972; Levelt, 1989). What one learns and stores in memory can be linked either with token (if one is remembering an individual) or with type (if one has learned a category). Proper names, insofar as they denote individuals (see also Macnamara, 1982), have only token reference and not type reference.

The Experimental Literature

Naturally occurring retrieval blocks seem to be much more frequent for proper names than for other kinds of words (Bolla, Lindgren, Bonaccorsi, & Blecker, 1991; Reason & Lucas, 1984; Young, Hay, & Ellis, 1985). This pattern was experimentally confirmed by Cohen and Faulkner (1986). An attempt to discover what makes proper names difficult to remember was undertaken by

McWeeny, Young, Hay, and Ellis (1986). In their experiment, subjects were asked to learn the names and occupations belonging to unfamiliar faces. The same word was presented sometimes as a name and sometimes as an occupation, so that imageability and meaningfulness were equated for the name recall condition and for the occupation recall condition. In spite of this, name recall was significantly poorer than recall of occupation with the somehow paradoxical result that a word like Baker presented as a name was harder to recall than the same word (baker) presented as an occupation (the Baker–baker paradox). Cohen (1990) further investigated this effect. Bearing in mind Kripke's (1980) emphasis on the weakness of the link between a name and its referent, she conducted two experiments that manipulated the meaningfulness of three types of information: proper names, occupations, and possessions. In the first experiment recall of proper names was in fact no better than recall of meaningless non-word possessions, and poorer than recall of meaningful possessions or meaningful occupations. In the second experiment Cohen was able to show how the Baker–baker paradox disappears if meaningful names are coupled with meaningless non-word occupations in the same context. She argued, therefore, that the recall of proper names is more difficult in everyday life because they are almost always treated as meaningless, and that people habitually ignore whatever meanings proper names may have because these meanings are irrelevant or conflict with actual person identity information.

These experiments, and many others, have been interpreted in the light of a model of face recognition developed by Bruce and Young (1986), which bears upon an analogy between the recognition of familiar faces and words first drawn by Bruce (1979; 1981; 1983). This model entails a sequence of functional components which is common to the recognition and naming of objects, faces, and words. The sequence comprises formation of an input code; activation of a face recognition unit; access to semantic information including a person's biographical and contextual information; and, finally, access to the person's name. This final node in the sequence can only be accessed via the semantic information and there is no direct link between faces and names. This model accounts for the fact that, although it is often the case that one does not seem to remember a name, but can remember biographical details about a person (Flude, Ellis & Kay, 1989, described this phenomenon magnified in an aphasic patient), the converse type of incident, in which the name is known, but biographical details cannot be recalled, appears to be extremely rare (Young, Hay & Ellis, 1985). Valentine, Bredart, Lawson, and Ward (1991) have recently proposed an extension of this model that is of direct interest for the present study (see Fig. 1).

The feature of interest is that, in the condition of naming from semantics, the model assumes a separate access of proper names (at least of people), and of common names, to the phonological output codes. The model is supported by the experimental observation that the effects of proper name familiarity and

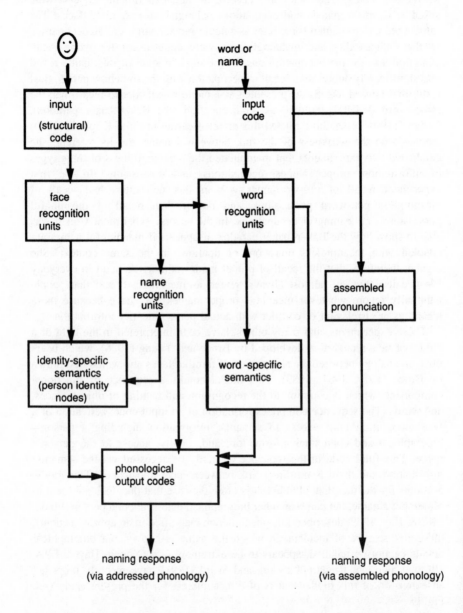

FIG. 1.   A functional model of face, name and word recognition, proposed by Valentine, Bredart, Lawson and Ward (1991). Note the separate access of names and words to the phonological output codes. Both addressed and assembled phonology are supposed to activate the naming response after the stage (not shown in Valentine et al's. figure) of realisation of a motor articulatory program.

frequency are analogous to the effects of word frequency in tasks (like nationality decision) that do not require access to memory for individuals. However, in tasks that do require access to memory for individuals, the effect of name frequency was analogous to the effect of distinctiveness in face recognition. According to the authors, these data are consistent with a framework in which it is assumed that names and words are represented by word recognition units, there being only one unit for every familiar word or name. The output of word recognition units that represent names connects to a set of name recognition units in which there is a unit for every familiar individual. Activation of name recognition units allows access to identity-specific semantics, which can also be accessed through the face recognition system. It would follow that, in production, proper names denoting individuals or individual entities, access phonological output codes from a special store containing identity-specific semantics rather than from the more general semantic store. For this reason, it should be noted, the model is in principle compatible with a dissociation in production of common and proper names, regardless of the direction of the dissociation.

Perhaps unsurprisingly, given all these findings, proper names have also been demonstrated to be vulnerable to the tip of the tongue (TOT) phenomenon in a recent study by Burke, MacKay, Worthley, and Wade (1991). Their explanation, which refers to an interactive activation theory of language production known as the Node Structure Theory (NST) (for a description see MacKay, 1987), is interesting and directly relevant for this study. According to NST, during normal, error-free, word finding the translation of thought into speech begins with activation of a propositional node representing a concept in the semantic system. Activating this node transmits priming to the lexical node, from which priming spreads to connected phonological nodes. When a TOT state occurs, a lexical node in the semantic system becomes activated, giving access to semantic information about the target word, but at least some phonological information remains inaccessible because insufficient priming is transmitted to enable activation of connected phonological nodes. In this framework, the lexical node for a common name (e.g. baker) would benefit by several converging semantic connections from the semantic system, thus being relatively invulnerable to TOT. The lexical node representing a proper name like a family name (e.g. Baker) is thought, instead, to be in a rather vulnerable position because it would be connected to semantic information only via propositional nodes for specific individuals ('John Baker', 'Mary Baker' etc.). These latter nodes may, indeed, receive even abundant converging semantic information about the individual, but the activation of the corresponding phonological node would still depend on the single connection link via the lexical node. Thus, even though the bearer of the name is highly familiar, their name (e.g. Baker) is more prone to TOT than, for instance, their occupation (e.g. baker).

The Neuropsychological Literature

The neuropsychological literature is very limited but extremely interesting. For tasks like matching, where the retrieval of the phonological form is not requested, or reading where it can be derived from the orthographic form, patients' studies converge in indicating a superiority in performance involving proper names in comparison to common ones. Superior reading of proper names compared with common ones by the right hemisphere was suggested by Saffran, Bogyo, Schwartz, and Marin (1980). They showed that proper names are read surprisingly well by deep dyslexics, and that they are read very well in the left visual field by normal readers. A better performance on familiar personal names in comparison to common names was reported by Van Lanker and Klein (1990) in four cases of global aphasia in the task of matching spoken or written names to photographs. According to these authors, qualities like familiarity and affectivity would allow some advantage for proper names over common ones in right hemisphere processing[1]. A particular category of proper names, names of places, was shown to be relatively preserved compared to other nouns in a few aphasics in the task of matching them to a map (Wapner & Gardner, 1979). Surprisingly well preserved spoken to written matching was shown by Warrington and McCarthy (1983) in a very severe global aphasic for certain types of proper names (famous people, countries, and cities). The authors argued that these proper names were distinguishable, along lines indicated by Miller and Johnson-Laird (1976), by their high probability of having a unique referent.

It is in naming tasks, however, where the phonological form is not provided and cannot easily be derived, that the more interesting phenomena concerning proper names have been reported. With the exception of McKenna and Warrington's (1978) case, where a limited number of high frequency names of countries seemed to be spared, all reported cases have shown a proper names deficit in comparison to names of other categories. McKenna and Warrington (1980) first described a selective anomia for persons' names. The deficit appeared to be equally severe when naming was from a picture or from a verbal description. In contrast, comprehension of the same names and knowledge about the people was demonstrated to be perfectly preserved.

Two other cases of proper name anomia, where the deficit extended to geographical names, were reported by Semenza and Zettin (1988; 1989). In the discussion of their first case, where they were speculating about the nature of category-specific aphasic disorders, they pointed out, following Kripke's (1980) views, that among the plausible determinants of proper name anomia was the special status of proper names as pure referring expressions. They pursued this hypothesis experimentally in their second case study, where they were able to

---

[1] Indeed Van Lanker and Klein take a less conservative position: what we report here is limited to what we would accept of their interpretation of their findings.

demonstrate that the patient could not learn arbitrary links between words (such as those that constitute the difficult items in the paired-associate learning test of the Wechsler Memory Scale) and could not name the titles of well known pieces of music. The patient also could not match numbers to hardware items, although this was a requirement of his job. Semenza and Zettin interpreted these findings as indicative of a problem in dealing with purely referential relations. This fact, in turn, would indirectly confirm the role of proper names as pure referring expressions.

Very recently Lucchelli and De Renzi (1992) further corroborated this conclusion in a study of yet another case of persons' names anomia. Their patient also had difficulty in learning arbitrarily paired associates like name–face pairs and number–colour pairs in comparison to learning occupation–face pairs. These last pairs are less arbitrary, on the assumption that the occupation represents a meaningful feature characterising the identity of a person (Cohen, 1990), whereas the surname bears the same arbitrary relation to a face as a number to a colour. Further evidence of an impairment in retrieving associations devoid of a semantic relation was provided by the patient's inability to recall previously well known telephone numbers (they also have no meaning).

A NEUROPSYCHOLOGICAL CASE

Although, as reported earlier, anomias for proper names with preservation of common ones have been described, as yet no case study is available featuring the opposite pattern of dissociation, i.e. a preservation of proper names within an otherwise generalised anomia. The case reported by McKenna and Warrington (1978) does not constitute a counterexample because the only proper names to be preserved were high frequency names of countries. However, an example of selective preservation of proper names will be discussed here. The interest of this case lies in the fact that it shows proper names to be virtually the only intelligible items in spontaneous production, despite a severe phonemic jargon. In constrained naming, the same finding emerged, but only when phonemic cueing was supplied.

Case Report

R.I., a right-handed farmer, 66 years old, with 5 years of education and some experience in small business suffered an ischemic attack, which led to an aphasia with mild hemiparesis and oral apraxia, in September 1988. A left parieto-occipital lesion could be demonstrated (CAT scan). His extremely severe aphasia concerned virtually only the production side and could be characterised as a phonemic jargon. Although otherwise cooperative, his awareness of the linguistic impairment probably contributed to his unwillingness to provide long pieces of spontaneous speech. R.I. was studied longitudinally in order to tap the evolution of his jargonaphasia and jargonagraphia (reported by Sgaramella, Semenza & Ellis, 1991) in September 1988, September 1989, and December 1990. The phenomena reported here appeared in this last period, during which the patient underwent testing in two consecutive weeks when his performance was virtually unaltered from one week to the other. A conspicuous presence of intact proper names (about 7% of all his word-like segments) in his spontaneous speech was indeed already present in September 1989. However, the constrained production of proper names was not tested then. At that time, intact proper names also appeared sporadically in his spontaneous writing which was otherwise affected by severe jargon. Between September 1989 and December 1990 his reading comprehension, which had been very good, and the mechanics of his writing underwent a severe deterioration. The cause of this deterioration is not clear, as no other signs of neurological illness showed up in this interval. Unfortunately, a few days after the last testing, R.I. suffered a further stroke, after which he showed a more severe hemiparesis and a dramatic loss of articulation capacities. His comprehension was also affected. No CAT scan is available after the second injury.

Spontaneous Speech.   Although produced with evident effort and at a slow rate, spontaneous speech was well articulated and consisted of monosyllabic segments which accounted for about 3/4 of the total speech segments. The remaining speech output consisted of word-like polysyllabic segments, the majority of which were either persons' names or literal paraphasias of persons' names (e.g. ''Petronill'', ''Rosalba''). For instance, in the longest single sample of uninterrupted speech (consisting of 209 segments) where R.I. was answering questions about his job, the only real words were: 49 persons' names (including 40 real names and 9 literal paraphasias of proper names) consisting of 11 different types; two numbers (''eight'' and ''five''); one adverb (intanto-while); one noun (barba-beard) that he repeated twice; and two literal paraphasias (scrita* instead of scritta-written; tuto* instead of tutto-all), consisting of the simplification of geminate phonemes. Most of the proper names he produced turned out to be those of relatives and friends. These names, as well as the few common ones, were not appropriate to the context but seemed to emerge rather randomly in the output. No recurrent utterances were found. All phonemes were present except /v/ and /f/ and /u/. The correlation of phoneme frequencies with normal frequencies was high ($r = 0.86$, $p > 0.0001$).

Automatic Series.   R.I. could start to count correctly as far as eight, but then he would resort to proper names and monosyllables or start the series anew from one. He could likewise start the days of the week or the months of the year (typically producing just the first two) and would then turn again to his jargon and proper names.

Repetition.   R.I. was unable to repeat the sounds of single letters (vowels or consonant sounds followed by *schwa*), although he was 4/20 correct in the repetition of CV syllables. He was unable to repeat single words (scoring 0/20) and proper names (0/20) including those he produced spontaneously or in naming conditions. However, he correctly echoed most of the endings of a word (the last one or two syllables) while the examiner was pronouncing it: he could not be prevented from doing this and would not wait until the examiner had finished pronouncing the word. For example, when asked to repeat the word 'tamburo' (drums) R.I. produced, along with the examiner, the ending "..ro*" or in repeating 'ventaglio' (fan) he produced "..aglio*". This behaviour was the same for both simple words and proper names: it was impossible to establish whether or not there was some advantage for proper names, as logic would suggest in consideration of his naming performance (see later section). This 'echo' effect virtually disappeared when repeating legal and illegal non-words (10 items), where he partially echoed just one ending that happened to be a real inflexional affix (*viomante** echoed "..nte*"). Other attempts to repeat (or rather echo) non-words did not bear any resemblance to the target (e.g. *'foldontu'** echoed "..lo"). He refused to repeat sentences.

Comprehension.   This was measured using the Milano Aphasia Battery (Basso, Capitani, & Vignolo, 1979). In a multiple choice paradigm, R.I. correctly matched 20/20 spoken words to one of four pictures when phonemic and semantic distractors were not included in the alternatives, and 16/20 when alternatives consisting of one phonological, one semantic, and one unrelated distractor, were systematically provided—e.g. cane (dog) being the target, pane (bread) was the phonological distractor, gatto (cat) was the semantic distractor, sedia (chair) was the unrelated distractor. His four errors consisted in pointing to one unrelated, one phonological, and two semantic distractors. These two 'semantic errors' involved confusion between two different musical instruments and between two different tools. He correctly executed 10/10 spoken orders of a complex sort (e.g. "fold a piece of paper and throw it into the basket"). He did not show any great difficulty (18/22) in matching spoken names to pictures of famous people, where the task was to pick the right one out of four persons sharing the same job (e.g. actors, politicians, popes) and of similar age. In the four instances where he failed, he managed to convey the idea that he really did not know the person and he refused to guess. He was not so efficient in recognising places on postcards except for his home-town, Rome, and Florence and Venice. It is very likely that this performance reflected his very low cultural level rather than a deficit. In non-testing everyday life situations R.I. appeared to have intact comprehension, responding correctly and confidently.

Reading aloud.   R.I. could read 2/20 single letters, 2/20 CV syllables, 0/20 real words, 0/20 non-words, and 0/10 sentences. When he failed, he produced series of monosyllables and some randomly chosen proper names. He was no better in reading single proper names (0/20).

Reading Comprehension. Reading comprehension of single words, as measured by a written word to pictures matching task, was 3/20 without distractors and 1/20 with distractors. R.I. could not execute written orders.

Writing. R.I.'s ability to write was very severely damaged. Even when the task was to copy single capital letters, very few items were recognisable at all. His performance was even worse in all other conditions such as dictation and spontaneous writing.

Constrained Naming. Constrained naming of objects (on confrontation or from definition) also elicited randomly produced monosyllables. Because of the remarkable abundance of well formed proper names in his spontaneous output, R.I. was also given naming tests for proper names on picture confrontation, including those of relatives and friends (10 items) and famous persons (22 items), and from definitions (10 items). Again he produced only randomly chosen monosyllables.

Naming was then tested in a cued condition where the cue consisted of the first sound of the name (a vowel or a consonant followed by a *schwa*). R.I.'s performance did not change in cued naming of very high frequency objects or animals (0/30 on confrontation and 0/15 from definitions) and when re-tested with the same items a week later his scores were unchanged. However, he scored 10/10 in cued naming of pictures of relatives and friends, and 18/22 in cued naming of pictures of famous persons (the same ones that he recognised in the comprehension test). He performed equally well a week later. The few errors were omissions, and appeared to reflect poor recognition of the items rather than a failure in name retrieval. In tests of naming proper names from definitions, aided by phonemic cueing, he scored 10/10 on both weeks.

R.I.'s poor geographical knowledge prevented full testing on geographical items. However, he could name (again only with a phonemic cue) the few items he was able to recognise or whose definition ('the capital of Italy') he was familiar with.

DISCUSSION

R.I.'s case seems to be relevant for a theory about the nature of proper names and the processes involved in their production. First of all it is important because it provides the complementary side of a double dissociation: selective spared production of proper names *vis à vis* the selective impairment of production already reported in literature.

R.I.'s case is not, however, isolated; another case of selective preservation of proper names in production has been recently observed (Warrington & Cipolotti, personal communication, December 1992). Formerly, the arguments outlined in the introduction might have led one to expect only a single dissociation, i.e. the one featured in proper name anomia. One might have argued, with abundant experimental support, that proper names, with only reference and no sense, are simply more difficult, or vulnerable to impairment. R.I.'s case shows that this view is too simplistic. Proper names may be (and, indeed, in general they are) more difficult to retrieve, but are also processed in a different way from common ones (hence the possibility of a double dissociation.

That this is the case, however paradoxical, should have been suspected when anomia for proper names (the 'expected' dissociation) was first described (Semenza & Zettin, 1988). Not the least remarkable feature of that case and of those that followed (Semenza & Zettin, 1989; Lucchelli & De Renzi, 1992) was their purity. At variance with the usually encountered anomias that tend to be relative rather than absolute, and where the deficit is not strictly confined to naming, described anomias for proper names had, in fact, an all-or-none character: virtually no proper name (at least of persons) could be retrieved by patients who succeeded in 100% of the cases with common ones. Different degrees of difficulty could not possibly explain a pattern where one's mother's name is forgotten and the name of abstract, uncommon words can be easily retrieved. Separate production mechanisms for proper and common names seem thus to be the only possible explanation for this phenomenon. Where and how this separation takes place in the course of processing is the next question to deal with. The findings on R.I. combined with those from patients with anomia for proper names allow, to some extent, an answer.

The locus of functional impairment(s) in R.I. should be considered first. His jargon does not result from a low level articulation disorder: despite visible efforts, his articulation is perfect. There is no clear evidence that the jargon originates in an impairment at the semantic level. His comprehension is, in fact, rather good: the few difficulties found with special testing cannot account for such a severely disturbed production. The deficit appears rather to lie in the input of both assembled and addressed phonology to the stage of the realisation of a motor articulatory program (Ellis & Young, 1988; Morton 1984; and particularly Monsell, 1989; and Nickels, 1992; for reference models). At this point, however, it is possible that stored phonological information about the lexical form to be produced (by definition unavailable for non-words) is, to a certain extent, effective in boosting production. This would happen in repetition (the echo effect for real words) and, in the particular case of proper names, when a phonemic cue is provided. It is likely that with enough acoustic phonemic information, the correct entry is located and then activated in a way able to trigger the articulatory program. Non-words would not benefit from activation in the lexicon and, therefore, are not even echoed. When no acoustic-phonemic help is provided, residual output would result in neologisms randomly interspersed in connected speech, with more readily available phonological forms of real words, in this case mainly proper names[2].

This account is very similar to that proposed, following Stemberger's (1985) model, by Kay and Ellis (1987) for their patient E.S.T. (see also Li & Williams, 1990, for a related view about the locus of the phonemic cueing effect). The two patients are substantially similar, even though R.I.'s jargon is more severe (let the emergence of correct proper names be set aside for a while). However, E.S.T., like R.I., has good comprehension, and his repetition is somewhat better for real words than for non-words. Like R.I., he is also helped by phonemic cueing in naming but, unfortunately, no cued naming tests for proper names were administered to E.S.T. Kay and Ellis (1987) pointed out that E.S.T.'s spontaneous speech shows that virtually all the words he uses in normal conversations are of high frequency and that the probability of his being able to name an object in constrained production is also strictly frequency related.

So, can the advantage of proper names in R.I. also be explained in terms of frequency? This may account for his spontaneous speech pattern. Indeed most of the names he produced were of family members and friends. However, if this is so, functors should also have appeared in his speech but they did not. Moreover, the frequency factor does not in itself explain the effect in the phonemic cueing condition, where R.I. was successful in providing names of people that, although well known, he presumably did not use frequently in everyday life. Other factors like salience and affect (see Van Lanker & Klein, 1990) may give some advantage to proper names, but such a clear-cut effect cannot be explained on these grounds (why 'Maradona' or 'Sophia Loren' yes, and 'cat' no?) The proper names advantage therefore needs a more complex explanation that has to take into account findings on previous patients.

One must remember that reported patients with proper names anomia (Semenza & Zettin 1988; 1989) show this same category-specific effect both in the oral and in the written modalities: this means that the defect determining anomia for proper names does not occur at the lexical level, but rather it occurs prior to the input to the phonological and to the orthographic lexicons (as these patients show perfect comprehension of proper names and retain plenty of semantic information on their bearers, the defect has to be at the output from an intact semantic system). By the logic of dissociations, then, these findings suggest that proper names access from the semantic system to the phonological lexicon (or to the phonological output codes, as in Fig.1) on a channel that is separate from the channel used by common ones. Converging evidence for such

---

[2] None of these forms has propositional value: even really existing lexical forms act rather as fillers seemingly in an attempt at compensation. This behaviour has been previously described and discussed by Butterworth 1979; 1985, and Panzeri, Semenza and Butterworth 1987: when active vocabulary is severely limited, spared elements emerge in some cases to make up for lexical difficulties.

a theory comes also from the recent work of Valentine et al. (1991), for the reasons mentioned in the introduction. If proper names and common names have separate channels, it would seem to follow that proper name anomias and common name anomias should be equally likely. Known cases of both kinds are, however, too few and far between for one to decide whether this is true. Moreover, if the two channels have different processing or resource demands, then the incidence of the two kinds of anomia may also be different.

Two explanations for R.I.'s performance can be considered at this point. According to the first, proper names are relatively spared because there is additional disturbance on the common nouns channel. In this case, R.I.'s disorder would be a mirror image of proper name anomias where the proper names channel seems to be cut out. By an extension of this view, one may imagine also that any sub-category of common names that happens to enjoy a relatively independent output from the semantic system may be selectively impaired or spared at this stage. Note that besides proper names, only very special categories like letters, colours, and body parts are reported in the literature as being selectively spared (Semenza, 1990). These considerations suggest that patients with a peripheral deficit analogous to R.I. (or E.S.T.) may, if properly tested, turn out to show other category-specific effects on phonemic cueing.

The second explanation does not need to postulate any disorder additional to the relatively peripheral one involving the input to the articulatory program. The proper names channel would be intrinsically more efficient when helped by a phonemic cueing because of the simple one-to-one relationship (token rather than type) that proper names entertain with their reference. This explanation does not, *prima facie*, fit with the intuition that processes based on rich, multidimensional sources of information would be those with greater efficiency. Nor does it fit with the large body of experimental findings.

However, the effect of phonemic cueing may be different on the two channels. Some evidence for this comes from a recent unpublished study[3] where aphasics' ability to name with both semantic and phonemic cueing was assessed for different semantic categories. A single patient was detected who showed a better response to semantic than to phonemic cueing for all categories (whereas most patients show the opposite pattern), except for the category of proper names, where he featured a much better performance with phonemic cueing. This latter finding suggests that patients who, like R.I. or E.S.T., have difficulty in activating the articulatory program, would benefit from phonemic cueing, especially when trying to retrieve proper names. Note that these two explanations are not mutually exclusive: they independently give rise to the same predictions.

---

[3] Corazza, G., (1992). *Effetti categoriali al cue fonemico e semantico: Particolarità dei nomi propri.* [Category effects in phonemic and semantic cueing: The particularity of proper names] Unpublished Graduate Thesis, University of Padova.

CONCLUSION

R.I.'s case provides further evidence of the special status proper names enjoy in comparison to common ones. This evidence converges with that brought by previous studies in indicating that what makes proper names special is the uniqueness of the relation they entertain with their reference. On the basis of this and other neuropsychological studies it is then proposed that pure referring—the specific semantic function of proper names—determines their peculiar processing way down to the phonological level.

Manuscript received 8 August 1992
Manuscript accepted 16 February 1993

REFERENCES

Basso, A., Capitani, E., & Vignolo, A. (1979). Influence of rehabilitation of language skills in aphasic patients. A controlled study. *Archives of Neurology*, *36*, 190–196.

Bolla, K.I., Lindgren, K.N., Bonaccorsi, C., & Blecker, M.L. (1991). Memory complaints in older adults. Fact or fiction? *Archives of Neurology*, *48*, 61–64.

Bruce, V. (1979). Searching for politicians: an information processing approach to face recognition. *Quarterly Journal of Experimental Psychology*, *31A*, 373–395.

Bruce, V. (1981). Visual and semantic effects in a serial word classification task. *Current Psychological Research*, *1*, 153–162.

Bruce, V. (1983). Visual and semantic effects in a serial word classification task. *Current Psychological Research*, *1*, 153–162.

Bruce, V. (1983). Recognizing faces. *Philosophical Transactions of the Royal Society of London, B 302*, 423–436.

Bruce, V. & Young, A. (1986). Understanding face recognition. *British Journal of Psychology*, *77*, 305–327.

Burke, D.M., MacKay, D.G., Worthley, J.S., & Wade, E. (1991). On the tip of the tongue: what causes word finding failures in young and older adults. *Journal of Memory and Language*, *30*, 542–579.

Butterworth, B. (1979). Hesitation and the production of verbal paraphasias and neologisms in jargon aphasia. *Brain and Language*, *8*, 133–161.

Butterworth, B. (1985). Jargon aphasia: processes and strategies. In S. Newman, & R. Epstein (Eds.), *Current perspectives in dysphasia*. Edinburgh: Churchill Livingstone.

Cohen, G. (1990). Why is it difficult to put names to faces? *British Journal of Psychology*, *81*, 287–297.

Cohen, G., & Faulkner, D. (1986). Memory for proper names: age differences in retrieval. *British Journal of Developmental Psychology*, *4*, 187–197.

Ellis, A.W., & Young, A.W. (1989). *Human cognitive neuropsychology*. (Pp.126–127; 118–119). Hove, UK: Lawrence Erlbaum Associates Ltd.

Flude, B.M., Ellis, A.W., & Kay, J. (1988). Face processing and name retrieval in an anomic aphasic: names are stored separately from semantic information about people. *Brain and Cognition*, *11*, 60–72.

Frege, G. (1892). Uber Sinn und Bedeutung. [On sense and meaning] In G. Patzig (Ed.) *Funktion, Begriff, Bedeutung* (pp.40–65). Gottingen: Vandenhoek und Ruprecht.

Jackendoff, R. (1983). *Semantics and cognition*. Cambridge, MA: MIT Press.

Katz, J. (1972). *Semantic theory*. NY: Harvey & Row.

Kay, J., & Ellis, A.W. (1987) A cognitive neuropsychological case study of anomia: implications for psychological models of word retrieval. *Brain, 110,* 613–629.

Kripke, S. (1980). *Naming and necessity.* Oxford: Basil Blackwell.

Levelt, W.J.M. (1989). *Speaking. From intention to articulation.* Cambridge, MA: MIT Press.

Li, E.C., & Williams, S.E. (1990). The effects of grammatical class and cue type on cueing responsiveness in aphasia. *Brain and Language, 38,* 48–60.

Lucchelli, F., & De Renzi, E. (1992). Proper name anomia. *Cortex, 28,* 221–230.

MacKay, D.G. (1987). *The organization of perception and action: a theory for language and other cognitive skills.* New York: Springer-Verlag.

Macnamara, J. (1982). *Names for things. A study of human learning.* Cambridge, MA: MIT Press.

McKenna, P., & Warrington, E.K. (1978). Category-specific naming preservation: a single case study. *Journal of Neurology, Neurosurgery and Psychiatry, 41,* 571–574.

McKenna, P., & Warrington, E.K. (1980) Testing for nominal dysphasia. *Journal of Neurology, Neurosurgery and Psychiatry, 43,* 781–788.

McWeeny, K.H., Young, A., Hay, D.C., & Ellis, A.W. (1987). Putting names to faces. *British Journal of Psychology, 78,* 143–144.

Mill, J.S. (1843). *A system of logic* (10th ed. 1879). London: Longmans.

Miller, G.A., & Johnson-Laird, P.N. (1976). *Language and perception.* Harvard: Harvard University Press.

Monsell, S. (1989). On the relation between lexical input and output pathways. In A. Allport, D. MacKay, W. Prinze, & E. Sheerer (Eds.), *Language perception and production: Shared versus mechanisms in listening, speaking, reading and writing.* London: Academic Press.

Morton, J. (1984). Naming. In S. Newman, & R. Epstein (Eds.) *Dysphasia.* Edinburgh: Churchill, Livingstone.

Nickels, L. (1992). The autocue? Self-generated phonemic cues in the treatment of a disorder of reading and naming. *Cognitive Neuropsychology, 9,* 155–182.

Panzeri, M., Semenza, C., & Butterworth, B. (1987). Compensatory processes in the evolution of severe jargon aphasia. *Neuropsychologia, 25,* 919–933.

Reason, J.T., & Lucas, D. (1984). Using cognitive diaries to investigate naturally occurring memory blocks. In J.E. Harris, & P.E. Morris (Eds.), *Everyday memory, actions and absentmindedness.* London: Academic Press.

Russell, B. (1905). On denoting. *Mind, 14,* 479–493.

Saffran, E.M. Bogyo, L.C., Schwartz, M.F., & Marin, O.S.M. (1980). Does deep dyslexia reflect right-hemisphere reading? In M. Coltheart, K. Patterson, & J.C. Marshall (Eds.) *Deep dyslexia.* London: Routledge & Kegan.

Searle, J.R. (1969). *Speech acts.* Cambridge: Cambridge University Press.

Searle, J.R. (1971). Semantics. In D.D. Steinberg & L.A. Jakobovitz (Eds.) *An interdisciplinary reader in philosophy, linguistics and psychology* (pp.134–144). Cambridge: Cambridge University Press.

Semenza, C. (1990). Disturbi semantico-lessicali nell'afasia. [Lexical-semantic disturbances in aphasia] In G. Denes, & L. Pizzamiglio (Eds.) *Manuale di neuropsicologia* (pp.325–364). Bologna: Zanichelli Editore.

Semenza, C., & Zettin, M. (1988). Generating proper names: a case of selective inability. *Cognitive Neuropsychology, 5,* (6), 711–721.

Semenza, C., & Zettin, M. (1989). Evidence from aphasia for the role of proper names as pure referring expressions. *Nature, 342,* (6250), 678–679.

Sgaramella, T.M., Semenza, C., & Ellis, A.W. (1991, May). *Independent evolution of jargon in speech and writing.* Poster presented at the TENNET II, Montreal.

Stemberger, J.P. (1985). An interactive model of language production. In A.W. Ellis (Ed.), *Progress in the psychology of language* (Vol.1). London: Lawrence Erlbaum Associates Ltd.

Valentine, T., Brédart, S., Lawson, R., & Ward, G. (1991). What is in a name? Access to information from people's names. *European Journal of Cognitive Psychology, 3*, 147–176.

Van Lanker, D., & Klein, K. (1990). Preserved recognition of familiar personal names in global aphasia. *Brain and Language, 39*, 511–529.

Warrington, E.K., & McCarthy, R.A. (1983). Category specific access dysphasia. *Brain*, 106, 859–878.

Wapner, W., & Gardner, H. (1979). A note on patterns of comprehension and recovery in global aphasia, *Journal of Speech and Hearing Research, 29*, 765–772.

Wittgenstein, L. (1922). *Tractatus Logico-philosophicus* (trans. C.K. Ogden). London.

Young, A., Hay, D.C., & Ellis, A.W. (1985). The faces that launched a thousand slips: everyday difficulties and errors in recognizing people. *British Journal of Psychology, 76*, 495–523.

Young, A., McWeeny, K.H., Ellis, A.W., & Hay, D.C. (1986). Naming and categorising faces and written names. *Quarterly Journal of Experimental Psychology, 38A*, 297–318.

MEMORY, 1993, *1* (4), 281–288

Selective Preservation of Place Names in an Aphasic Patient: A Short Report

Elizabeth K. Warrington and Frances Clegg

The National Hospital for Neurology and Neurosurgery, London, UK

This report describes the case of a severely aphasic patient who shows selective preservation for the names of countries.

INTRODUCTION

In the literature describing category effects in naming, the documentation of a selective impairment for proper names is not uncommon. McKenna and Warrington (1980), and Lucchelli and De Renzi (1992) document two cases in which there has been a loss of proper names for specific people only; Semenza and Zettin (1988; 1989) describe two cases in which the naming of specific people, cities, rivers, countries, and mountains was impaired in the context of preserved comprehension. The converse, islands of preservation along categorical dimensions, is less common. Such cases as have been documented seem to affect proper names. These can be subdivided, and even a single class may have the status of selective preservation, that of names of countries. This is such a rare phenomenon however, that there is only one case described in the literature, that of F.C. (McKenna & Warrington, 1978; but see also Cipolotti, McNeil, & Warrington, this issue). This paper describes a second case in which an aphasic patient shows selective preservation for names of countries.

CASE REPORT

A.F., a 57-year-old company director was admitted to the National Hospital in 1989 under the care of Professor Anita Harding for investigation of progressive memory and language impairment. Neurological examination was normal apart from the cognitive changes to be described shortly. The only investigation of

Requests for reprints should be sent to Professor Elizabeth K. Warrington, Psychology Department, National Hospital for Neurology and Neurosurgery, Queen Square, London WC1N 3BG, UK.

We are grateful to Professor Anita Harding and Doctor Martin Rossor for permission to investigate the patient under their care and to report the findings. We also wish to thank Ms Jane McNeil and Doctor Luke Kartsounis for their assistance in the clinical assessment.

note was a CT scan performed in 1989, which showed extensive cortical and cerebellar atrophy, most prominent in the left temporal region. A.F. was transferred to the care of Dr. Martin Rossor and continues to attend out-patient clinics at regular intervals. The provisional diagnosis is that of progressive cortical degeneration.

Neuropsychological Assessment

When first assessed in the Psychology Department, on a shortened form of the WAIS-R (Warrington, James, & Maciejewski, 1986) A.F. obtained a Verbal IQ of 82 and a Performance IQ of 114. All verbal subtest scores were below the average range. His Picture Completion and Picture Arrangement subtest scores were average and dull average respectively, but an almost perfect score on the Block Design subtest raised his pro-rated Performance IQ substantially. On Raven's Advanced Progressive Matrices, Set I (Raven, 1962), his score of 9/12 on this non-verbal reasoning test was above average for his age (Warrington, 1984).

Although he obtained only a dull average score on the Arithmetic subtest of the WAIS-R, on an arithmetic test which focuses on adding and subtracting at speed (Jackson & Warrington, 1986), his score of 16/24 lay at the 75th percentile.

His spontaneous speech was fluent and voluble, although often circumlocutory and with stereotypic phrases. However, on the Graded Naming Test (GNT, McKenna & Warrington 1983), he failed to name any items, and on the easier Oldfield Picture Naming Test (Oldfield & Wingfield 1965), he named only 7/30 common objects.

On the British Picture Vocabulary Scale (BPVS) for single word comprehension, his raw score of 54 was below the first percentile for a young adult, indicating a marked language comprehension deficit (Dunn, Dunn, & Whetton, 1982). His reading skills had deteriorated considerably, and it was evident that his score of 4/50 on the National Adult Reading Test (NART, Nelson, 1982) in no way reflected his pre-morbid level of functioning, which, from his occupational background, was evidently well above average.

On the Recognition Memory Test (RMT) for faces, in which the patient is first shown 50 unfamiliar male faces one by one, and then asked to point to each one when it is presented together with a 'distractor' face (Warrington, 1984), he obtained an average score. Reading difficulties precluded the administration of the verbal version. When he was shown a set of 12 famous faces, although he recognised 6 of them (as evidenced by his account of their occupation etc), he could name only 1.

He completed the Fragmented Letters Test from the Visual Object and Space Perception Battery (VOSP) without error, but his dysphasia precluded administration of the animal and objects silhouettes tests in this battery (Warrington & James 1991).

In summary, when first seen, his verbal intellectual skills had deteriorated to a level that was well below average. His non-verbal skills also showed some deterioration, but with the exception of the Block Design subtest from the WAIS-R, which lay at the 95th percentile. He had a marked nominal dysphasia, was dyslexic and had a verbal comprehension deficit. However, his visual memory and perceptual skills were intact.

Reassessment

When he was reassessed 18 months later, his verbal comprehension had deteriorated to such a point that he failed to grasp the content or the requirements of the majority of tests. On the BPVS he failed to achieve even a basal level, he was unable to read any words on the NART, and his expressive speech had become sparse and repetitive. He failed to name any item on the simple Oldfield Picture Naming test. His wife reported that he was only able to use first names for a few immediate members of the family.

On verbal subtests of the WAIS-R he managed the first three items on the Arithmetic subtest, and was able to repeat four digits forwards. On the performance subtests, Picture Arrangement was beyond him, but his raw score on Picture Completion was five. But once again he successfully completed the Block Design test, only failing to obtain a perfect score on two items. His score on Raven's Advanced Matrices Set I had dropped to 5/12, an average level.

His score on the arithmetic test (Jackson & Warrington, 1986) had also dropped to an average level (19/24). However he could still read and write arabic numerals, count simple arrays of dots, and identify two digit numbers from arrays of numbers.

That his perceptual skills were intact was demonstrated by his score of 18/20 on the Object Decision Test from the Visual Object and Space Perception Battery. This test does not involve any language skills, but requires the patient simply to point to the 'real' object silhouette from an array of four in which three are non-objects.

By contrast, he completely failed a test in which he was required to point to one famous face from an array of three faces in which two were nonentity distractor items. He did not appear to recognise any of them, which indicates a degree of prosopagnosia.

To summarise his cognitive status at the time of this study, A.F. had developed a severe global dysphasia in which he had become almost mute and showed extremely impaired verbal comprehension. However his arithmetical and perceptual skills (except for face perception) were relatively well preserved, and on non-verbal problem solving tasks his performance was in the average or above average range.

'Nonograms'

While he was an inpatient at the hospital, A.F. inadvertently demonstrated how well preserved his visuo-spatial skills were. On two successive weekend stays he completed two 'nonograms', complex visuo–spatial–numerical tests of 'logic and deduction', as published weekly in a Sunday newspaper. They comprise a blank grid which might typically contain hundreds of small cells, the horizontal and vertical axes being labelled with numbers which enable the reader to deduce which squares should be shaded in. When the shading is completed, the emergent silhouette corresponds to the cryptic title of the nonogram. One of the nonograms that A.F. completed (perfectly) as an inpatient, "sailing", is reproduced in Fig. 1.

Topographical Knowledge

When he was first seen, AF had mentioned that much of his career had involved travelling abroad, and some details of places he had visited were noted at this

Nonogram 97 - SAILING

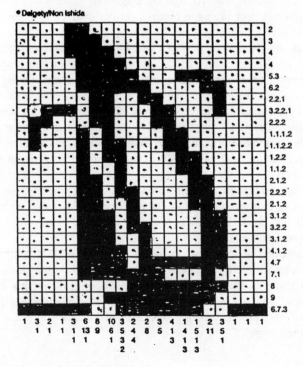

FIG. 1. 'Nonogram' successfully completed by A.F.

time. As his speech dwindled, the subject of travel formed the core of his utterances. He managed to indicate that he could recall the appearance of many of the cities he had visited, and with some effort was able to name several. When he was shown photographs taken from holiday brochures, or postcards, he correctly located on an outline map of the world all 10 specific buildings (such as the Taj Mahal or the Eiffel Tower), and three of the six cities. In this context it should be noted that he was never observed to use people's names.

At the time of reassessment, when A.F. was handed an atlas, he spontaneously opened it and pointed to countries and cities which he had visited, for instance North America, Singapore, and Hong Kong. Occasionally he was also able to give the name of the place indicated. It was this ability to give the names of some places that stood in such marked contrast to his inability to name even the most common everyday items, such as a chair or a comb.

EXPERIMENTAL INVESTIGATION

In many respects A.F. resembled the anomic patient F.C. whose preservation of the semantic category of countries was reported by McKenna and Warrington in 1978. Using the same test materials as those used with F.C., the aim was to establish whether this patient also had a category-specific selective preservation of country names.

Materials

Ten items from each of five categories of names were used—body parts, colours, animals, objects, and countries. All were of high frequency (A or AA, Thorndike & Lorge, 1944). The 10 countries were shown by means of a clear outline map, and the body parts, animals, and objects were illustrated by clear line drawings. The colours were depicted with colour patches approximately one inch square.

Procedure

Two of the three test conditions used by McKenna and Warrington (1978) in their investigation of F.C. were used; naming to visual confrontation and comprehension of the spoken word through word–picture matching.

Under the confrontation naming condition, the 50 items were presented singly across the desk using a Latin Square Design to control for category order effects. Presentation was untimed, and responses scored as correct or incorrect. In the comprehension condition of word–picture matching, the 10 items from one category were placed in an array and A.F. was required to point to each after its name was spoken. There were no time limits, and responses were scored as either correct or incorrect. These procedures were carried out twice with A.F., with a two day interval between the trials.

TABLE 1
Correct Responses

	Colours	Objects	Countries	Body Parts	Animals	Total
Naming (first trial)	0	0	7	0	0	7
Naming (second trial)	2	1	7	0	0	10
Naming (totals)	2	1	14	0	0	17
Comprehension (first trial)	8	3	10	5	1	27
Comprehension (second trial)	7	3	7	9	0	26
Comprehension (totals)	15	6	17	14	1	53

Results

The number of correct responses for the two presentation conditions in both trials is shown in Table 1.

A chi^2 test carried out on the naming scores (errors $\times$ categories) was significant ($X^2 = 10.05$, $df = 4$, $P < 0.05$). Examination of the data reveals that this result is entirely due to the superiority of A.F.'s ability to name countries. A chi^2 test carried out on the comprehension scores (items correct $\times$ categories) was also significant ($X^2 = 17.46$, $df = 4$, $P < 0.05$), although the interpretation is less clear-cut. His highest score was also in the country category, but his ability to recognise the names of colours and body parts was similar, all three categories showing only relatively mild impairment. However he had more difficulty in recognising object and animal names, both categories being impaired.

DISCUSSION

The results of this study confirm that A.F. showed a specific preservation of naming in the context of a severe anomia. The category of names preserved is that of countries, and to our knowledge A.F. is only the second case in which this pattern of performance has been documented.

In some respects, A.F.'s preserved category is even more selective than that of the original case, F.C., who also managed to name several body parts (McKenna & Warrington, 1978). Furthermore, except for body parts, F.C. was generally successful in comprehending stimuli through word–picture matching. But his results were unusual in that for body parts his naming score exceeded his comprehension score. In the case of A.F. there are no categories in which naming scores exceed comprehension scores.

At the time this investigation was carried out, clinical considerations precluded more extensive assessment of proper names. However there was limited evidence that names of people were *not* a preserved category; at the time of the first assessment, he had only managed to name one famous person, and when enquiries were made subsequently, his wife reported that for a considerable period he had only used first names for the most immediate members of his family. Finally, his face recognition skills also appeared to be impaired.

There is one other noteworthy feature in this case, besides the selective preservation of place names. This is that many non-verbal skills also show remarkable preservation. It has been known for over a century that some cognitive skills remain preserved in patients with a grave degree of language impairment. The two patients with jargon aphasia reported by Kinsbourne and Warrington (1963) are somewhat similar to A.F., in that both were severely incapacitated in the use of words, but nevertheless obtained average or above average scores on Raven's Progressive Matrices and the majority of WAIS Performance subtests. Case 6 in the report on six patients with syndromes of progressive aphasia (Tyrrell, Warrington, Frackowiak, & Rossor, 1990) also obtained an above average score on the Matrices long after he had ceased to obtain any score at all on verbal subtests of the WAIS. In the case of A.F., when assessment had become almost impossible due to his inability to comprehend test instructions, it is likely that his performance on the Matrices and Block Design tests was aided by his initial recall of the test requirement.

There is good evidence of preservation of right hemisphere skills in A.F. Rather than suggesting that the place names are an island of preservation in his verbal knowledge base, it might be plausible to speculate that these referents, together with his topographical knowledge, share a common neurological substrate in the right hemisphere, and possibly have a privileged access to phonology.

Manuscript received 30 January 1993
Manuscript accepted 25 March 1993

REFERENCES

Cipolotti, L., McNeil, J., & Warrington, E.K. (this issue). Spared written naming of proper names: A case report. *Memory*.

Dunn, L.M., Dunn, L.M., & Whetton, C. (1982). *British Picture Vocabulary Scale*. Windsor, UK: NFER-Nelson.

Jackson, M., & Warrington, E.K. (1986). Arithmetic skills in patients with unilateral cerebral lesions. *Cortex, 22*, 610–620.

Kinsbourne, M., & Warrington, E.K. (1963). Jargon aphasia. *Neuropsychologica, 1*, 27–37.
Lucchelli, F., & de Renzi, E. (1992). Proper name anomia. *Cortex, 28*, 221–230.
McKenna, P., & Warrington, E.K. (1978). Category specific naming preservation: A single case study. *Journal of Neurology, Neurosurgery and Psychiatry, 41*, 571– 574.
McKenna, P., & Warrington, E.K. (1980). Testing for nominal dysphasia. *Journal of Neurology, Neurosurgery and Psychiatry, 43*, 781–788.
McKenna, P., & Warrington, E.K. (1983). *The Graded Naming Test.* Windsor, UK: Nelson.
Nelson, H.E. (1982). *The National Adult Reading Test.* Windsor, UK: NFER-Nelson.
Oldfield, R.C., & Wingfield, A. (1965). Response latencies in naming objects. *Quarterly Journal of Experimental Psychology, 17*, 273–281.
Raven, J.C. (1962). *Advanced Progressive Matrices.* London: H.K. Lewis.
Semenza, C., & Zettin, M. (1988). Generating proper names: A case of selective inability. *Cognitive Neuropsychology, 5*, 711–721.
Semenza, C., & Zettin, M. (1989). Evidence from aphasia for the role of proper names as pure referring expressions. *Nature, 342*, 678–679.
Thorndike, E.L., & Lorge, I. (1944). *The Teacher's Word Book of 30,000 Words.* New York: Teachers' College Press.
Tyrrell, P.J., Warrington, E.K., Frackowiak, R.S.J., & Rossor, M.N. (1990). Heterogeneity in progressive aphasia due to focal cortical atrophy. *Brain, 113*, 1321–1336.
Warrington, E.K. (1984). *Recognition Memory Test.* Windsor, UK: NFER-Nelson.
Warrington, E.K., & James, M. (1991). *Visual Object and Space Perception Battery.* Bury St. Edmunds, UK: Thames Valley Test Company.
Warrington, E.K., James, M., & Maciejewski, C. (1986). The WAIS as a lateralising and localising diagnostic instrument: A study of 656 patients with unilateral cerebral lesions. *Neuropsychologia, 24*, 223–239.

MEMORY, 1993, *1* (4), 289–311

Spared Written Naming of Proper Nouns: A Case Report

Lisa Cipolotti, Jane E. McNeil, and Elizabeth K. Warrington

The National Hospital for Neurology and Neurosurgery, London, UK

In this study we describe an investigation into the residual written word retrieval skills of M.E.D., a patient with a severe aphasia. M.E.D.'s performance on written naming and writing to dictation tasks showed a distinctive pattern of performance across semantic categories. The patient's ability to write the names of countries and famous people was consistently superior to her ability to write the names of objects. These results could be considered as indicative of a double dissociation in the proper nouns category, as there are already patients on record who have a selective deficit in retrieving proper nouns.

INTRODUCTION

The ability to retrieve certain categories of words can be selectively impaired or preserved. In the aphasia literature many examples of category-specific naming difficulties have been studied since the pioneering work of Goodglass, Klein, Carey, and Jones (1966). Over the past few years, a particular category, that of proper nouns, has been the focus of a number of experimental studies. There have been four cases described with particularly striking category impairments in their oral retrieval of proper nouns that contrasted with their well maintained performance in naming various items from different categories (e.g. objects, fruits and vegetables, body parts, means of transport, colours etc; see Luchelli & De Renzi 1992; McKenna & Warrington 1980; Semenza & Zettin 1988, 1989). These patients with a selective proper noun anomia showed different patterns of performance in retrieving particular categories of words within the broad class of proper nouns. The two patients described by Semenza and Zettin had an impairment in the retrieval of all classes of proper nouns including famous people, cities and countries, mountains and rivers. The patients described by McKenna and Warrington, and Luchelli and De Renzi both had an oral anomia

---

Requests for reprints should be sent to Lisa Cipolotti, Psychology Department, National Hospital for Neurology and Neurosurgery, Queen Square, London, WC1N 3BG, UK.

We wish to thank Dr. P. Rudge for his permission to investigate M.E.D., a patient under his care, and to report our findings.

290 CIPOLOTTI, McNEIL, WARRINGTON

restricted to famous people's names with the preservation of the oral retrieval of place names.

Examples of the selective sparing of proper nouns have been described in reading aloud tasks. Superior reading of proper nouns when compared with common nouns has been documented in deep dyslexic patients by Saffran, Bogyo, Schwartz, and Marin (1980). Examples of the selective sparing of proper nouns in comprehension tasks have also been reported. Warrington and McCarthy (1987) described a patient with a grave global aphasia who, when tested using word–picture matching tasks, had no difficulty with proper nouns (famous people's names, countries and cities) along with food, and living things, whereas her performance for common nouns and ordinary people's names was severely impaired. In line with this, Van Lanker and Klein (1990) reported four global aphasics with a superior performance for proper nouns when compared with common nouns in word–picture matching tasks.

The selective preservation of oral naming of proper nouns is more rare. McKenna and Warrington (1978) reported a patient with a selective preservation of the ability to retrieve orally a single class of proper nouns, that of names of countries. This patient demonstrated an ability to orally retrieve the names of countries together with a global impairment in oral retrieval of common nouns (objects, animals, colours, and body parts). This finding has recently been replicated in another severely aphasic patient who shows the same selective preservation for names of countries (see Warrington & Clegg, this issue).

The studies reviewed above focused on the ability to read, comprehend, or orally name proper nouns. There are only a few indications that category-specific disorders can manifest themselves in written naming. Recently, Hillis and Caramazza (1991) reported an example of a double dissociation between living and nonliving things in two patients. One patient showed preserved oral and written naming of animals when compared with other common object categories. The other patient showed the opposite pattern, namely the impairment of oral and written naming of animals with the relative sparing of the ability to name other common object categories. In both patients the comprehension of words in the semantic category of animals paralleled their naming performance (i.e. selectively spared in the first case and selectively impaired in the second case). In writing to dictation tasks there are a number of examples of category-specific impairments that are affected by parts of speech, lexicality, and concreteness (Baxter & Warrington, 1985; Bub & Kertesz, 1982; Kremin, 1987; Roeltgen, Rothi, & Heilman, 1986; Shallice, 1981). However, an example of a selective preservation of proper nouns in written naming and/or writing to dictation has never been documented.

In this paper we describe a severely aphasic patient who provides an example of a remarkable selective preservation of written naming and writing to dictation in one category, proper nouns. Within the broad class of proper nouns, the patient was able to retrieve the names of countries and famous people's names.

The sparing of this particular type of word (i.e. famous people's names) has not previously been documented.

CASE REPORT

M.E.D., a 63 year old woman, a professional artist, was admitted to the National Hospital on 6 July 1992 under the care of Dr. Rudge. The patient was referred from the Royal Marsden Hospital for evaluation of her progressive aphasia. M.E.D. had long standing follicular lymphoma which was first diagnosed in 1960 and which has been treated over the years with local radiotherapy and occasional courses of chlorambucil.

In June 1992, she started to complain of progressive language difficulties. On neurological examination she had a marked expressive aphasia and minor right sided signs. A CT scan (9 July, 1992) showed a left posterior fronto-parietal low density lesion and two additional small low density areas in the left frontal lobe. A MRI (July, 1992) showed an abnormal signal in the left posterior temporal and parietal lobes. There was a separate small focus of high signal in the left thalamus. There was also scattered white matter foci bilaterally which were not specific. She died on 5 August, 1992. The histological and neuropathological findings were compatible with the clinical diagnosis of progressive multifocal leucoencephalopathy.

NEUROPSYCHOLOGICAL ASSESSMENT

M.E.D. was referred on 7 July 1992 to the Psychology Department for a more detailed assessment of her dysphasia and other cognitive deficits. She was tested every day until her discharge on 17 July 1992. During this period M.E.D. remained alert and cooperative, although her language functions noticeably deteriorated.

She was unable to attempt any of the verbal subtests of the WAIS-R, and on the performance subtests she completely failed the Block design subtest (scaled score 0) and performed poorly on the Picture Arrangement and Picture Completion subtests (scaled score 8 and 7 respectively). On the Advanced Progressive Matrices Set A, she scored within the normal range (5/12) (Warrington, 1984). On a visuoperceptual test, Object Decision Silhouettes Test (from the VOSP, Warrington & James, 1991), her performance was satisfactory (17/20).

Language Functions

Speech Production.   When first assessed, her spontaneous speech was non fluent, with articulatory difficulties. There was a marked reduction in phrase length and syntactic complexity that gave the patient's speech a 'telegraphic' quality. Verbs, function words, and grammatical inflections were frequently omitted or, more rarely, incorrectly used. Phonetic and/or phonological paraphasias were noted, whereas semantic paraphasias seemed absent. In her spontaneous speech, long pauses were present indicating a marked word-finding difficulty. M.E.D.'s spontaneous speech appeared to be deteriorating quite rapidly. When she was discharged from the Hospital her verbal utterances were restricted to a few simple stereotyped phrases.

On initial assessment (7 July 1992) she was able to reliably repeat single letters and words. At this time she was also able to repeat 8/8 two-syllable nonwords correctly. However, her repetition abilities deteriorated very rapidly during the investigation and by 13 July repetition was no longer viable. A similar pattern was observed with her oral naming. When first seen (7 July 1992) she was able to name 2/30 objects from the graded naming test (GNT, McKenna & Warrington, 1980). No semantic errors were noted. However, her oral naming also rapidly deteriorated so that by 13 July the patient was almost totally unable to complete even the simplest oral naming tasks.

Language Comprehension.   Her single word comprehension was evaluated using a spoken word to picture matching task. The same test materials as those used by McKenna and Warrington (1978) and Warrington and Clegg (this issue) were used. Ten items from each of five categories of names were used: body parts, colours, animals, objects and countries. The 10 items from one category were placed in an array and M.E.D. was required to point to a given item after its name was spoken. There were no time limits and responses were scored as either correct or incorrect. M.E.D.'s performance was virtually perfect for all five categories, indicating a largely preserved comprehension of spoken words. She scored 10/10 correct responses respectively for the categories of body parts, objects, animals, and countries and 8/10 correct responses for the category of colours.

Reading.   Her literacy skills were also compromised. In addition to her writing difficulties, which will be described in detail below, she had marked difficulties in reading aloud. She was only able to read aloud 5 out of 12 single letters and 5 out of 16 of the easiest words from the Schonell graded reading test (Schonell, 1942). Her errors were either omissions of response or phonological paralexias (e.g. when asked to read milk she responded "milt"). Semantic errors were never recorded. When she failed to give an answer she often spontaneously drew a picture of the item she was unable to read (e.g. instead of reading aloud "clock" she drew a picture of a clock). As with her other spoken language skills these abilities deteriorated to such an extent that she could no longer perform oral reading tasks. Her comprehension of single written words was remarkably well maintained (see McNeil, Cipolotti, & Warrington, in press, for a more detailed report on her performance on written word comprehension tests).

Calculation. Her calculation skills were severely impaired. M.E.D. could read aloud single arabic numerals (10/10), but she failed in reading aloud multidigit arabic numerals (10/20). Similarly, she could write to dictation single arabic numerals (10/10), but she was impaired in writing to dictation multidigit arabic numerals (7/15). Her performance on an arabic numeral cardinality judgment task was well preserved (20/20). On tasks of simple oral addition, subtraction, and multiplication her performance was very impaired.

Writing to Dictation. M.E.D.'s ability to write letters, numbers, and words to dictation was tested as follows.

1. *Letters.* M.E.D. correctly wrote 18 out of 22 single letter-names to dictation. The letters were all well-formed and the four errors were letter substitutions.

2. *Arabic numerals.* M.E.D. was asked to write 30 arabic numerals which consisted of the following: the numbers 1–9; 10 numbers from 10–99; and 10 numbers from 100–999. Her performance was flawless when writing single digit arabic numerals. She made two syntactic errors (e.g. stimulus "forty" response 14) and one lexical error (e.g. stimulus "thirty five" response 38) when writing arabic numerals of two digits. She made five lexical errors when writing arabic numerals of three digits (e.g. stimulus "two hundred" response 400).

3. *Words.* On a graded spelling test (Baxter, 1987) M.E.D. scored 2 out of the first 10. Her ability to write to dictation high frequency common nouns from the Schonell Graded Spelling Test (Schonell, 1942) was also impaired. She could only write 6 out of 15 words correctly.

4. *Nonwords.* M.E.D. was asked to write 10 monosyllabic nonwords of three or five letters (Barry & Seymour, 1988). Her performance was extremely impaired; none of her responses were correct. One of her errors was an omission. The other remaining nine errors were neologisms, which were visually dissimilar to the target nonword (e.g. stimulus "turve" response *entru*).

In summary, M.E.D.'s ability to write either at the level of single letters or single words was impaired. It is in this context that we report our investigation of her ability to write to dictation and name in the written modality proper and common nouns.

EXPERIMENTAL INVESTIGATION

It was observed that M.E.D. was able to write the names of the various countries and places where she had lived without any difficulty (e.g. *Montreal, Canada, Paris, New York, London*). When she was trying to communicate where she was living she was able to write *Brompton...Knightbridge...Harrods*. However, she was unable to write very frequent common words like *house* and *road*. Indeed, on occasion she resorted to writing country and people's names as a means of communication (e.g. *Dior, Cardin, Julie Andrew*). In order to explore these observations more carefully the following investigations were completed.

Test 1: Written Naming of the Oldfield Pictures and Maps of Well-known Countries

M.E.D.'s ability to write the names of maps of well known countries (McKenna & Warrington, 1978; Warrington & Clegg, this issue) and the names of objects from the Oldfield Naming Test (ONT) was tested on two different days (8.7.92 and 9.7.92) and on three different occasions. On the first day (8.7.92) the tests were administered in the following order: in the morning, the ONT first then the maps. In the afternoon, the ONT in oral naming followed by written naming. The maps were not re-examined in this session. On the second day (9.7.92) the tests were administered in the following order: the maps first, then the ONT. The frequency of the items belonging to the countries category varied over a wide range (from AA to 14 as estimated by Thorndike & Lorge, 1944). The frequency of the ONT items also varied over a wide range (from AA to 0.83 as estimated by Thorndike & Lorge, 1944). See Appendix 1 for the stimuli used on 8.7.92, and Appendix 2 for the stimuli used on 9.7.92.

On the first examination (8.7.92; morning), M.E.D. scored 0 out of 10 writing the ONT names, and 8 out of 10 writing the names of the countries. It was observed that when M.E.D. was failing to retrieve the written name of an object, she gave evidence of knowing the object shown in the picture. For example, she might point to a real object and/or draw a picture (i.e. *shoe*: she pointed to her shoe and then she drew a picture of a shoe; *watch*: she showed her watch). All her failures on the ONT were omissions (failures to offer any sort of attempt at the spelling) and her two errors on the maps of well-known countries test involved grapheme deletion (e.g. stimulus Ireland response *Ireand*) and a semantic substitution combined with a grapheme omission (e.g. stimulus Germany response *Holand*). M.E.D.'s performance cannot be explained as a product of word frequency, as at least 7 out of 10 of the ONT items shared almost the same frequency counts as the well-known names of countries (see Appendix 1 for frequency count and for the corpus of errors).

On the second examination (8.7.92; afternoon), M.E.D. scored 6 out of 14 in orally naming the ONT items, and 1 out of 14 in writing the ONT names. When she was trying to orally name the ONT items, her errors consisted of unsuccessful phonological approximations to the target words (e.g. for the word "key" M.E.D.'s answer was: "ki...kia"). Semantic errors and omissions were absent. When retrieving the written names of the ONT objects, her failures consisted of eight omissions, two visual approximations (e.g. glove–*gluve*) and three miscellaneous errors (e.g. watch–*Awar*). The corpus of errors is given in Appendix 1.

On the third examination (9.7.92) her performance appeared somewhat improved. In this examination a larger number (*n* = 24) of items from the ONT was administered. The same number (as in the previous examinations) of items with high frequency names were present, however there was a larger number of items with low frequency names. M.E.D. was able to write correctly the names of 9 out of 24 objects from the ONT (38% overall correct answers) and 9 out of 10 country maps. This discrepancy between writing the names of objects of the ONT and the well-known countries cannot be reduced to a word length effect. Considering only a subset of names matched for length (5–8 letters) her score was 5 out of 13 for the Oldfield pictures, and 9 out of 10 for the maps of well-known countries.

Of the total 15 incorrect responses that M.E.D. gave in the ONT, only three were semantic errors (e.g. cigarette–*cigar*). To four pictures, M.E.D. was unable to offer any response (e.g. watch), although she was able to give evidence of knowing the object shown in the picture (e.g. for the picture of a syringe, she pantomimed the use). The remaining eight errors were visual approximations consisting of: grapheme substitution (n=4) (e.g. boat–*poat*); grapheme deletion (n=1) (e.g. drum–*dum*); grapheme insertion (n=1) (e.g. bagpipes–*bag-p-pipe*); and misordering (n=1) (e.g. windmill–*mill winds*). The corpus of errors is given in Appendix 2.

Furthermore, it was observed that M.E.D. sometimes substituted a proper name for a common name. For example, when attempting to name the picture of a *typewriter* she wrote its commercial name *Olivetti*. It also appeared that M.E.D. was able to retrieve the orthographic form of low frequency object names at least as easily as the high frequency object names. Her nine correct responses were in fact distributed as follows: three were AA or A words, two were words with a frequency from 43 to 22, and four were words with a frequency from 20 to 0.83 (see Appendix 2). Indeed it was remarkable that she failed to give any spelling for the picture of a watch, and misspelt *shoe*, but succeeded in writing low frequency words like *scissors* and *anvil*. In order to explore these observations in more detail the following tests were devised.

Test 2: Writing Naming of Graded Difficulty Common Nouns and Proper Nouns (10.7.92)

The observations of the first test prompted us to study M.E.D.'s ability to write the names of items from two major semantic categories; common nouns and proper nouns. McKenna and Warrington (1980) have constructed and standardised graded difficulty naming tests (GNT) based on this category distinction. The common nouns test comprises 30 line drawings of items consisting of 26 objects and 4 animals. The proper nouns test consists of 24 photographs of famous people (e.g. Virginia Woolf and Lenin), two maps (e.g. Italy and South America) and four photographs of famous places (e.g. Parthenon and Taj Mahal). The items from the proper and common nouns test are all of very low frequency (see Appendix 3) and were designed to be difficult for the average subjects. McKenna and Warrington (1980) showed that, in their standardisation sample, the mean score on the common nouns test was significantly higher than the mean score on the proper nouns test.

M.E.D. attempted to write the names of the common nouns and then, after a break, the proper nouns. She produced the correct written names to 7 of the 30 object line drawings (over 3 SDs below the mean of the standardisation sample; Mean = 22.54, SD = 4.3) and 19 of the 30 proper nouns (which is very close to the Mean of the sample; Mean = 20.32, SD = 5.8). This result shows that M.E.D.'s ability to produce the written form of proper nouns is far superior to her ability to produce the written form of common nouns. In addition, her ability to retrieve the written form of low frequency common nouns from the GNT did not appear to be worse than her ability to retrieve the written form of high frequency common nouns from the ONT (see Test 1).

The errors included: omission of response; semantic errors (e.g. Castro–*Cuba*); visual approximation errors consisting of partial lexical knowledge (e.g. Disraeli–*Dis*) or grapheme deletions and substitutions (e.g. shuttlecock–*sculac*); misordering of graphemes (e.g. Mao–*Moa*); and others (e.g. leotard–*cut*). The corpus of errors is given in Appendix 3. A detailed error analysis will be given below.

Test 3: Comparison of Naming, Comprehension, and Repetition for Different Categories (13.7.92)

The results of Test 2 confirmed that M.E.D.'s performance might be characterised by a category-specific preservation of written naming. M.E.D.'s naming of proper nouns appeared superior to her naming of common nouns. In this experiment a task was designed which permitted a more thorough investigation of her residual verbal capacities.

Materials. There were three categories of nouns: 10 maps of well-known countries (previously used in Test 1); 10 photographs of famous people (previously used in Test 2); and the first 10 items from the ONT (see Appendix 4).

Procedure. There were four conditions of testing: written and oral naming, comprehension, and repetition. She completed all conditions on the same session of the same day. Oral and written naming were tested first using an ABBA design to control for category order effects. Subsequently word repetition and spoken word–picture matching were tested for the same items. Within each of the naming and repetition tasks the stimuli were presented in blocks of five items from each category. In the naming tasks, M.E.D. was asked to say or to write the name corresponding to the picture. Each response was scored correct or incorrect. In the word repetition task, the examiner said each word once and the patient was asked to repeat the stimulus immediately after the examiner. In the spoken word–picture matching task, the pictures of the 10 items from a single category were presented in an array. Each name was spoken by the examiner and M.E.D. was required to point to the named item. The order of testing recognition of the 10 items for each category was as follows: names of famous people, object names, and country names.

Results.   The number of correct responses for each condition for each of the three categories are given in Table 1.

A differential effect of both category and condition of testing was demonstrated. M.E.D.'s performance on matching spoken words to pictures was at ceiling for all three categories. By contrast, her oral naming performance was very impaired for all categories, and her performance on the repetition task was weak, but above floor level, for all three categories. However, in the written naming condition there was clearly a category effect. M.E.D. made only one error with the country names, and only two errors with the famous people names, whereas her performance with the object names was very poor (seven errors). This finding clearly corroborates the results of Tests 1 and 2, and provides further evidence of a specific preservation of one category, in this case proper nouns.

M.E.D.'s latency of response (in seconds) was recorded from the time she initiated the first response. Her average speed (all responses other than omissions) for the three categories in the writing tasks are given in Table 2.

It is clear that her response latencies for object names were very much slower than for famous people and country names. Her performance on oral naming and

TABLE 1
Oral and Written Naming, Comprehension and Repetition: Number Correct and Percentage Correct

	Object	Countries	Famous People
Oral naming	1/10	0/10	1/10
%	10	0	10
Written naming	3/10	9/10	8/10
%	30	90	80
Matching spoken words to pictures	10/10	10/10	10/10
%	100	100	100
Repetition	3/10	5/10	4/10
%	30	50	40

Number correct and percentage of total number of errors for common nouns (items from the ONT) and proper nouns (items from the GNT and maps).

TABLE 2
Mean Response Latency ($\bar{X}$RT) in Seconds and Standard
Deviation (SD) for Written Naming and Writing to Dictation Tasks

	$\bar{X}$RT	SD
Written Naming		
Objects	21.7	11.5
Famous people	5.8	4.6
Countries	5.5	2.8
Writing to Dictation		
Objects	22.3	9.0
Famous people	8.6	4.4
Countries	6.0	2.2

repetition tasks was very sparse, providing insufficient data for response latency or for an error analysis. Therefore, only a detailed analysis of her errors in the written naming task will be given. The corpus of errors is given in Appendix 4.

Test 4: Writing to Dictation the Names of Objects (ONT), Low Frequency Common and Proper Nouns (GNT), and Well-known Countries (13.7.92)

The results of the previous three tests demonstrated that M.E.D.'s written naming performance was characterised by a category-specific preservation of proper nouns. Furthermore, the results of both Tests 1 and 2 showed that M.E.D.'s ability to retrieve the written names of low frequency objects was unexpectedly partially preserved, and certainly no worse than her ability to write the names of high frequency objects. To obtain further support for these findings, M.E.D. was asked to write to dictation the names of 10 objects from the ONT, the names of 10 well known countries previously used in Tests 1 and 3, and the names of 10 famous people's names, previously used in Tests 2 and 3. The words of the three categories were alternated in blocks of five items for each category to control for category order effects. Subsequently the 30 low frequency object names from the GNT were spoken aloud for written response. Each response was scored correct or incorrect.

Results.   The number of correct responses for each of the four categories are given in Table 3.

M.E.D.'s ability to write the names of countries and famous people to dictation appeared well preserved in comparison to her ability to write common nouns to dictation. Furthermore, M.E.D.'s ability to write to dictation low frequency object names was relatively preserved considering her severe

TABLE 3
Performance on Writing to Dictation

	No. Correct	% Correct
Objects from the ONT	1/10	10
Objects from the GNT	14/30	46.6
Countries	10/10	100
Famous people	7/10	70

Number correct and percentage of total number of errors for common
nouns (items from the ONT and the GNT) and proper nouns (items
from the GNT and maps).

impairment in writing high frequency object names. The corpus of errors is
given in Appendix 5 and a detailed error analysis follows.

Error Analysis

The corpus of errors obtained in the written naming and dictation tasks obtained
in the four tests have been classified as follows:

1. Omissions: when the patient failed to give an answer or she produced only
one or two letters (e.g. corkscrew-c).
2. Semantic errors, when the patient wrote an incorrect name that was
semantically related to the correct name. 'Degraded' semantic responses in
which M.E.D. produced an incorrect name that was semantically related to the
correct name but was also misspelt (e.g. Canute–Aifed) were included in this
category.
3. Visual approximation to the target: when partial knowledge of the correct
spelling of the target word was demonstrated (e.g. Mona Lisa–Moni.... Mona;
anteater–ant).
4. Miscellaneous: In this case there was no detectable relation with the target
words (e.g. periscope–pejin). Table 4 shows the error distribution.
As shown in Table 4, there was a different pattern of errors for proper nouns
and common nouns. Generally, it appeared that when M.E.D. attempted to
produce a proper noun the errors took the form of incorrect attempts at words
that showed substantial knowledge of the target's spelling (50% of the total
errors) (e.g. Maji Tahal for Taj Mahal). In contrast, when M.E.D. attempted to
write object nouns the most frequent type of failure was either omission (45.5%
of the total errors) or the production of a response totally dissimilar to the target
(13.2% of the total errors), as for example the response cut for the picture

TABLE 4
The Distribution of Errors in Written Naming

	Proper Nouns	Common Nouns
Omission	1	31
%	(6.2)	(45.5)
Semantic errors	7	12
%	(43.7)	(17.6)
Visual approximation	8	16
%	(50)	(23.5)
Miscellaneous	0	9
%		(13.2)

Number correct and percentage of total number of errors for common
nouns (items from the ONT and GNT) and proper nouns (items from
the GNT and maps).

leotard. The percentage of semantic errors in the two categories did appear to
differ (43.7% of the total errors for the proper names category and 17.6% of the
total errors for the object names category). However, it is important to note that
the majority of the semantic errors were substitutions of proper names for object
names (e.g. *Wizard of Oz* for scarecrow, or *Chinese* for chopsticks) or
substitutions of proper names for other proper names (e.g. *Robin Hood* for King
Harold).

A similar pattern of errors emerged in the writing to dictation tasks. When
M.E.D. was trying to write a common name she frequently failed to give any
response (68% of the total errors) or gave an incorrect response bearing no
visual or semantic similarity with the target word (12% of the total errors) as for
example the response *culat* for the spoken word *glove*. She occasionally
produced semantic errors (8% of the total errors). For example, when attempting
to write to dictation the word chopsticks she wrote *Chinese*. There were also
visual approximation errors (12% of the total errors, e.g. "anteater"–*ant*).
However, when she was trying to write proper nouns there were very few errors.
Interestingly, a semantic error was also recorded in this task (e.g. "Elizabeth
I"–*Mary of Scotland*). The other two errors were visual approximations (e.g.
"Napoleon"–*Nato n ol*). Table 5 shows the error distribution.

These results parallel the error analysis of the written naming errors. When
M.E.D. was attempting to produce a proper noun, the few errors showed
substantial knowledge of the target's spelling. However, when she was
attempting to write common nouns the most frequent errors were response
omissions.

TABLE 5
The Distribution of Errors in Writing to Dictation

	Proper Nouns	Common Nouns
Omission	0	17
%		(68)
Semantic errors	1	2
%		(8)
Visual approximation	2	3
%		(12)
Miscellaneous	0	3
%	0	(12)

Number correct and percentage of total number of errors for common
nouns (items from the ONT and GNT) and proper nouns (items from
the GNT and maps).

DISCUSSION

In this study we have described an investigation of the residual word retrieval
skills of a severely aphasic patient. It was found that the patient's word retrieval
abilities were dependent on the form of output. Spoken word retrieval was
compromised whatever the type of input (i.e. spoken words or pictures). In
contrast, written word retrieval was relatively spared for both writing to
dictation and written naming tasks. In summary:

1. M.E.D. was impaired in writing nonwords. This deficit is indicative of
damage to the phoneme-to-grapheme conversion component of the spelling
process. It is therefore assumed that in her case lexical and semantic processing
is required for written output to occur.

2. There was a distinctive pattern of performance across semantic categories.
M.E.D.'s ability to write the names of countries and famous people was
consistently superior to her ability to write the names of objects. This impaired
ability to retrieve common nouns was not a trivial effect of word length, as her
writing of proper nouns was better than object nouns matched for length. The
preservation of the proper nouns category could be considered as indicative of a
double dissociation in the proper nouns category, as several patients are on record
who showed a selective deficit in retrieving well-known people's names (Luchelli
& De Renzi, 1992; McKenna & Warrington, 1980) or in retrieving well-known
people's names and country names (Semenza & Zettin, 1988; 1989).

3. M.E.D. made semantic errors in both written naming and writing to
dictation, not only for proper nouns but also for common nouns. In addition,

some of M.E.D.'s responses were visual approximations to the target. A higher proportion of these errors occurred when the stimuli were proper nouns rather than common nouns. This pattern of results suggests that, at least for the proper nouns category, when the correct orthography could not be retrieved, there was a partial knowledge of the target spelling. Furthermore, there was a higher proportion of omission errors for the common nouns than for proper nouns.

4. M.E.D.'s ability to write the names of low frequency objects was relatively spared as compared with her very impaired ability to write the names of high frequency objects. This finding is unexpected considering those studies that have shown in patients the normal advantage for spelling (as well as reading and naming) high frequency as compared with low frequency common nouns (e.g. Baxter & Warrington, 1985; Newcombe, Oldfield & Wingfield, 1965; Rochford & Williams, 1965; Seymour and Pordas, 1980; and see papers in Patterson, Marshall, & Coltheart, 1985).

We have evidence that M.E.D. could spell a small vocabulary of country names and a small vocabulary of famous people's names fairly accurately. The majority of object names were spelt very inaccurately. These observations raise two issues of theoretical interest: at what level in the system does M.E.D.'s spelling deficit arise, and what is the significance of the category effects.

In discussing the candidates for the locus of M.E.D.'s impairment, we assume that M.E.D.'s residual written naming and writing to dictation skills require semantic representations, orthographic representations, and an access process that mediates between them. In this, we subscribe to a model that implies that written naming and writing to dictation could be supported by the use of a direct route from the semantic representations to the orthographic representations, which bypasses the phonological representations (see Ellis, 1982; Ellis & Young, 1988; Morton, 1980). Indeed the qualitative and quantitative similarities between M.E.D.'s performance in written naming and in writing to dictation tasks provide support for such a model.

First we must consider whether the locus of impairment responsible for M.E.D.'s unusual pattern of preserved and impaired spelling abilities is in the semantic representations. Her comprehension of object names, which she could not write, appears to be well preserved and she could correctly match spoken words to pictures. Furthermore, in the naming tasks when she failed to retrieve the written name of an object, she frequently gave evidence of knowing the object shown in the picture. In addition, some of the errors she made when trying to write common nouns also seemed to indicate largely preserved comprehension of these items. For example, when attempting to name the picture of a basket, she wrote instead *backet*, and when attempting to name the picture of a kangaroo, she wrote instead *Kang*. It is implausible to suggest that errors such as these are due to defective comprehension of the to-be-named item. In addition, if the semantic errors produced by M.E.D. were the result of damage to the semantic representations, then she should have made semantic errors in comprehension tasks and in tasks involving oral output. However, as we reported earlier, M.E.D. did not make any errors in comprehension tasks requiring her to match spoken words to pictures. Given the rapid progressive decline of her language skills it was unfortunately not possible to formally test her performance on reading aloud and oral naming tasks. However, in the few sparse observations that we made initially, semantic errors were never detected in her residual oral naming and reading aloud. Indeed our observations provide evidence for Caramazza and Hillis's (1990) argument that semantic errors may arise at the level of the phonological and/or orthographical representations.

If we are right in rejecting a semantic representation account of M.E.D.'s impairment then we are led to argue that the only plausible candidate would be damage to the orthographic representations or to the process by which these are accessed.

During our investigations, the severity of her dysphasia increased, and, at a stage when she was no longer able to write at all, her comprehension became implicated. A similar pattern of preserved and of impaired categories in her comprehension emerged using word picture matching tests (see McNeil et al., in press). Thus, in comprehension tasks a selective preservation of famous people's names and country names was documented. It is necessary, therefore, to consider why a category specific deficit demonstrated at an output level in writing tasks reoccurs later in comprehension tasks. Is this conjunction accidental or principled? If it is principled, how do we account for a double deficit affecting almost the same categories?

One suggestion is that the proper nouns have properties that require common computational procedures underpinning the accessing of the semantic representations and the orthographic and/or phonological representations. There is already evidence that the computational procedures responsible for accessing semantic and orthographic and/or phonological representations of common nouns can be independent of those of proper nouns. Several patients have been found who show selective sparing of access to the semantic representations for proper nouns but impaired access to common nouns (Van Lanker Klein, 1990; Warrington & McCarthy, 1987). Furthermore, patients with a selective proper noun anomia can have intact proper noun semantic representations (Luchelli & De Renzi, 1992; McKenna & Warrington, 1980; Semenza & Zettin 1988; 1989). It is proposed that these common computational procedures have two roles: they access the relevant representations in the semantic system and they activate the orthographic system in preparation for the incoming semantic representations. It is suggested that M.E.D.'s deficit would be in the common noun computational procedures involved in both accessing semantic and activating orthographic representations.

We turn now to the significance of the category effects: if proper and common nouns involve different kinds of computational procedures, the properties which make proper nouns different from common nouns must be specified. One obvious difference between proper nouns and common nouns is that common nouns designate all the entities sharing a set of attributes, whereas proper nouns have a single high probability referent. Furthermore, in the case of names of famous people and of countries, they have an unambiguous referent that is independent of the context. Following this distinction, the preservation of the proper noun category in our patient might be explained as a consequence of the closer and more direct links that proper noun have with their unique invariant referent. These special and unique properties may require different and dedicated computational procedures both in the semantic representations and in the orthographic representations.

We also wish to suggest that there are other differentiating features between proper nouns and common nouns. Proper nouns are acquired later in life than common nouns. Indeed, there are studies indicating that one of the factors affecting the ability to retrieve words is their age of acquisition (Rochford & Williams, 1962). Furthermore, proper nouns might not only be acquired later in life, but there might be different ways in which these words and their meanings are learnt. For example, Johnson-Laird (1983) has suggested that low frequency common nouns are learnt verbally by definition, whereas high frequency common nouns are more likely to be acquired by other, more direct, means. Proper nouns may be verbally acquired like low frequency common nouns; that is, by definition. If they can be acquired as definitions, their meanings are more likely to be circumscribed and crystallised, because their definitions will prevent them from taking on radically new meanings. Perhaps, in this context, it should be remembered that M.E.D. showed a lack of the normally robust frequency effect in addition to her selective preservation of proper nouns. Low frequency common nouns are also learnt later in life. They, too, may enjoy a more circumscribed and crystallised meaning than high frequency common nouns.

However, the question remains to be answered as to whether there is an inevitable conjunction of the selective preservation of proper nouns and the lack of a high frequency effect for common nouns. Further cases will establish whether there is a meaningful relationship between the procedures for retrieving proper names and low frequency common nouns.

Manuscript received 20 January 1993
Manuscript accepted 30 April 1993

REFERENCES

Barry, C., & Seymour, P.H.K. (1988). Lexical priming and sound-to-spelling contingency effects in nonword spelling. *The Quarterly Journal of Experimental Psychology, 40A (1)*, 5–40.

Baxter, D.M., & Warrington, E.K. (1985). Category-specific phonological dysgraphia. *Neuropsychologia*, 23, 653–666.

Baxter-Versi, D.M. (1987). *Acquired spelling disorders.* Unpublished doctoral dissertation, London University, London.

Bub, D., & Kertesz, A. (1982). Deep agraphia. *Brain and Language*, 17, 146–165.

Caramazza, A., & Hillis, A.E. (1990). Where do semantic errors come from? *Cortex*, 26, 95–122.

Ellis, A.W. (1982). Spelling and writing (and reading and speaking). In A.W. Ellis (Ed.), *Normality and pathology in cognitive functions.* London: Academic Press.

Ellis, A.W., & Young, A.W. (1988). *Human cognitive neuropsychology.* London: Lawrence Erlbaum Associates Ltd.

Goodglass, H., Klein, B., Carey, P., & Jones, K. (1966). Specific semantic word categories in aphasia. *Cortex*, 2, 74–89.

Hillis, A.E., & Caramazza, A. (1991). Category-specific naming and comprehension impairment: a double dissociation. *Brain*, 114, 2081–2094.

Johnson-Laird, P.N. (1983). *Mental models.* Cambridge: Cambridge University Press.

Kremin, H. (1987). Is there more than ah-oh-oh? Alternative strategies for writing and repeating lexically. In M. Coltheart, R. Sartori, & R. Job (Eds.), *The cognitive neuropsychology of language.* (pp. 295–335). London: Lawrence Erlbaum Associates Ltd.

Luchelli, F., & De Renzi, E. (1992). Proper name anomia. *Cortex*, 28, 221–230.

McKenna, P., & Warrington, E.K. (1978). Category-specific naming preservation: a single case study. *Journal of Neurology, Neurosurgery and Psychiatry*, 41, 571–574.

McKenna, P., & Warrington, E.K. (1980). Testing for nominal dysphasia. *Journal of Neurology, Neurosurgery and Psychiatry*, 43, 781–788.

McNeil, J.E., Cipolotti, L., & Warrington, E.M. (in press). Accessibility of proper names. *Neuropsychologia.*

Morton, J. (1980). The logogen model and orthographic structure. In U. Frith (Ed.), *Cognitive processes in spelling.* London: Academic Press.

Newcombe, F., Oldfield, R.C., & Wingfield, A. (1965). Object naming by dysphasic patients. *Nature (London)*, 207, 1217–1218.

Patterson, K., Marshall, J.C., & Coltheart, M. (1985). *Surface dyslexia.* London: Lawrence Erlbaum Associates Ltd.

Rochford, G., & Williams, M. (1962). Studies in the development and breakdown of the use of names. *Journal of Neurology, Neurosurgery and Psychiatry*, 25, 222–233.

Rochford, G., & Williams, M. (1965). The development and breakdown of the use of names. Part IV. The effects of word frequency. *Journal of Neurology, Neurosurgery and Psychiatry*, 28, 407–433.

Roeltgen, D.P., Rothi, L.J., & Heilman, K.M. (1986). Linguistic semantic agraphia: A dissociation of the spelling system from semantics. *Brain and Language*, 27, 257–280.

Saffran, E.M., Bogyo, L.C., Schwartz, M.F., & Marin, O.S.M. (1980). Does deep dyslexia reflect right-hemisphere reading? In M. Coltheart, K. Patterson, & J.C. Marshall (Eds.), *Deep dyslexia.* London: Routledge & Kegan.

Schonell, F.J. (1942). *Backwardness in basic subjects.* Edinburgh: Oliver & Boyd.

Semenza, C., & Zettin, M. (1988). Generating proper names: a case of selective inability. *Cognitive Neuropsychology*, 5, 711–721.

Semenza, C., & Zettin, M. (1989). Evidence from aphasia for the role of proper names as pure referring expressions. *Nature*, 342, 678–679.

Seymour, P.H.K., & Pordas, C.D. (1980). Lexical and non-lexical processing of spelling in dyslexia. In U. Frith (Ed.), *Cognitive processes in spelling.* London: Academic Press.

Shallice, T. (1981). Phonological agraphia and the lexical route in writing. *Brain*, 104, 413–429.

Thorndike, E.L., & Lorge, I. (1944). *The teachers' word book of 30,000 words.* New York: Teachers College Press, Columbia University.

Van Lanker, D., & Klein, K. (1990). Preserved recognition of familiar personal names in global aphasia. *Brain and Language, 39,* 511–529.

Warrington, E.K. (1984). *Recognition memory test.* Windsor, UK: NFER-Nelson.

Warrington, E.K., & Clegg, F. (this issue). Selective preservation of place names in an aphasic patient: A short report. *Memory.*

Warrington, E.K., & James, M. (1991). *The visual object and space perception battery.* UK: Thames Valley Test Battery.

Warrington, E.K., & McCarthy, R.A. (1987). Categories of knowledge: Further fractionations and an attempted integration. *Brain, 110,* 1273–1296.

APPENDIX 1

8.7.92 Test 1: Morning, first assessment. Written naming.

Oldfield picture names				*Maps of well known countries*			
Stimulus	R.	E.T.	T.L.	Stimulus	R.	E.T.	T.L.
Watch	—	O.	AA	America	✓		AA
Basket	—	O.	A	England	✓		AA
Clock	—	O.	A	France	✓		AA
Key	—	O.	A	Germany	Holand	S.	AA
Glove	—	O.	43	Spain	✓		A
Drum	—	O.	40	India	✓		46
Tap	—	O.	32	Italy	✓		41
Anchor	—	O.	26	Scotland	✓		30
Cigarette	—	O.	22	Wales	✓		15
Screw	—	O.	20	Ireland	Ireand	V.A.	14

8.7.92 Test 1: Afternoon, second assessment. ONT: Written and Oral naming.

	Oral naming		*Written naming*		
Stimulus	R.	E.T.	R.	E.T.	T.L.
Watch	fol	M.	awar	M.	AA
Book	b	P.A.	✓		AA
Boat	✓		—	O.	AA
Shoe	✓		—	O.	AA
Chair	✓		—	O.	AA
Key	ki..kia	P.A.	—	O.	A
Basket	✓		—	O.	A
Glove	Kuel	M.	gluve	V.A.	43
Drum	✓		—	O.	40
Tap	t..ta	P.A.	eaut	M.	32
Anchor	fok..foks	M.	—	O.	26
Cigarette	—		cizabet	V.A.	22
Comb	✓		—	O.	19
Scissors	kukel	M.	schilline	M.	8

T.L. = Thorndike and Lorge (1944) word frequency count. AA refers to >100 per million, A refers to >50 per million but <100 per million. * = frequency count not reported. R. = response. E.T. = error type. — = no response. O. = omission error. S. = semantic error. V.A. = visual approximation. M. = miscellaneous. P.A. = phonological approximation.

APPENDIX 2

9.7.92 Test 1: Third assessment. Written naming.

Oldfield picture names				Maps of well known countries			
Stimulus	R.	E.T.	T.L.	Stimulus	R.	E.T.	T.L.
Book	✓		AA	England	✓		AA
Chair	✓		AA	France	✓		AA
Watch	—	O.	AA	Germany	Holland	S.	AA
Boat	poat	V.A.	AA	America	✓		AA
Shoe	sholk	V.A.	AA	Spain	✓		A
Key	✓		A	India	✓		46
Basket	baseuit	V.A.	A	Italy	✓		41
Glove	gaunt	S.	43	Scotland	✓		30
Drum	dum	V.A.	40	Wales	✓		15
Tap	✓		32	Ireland	✓		14
Anchor	✓		26				
Cigarette	cigare	S.	22				
Screw	✓		20				
Comb	✓		19				
Typewriter	olivetti	S.	12				
Windmill	millwind	V.A.	11				
Microscope	micno	V.A.	9				
Scissors	✓		8				
Dice	—	O.	8				
Anvil	✓		7				
Horseshoe	—	O.	4				
Octopus	octup	V.A.	2				
Bagpipes	pipe-bag	V.A.	1				
Syringe	—	O.	0.83				

T.L. = Thorndike and Lorge (1944) word frequency count. AA refers to >100 per million, A refers to >50 per million but <100 per million. * = frequency count not reported. R. = response. E.T. = error type. — = no response. O. = omission error. S. = semantic error. V.A. = visual approximation. M. = miscellaneous.

APPENDIX 3

10.7.92 Test 2: Written naming of graded difficulty common nouns and proper nouns.

Stimulus	R.	E.T.	T.L.
shuttlecock	sculac	M.	15
retort	—	O.	15
turtle	✓		13
boar	truffed	S.	11
bellows	fires	S.	8
radius	✓		6
cowl	—	O.	5
buoy	—	O.	5
kangaroo	Kang	V.A.	2
handcuffs	cuff fists	S.	2
centaur	✓		2
scarecrow	Wizard of oz	S.	1
thimble	✓		1
corkscrew	screws	V.A.	1
sundial	sunflake	S.	1
monocle	✓		1
pagoda	kew	S.	1
mitre	pope	S.	<1
sextant	greeninch	S.	<1
periscope	Pejin	M.	<1
blinkers	—	O.	<1
anteater	—	O.	<1
sporran	✓		*
tutu	✓		*
leotard	cut	M.	*
trampoline	lam	M.	*
tweezers	—	O.	*
tassle	Horse....bell	M.	*
chopsticks	chown palw	V.A.	*
yashmak	masu	M.	*
South America	✓		AA
Lincoln	✓		A
Italy	✓		41
Shakespeare	Shaki kuep	V.A.	24
Napoleon	✓		19
King Harold	Robin Hood	S.	12
Hitler	✓		7
Parthenon	Athens	S.	2
Disraeli	Dis	V.A.	2
Marx	✓		2
Ghandi	✓		1
Eros	✓		1
Canute	Aifed	S.	1
Lenin	✓		1
Eiffel Tower	✓		<1

Stimulus	R.	E.T.	T.L.
Kremlin	✓		<1
Taj Mahal	Maji Tahal	V.A.	*
Mao Tse Tung	Moa	V.A.	*
Castro	Cuba	S.	*
Rasputin	Raptio	V.A.	*
Trotsky	Trojst	V.A.	*
Virginia Woolf	✓		*
Henry VIII	✓		*
Elizabeth 1	✓		*
Louis Armstrong	✓		*
Joan of Arc	✓		*
Lawrence of Arabia	✓		*
Q. Victoria	✓		*
Florence Nightingale	—	O.	*
Mona Lisa	✓		*

T.L. = Thorndike and Lorge (1944) word frequency count. AA refers to >100 per million, A refers to >50 per million but <100 per million. * = frequency count not reported. R. = response. E.T. = error type. — = no response. O. = omission error. S. = semantic error. V.A. = visual approximation. M. = miscellaneous.

APPENDIX 4

13.7.92 Test 3: Written naming of well-known proper names of countries and famous people, objects names from the ONT and from the GNT.

Stimulus	R.	E.T.	T.L.
America	✓		AA
England	✓		AA
Germany	Holland	S.	AA
France	✓		AA
Spain	✓		A
India	✓		46
Italy	✓		41
Scotland	✓		30
Wales	✓		15
Ireland	✓		14
Napoleon	✓		19
Hitler	✓		7
Ghandi	✓		1
Joan of Arc	✓		*
Lawrence of Arabia	T.H.		*
Q. Victoria	✓		*
Mona Lisa	Moni	V.A.	*
Elizabeth 1	✓		*
Henry VII	✓		*
Louis Armstrong	✓		*

Stimulus	R.	E.T.	T.L.
Basket	Backet	V.A.	A
Clock	—	O.	A
Key	✓		A
Glove	✓		43
Drum	—	O.	40
Tap	✓		32
Anchor	—	O.	26
Cigarette	cicar	V.A.	22
Screw	scum	V.A.	20
Typewriter	olvilla	S.	12

T.L. = Thorndike and Lorge (1944) word frequency count. AA refers to >100 per million, A refers to >50 per million but <100 per million. * = frequency count not reported. R. = response. E.T. = error type. — = no response. O. = omission error. S. = semantic error. V.A. = visual approximation. M. = miscellaneous.

APPENDIX 5

13.7.92 Test 4: Writing to dictation of well-known proper names of countries and famous people, objects names from the ONT and from the GNT.

Stimulus	R.	E.T.	T.L.
America	✓		AA
England	✓		AA
Germany	✓		AA
France	✓		AA
Spain	✓		A
India	✓		46
Italy	✓		41
Scotland	✓		30
Wales	✓		15
Ireland	✓		14
Napoleon	Nato n ol	V.A.	19
Hitler	✓		7
Ghandi	✓		1
Joan of Arc	✓		*
Lawrence of Arabia	✓		*
Q. Victoria	✓		*
Mona Lisa	Moni...Mona	V.A.	*
Elizabeth 1	Mary of Scotland	S.	*
Henry VIII	✓		*
Louis Armstrong	✓		*
Basket	Backet	V.A.	A
Clock	—	O.	A
Key	✓		A
Glove	culat	M.	43

Stimulus	R.	E.T.	T.L.
Drum	—	O.	40
Tap	—	O.	32
Anchor	—	O.	26
Cigarette	cigatte	V.A.	22
Screw	—	O.	20
Typewriter	oliva	S.	12
shuttlecock	—	O.	15
retort	restia	M.	15
turtle	tu	O.	13
boar	—	O.	11
bellows	✓		8
radius	✓		6
cowl	✓		5
buoy	✓		5
kangaroo	✓		2
handcuffs	—	O.	2
centaur	—	O.	2
scarecrow	—	O.	1
thimble	✓		1
corkscrew	c	O.	1
sundial	✓		1
monocle	✓		1
pagoda	✓		1
mitre	✓		<1
sextant	—	O.	<1
periscope	pegino	V.A.	<1
blinkers	✓		<1
anteater	—	O.	<1
sporran	✓		*
tutu	✓		*
leotard	lep ope	M.	*
trampoline	—	O.	*
tweezers	✓		*
tassle	—	O.	*
chopsticks	chinese	S.	*
yashmak	—	O.	*

T.L. = Thorndike and Lorge (1944) word frequency count. AA refers to >100 per million, A refers to >50 per million but <100 per million. * = frequency count not reported. R. = response. E.T. = error type. — = no response. O. = omission error. S. = semantic error. V.A. = visual approximation. M. = miscellaneous.

MEMORY, 1993, *1* (4), 313–328

Selective Preservation of a Lexical Category in Aphasia: Dissociations in Comprehension of Body Parts and Geographical Place Names Following Focal Brain Lesion

Harold Goodglass
Boston University School of Medicine, USA

Arthur Wingfield
Brandeis University, USA

The selective dissociation of memory for proper names is discussed in the context of a review of dissociations involving broadly defined *vs* narrowly defined semantic categories in brain damaged adults. Two narrowly defined categories for which dissociations have been reported are body parts (selectively impaired in comprehension) and geographical place names (selectively preserved in comprehension). In this study, 167 aphasic patients were tested for their ability to correctly identify body parts and map locations from spoken names, relative to a baseline for correct responses on general word discrimination (object identification). Wernicke's aphasics and Global aphasics both had significantly more success in pointing to named map locations and significantly worse performance in pointing to named body parts than they had in selecting other objects from multiple choice. Anomic aphasics showed precisely the opposite pattern of results. Other aphasic subgroups (Broca's aphasics, Mixed Nonfluent aphasics, Conduction aphasics, Transcortical Motor and Transcortical Sensory aphasics, and Mixed Fluent aphasics) did not show significant deviations in either direction. We suggest that the selective preservation for place names may be related to their status as proper names.

INTRODUCTION

Investigations of brain-injured individuals have brought to light a range of dissociations in naming or comprehension that are limited to words of a particular category. Categories vulnerable to such dissociations have widely

Requests for reprints should be sent to Dr. Harold Goodglass, Aphasia Research Center, Boston VA Medical Center, 150 South Huntington Avenue, Boston, MA 02130, USA.

This research was supported by PHS Grants DC 00081 and AG 04517 from the National Institutes of Health. We thank Merri Rosen for Assistance in the latter stages of this project.

varying criteria. They include broad semantic categories like animate *vs* inanimate objects (Warrington & McCarthy, 1983; Warrington & Shallice, 1984); narrower groupings like body-part names (Dennis, 1976; McKenna & Warrington, 1978), or fruits and vegetables (Hart, Berndt, & Caramazza, 1985); particular symbol systems, such as numbers or letters (Goodglass, Klein, Carey, & Jones, 1966); and linguistically defined criteria such as common *vs* proper names (Semenza & Zettin, 1989). In this paper we present new observations concerning opposite types of dissociations in two narrow categories: body parts and geographical place names. As the latter are proper names, we consider whether selective preservation or loss may be related to this property.

When one speaks of difficulty in memory for proper names, the operation referred to is usually the retrieval of the name for a particular unique referent. This is an important point to make, because in the few reported cases of selective retrieval difficulty for proper names, it is only the referential function that is impaired (Semenza & Zettin, 1989). The patient who is affected has no abnormality in retrieving names (e.g. "boys' names") as a list, so long as these names do not have to be retrieved as specific names for particular persons.

Lucchelli and De Renzi (1992) report a case of a patient who, after a left thalamic infarction, recovered from a mild general naming and verbal memory deficit, but who was left with a proper-name anomia specific to people's names. The fact that he could readily supply biographical information, either from a picture of the person or a verbal description, suggests that the identity of the person was not lost; he could also match the spoken name to the correct photograph. To Lucchelli and De Renzi, the deficit thus appeared to be one of access to the phonological output system in an otherwise preserved semantic system. Although this apparent fractionation of proper-name performance is extreme, Lucchelli and De Renzi correctly note that difficulty in proper-name finding is virtually a hallmark of normal aging. Difficulty with proper names represents, in healthy elderly adults, one of the most common memory complaints (Cohen & Faulkner, 1986).

It is probably appropriate to treat dissociations affecting word retrieval and those affecting word comprehension under the single heading of category-specific dissociations of lexical processing. This heading would include either the selective impairment or the selective sparing of the category or categories involved. The reason for such inclusiveness is that selective dissociations have been observed for a limited set of specific category types; categories from this set that are selectively impaired for auditory comprehension in some individuals may appear as selectively preserved for production in others (e.g. body part names [Goodglass & Budin, 1988]). In some cases, these dissociations may affect performance in a single modality (e.g. naming); in other cases they may be shown to extend across many modalities, suggesting a category-specific disorder of semantic knowledge (Warrington, 1975; Warrington & McCarthy, 1987). This has led to the conclusion that there are both category-specific and modality-specific meaning systems (McCarthy & Warrington, 1988; 1990).

One must acknowledge that the selection of objects or symbols to represent various categories could accidentally produce exemplars that happen to be more difficult or uncommon than exemplars chosen to represent some other category. This is an important caution, given that object–name frequency is known to influence naming ability in normal subjects (Goodglass, Theurkauf, & Wingfield, 1984; Wingfield, 1968) as well as in aphasic patients (Newcombe, Oldfield, & Wingfield, 1965; Newcombe, Oldfield, Ratcliff, & Wingfield, 1971). Concept familiarity and visual complexity of the object pictures chosen to represent object categories can also have effects (Stewart, Parkin, & Hunkin, 1992). As we have argued elsewhere, however, (Goodglass, Wingfield, Hyde, & Theurkauf, 1986), the sheer number of reported cases that manifest dissociations within the same set of categories makes such frequency-based or object-representation explanations unlikely.

In spite of the commonalities among category based lexical dissociations, they almost certainly represent the effects of different mechanisms. In the case of the broad categories 'animate' *vs* 'inanimate', Warrington and McCarthy (1987) suggest that the distinctions may depend on the sensory input modality that is most salient to the meaning representation of the item. In fact, some semantic category-specific dissociations have been found to be confined to a single mode of stimulation, such as the case of optic anomia for animals, reported by Hart and Gordon (1992). Obviously, an account in terms of sensory modality would not explain why Warrington and McCarthy's (1987) patient could select 18 out of 18 orally named countries from a multiple choice of six written words in each trial, but could select only 4 of 18 boys' names in the same type of task.

In the present study we focused on two category-based dissociations that have previously been reported: the selective preservation of the comprehension of geographical place names, and the selective impairment for the comprehension of body-part names. Impairment in the ability to point correctly to parts of one's body was originally described in the context of a breakdown of a somatosensory body schema (Munk, 1890). Pick's assignment of the term 'autotopagnosia' to such failures defines them as due to a lack of appreciation of body topology. In their review, Poeck and Orgass (1971) point out that most of the described cases were aphasic patients and that it remained to be shown that their disorder was not purely one of language comprehension, rather than of body schema. Subsequent studies of aphasic patients by Assal and Buttet (1973), Semenza and Goodglass (1985), and Goodglass and Budin (1988), made it clear that selective impairment in identifying body parts from the spoken name by aphasics is a purely language disorder, unrelated to any impairment in the nonverbal awareness of body parts. The latter authors demonstrated that their patient could perform perfectly when the words were presented in writing. He could also point to the proper location for named clothing articles on an unclothed outline manikin, after having failed to identify the corresponding body parts (e.g. collar *vs* neck; belt *vs* waist; sock *vs* foot).

Selectively preserved comprehension of geographical place names was first reported by Wapner and Gardner (1979), and later confirmed by Goodglass and Butters (1988). Relatively preserved ability to name countries, in contrast to animals, colours, and common objects, along with perfectly preserved auditory comprehension of names of countries was reported by McKenna and Warrington (1978). Goodglass and Butters (1988) found that Broca's, Wernicke's, Global, and Conduction aphasics had a preponderance of superior performance on geographical place names, in comparison with their success on body-part identification from their spoken names. The differences in performance were most extreme in the case of Wernicke's and Global aphasics. Anomic aphasics, on the other hand, had a very marked superiority for comprehension of body-part names over geographical place names (Goodglass & Butters, 1988). In the present study we used a new and larger sample of aphasic patients, and compared patients' performance on the two target categories with their performance on the comprehension of assorted object names, a measure that served as a neutral reference point.

By such criteria as word-frequency and age of acquisition, one would assume that body-part names are an easier set for comprehension than are geographical place names. The mode of testing for these two word categories is similar; both require the subject to identify a referent by pointing to its location. Although the response for body parts involves pointing to one's body, investigators have reported similar levels of performance when subjects pointed to a drawn manikin (Semenza & Goodglass, 1985). (See also Benedet & Goodglass, 1989, for parallels between pointing to body parts and selecting cut-out body parts.) In considering the analogies between the map and body part location tasks, one must not overlook the fact that impairments related to extrapersonal space may be dissociated from those involving one's own body (Newcombe & Ratcliff, 1990; Semmes, Weinstein, Ghent, & Teuber, 1963).

The performance of normal subjects provides a useful index of the relative difficulty of the several tests in the absence of any language comprehension disorders. Borod, Goodglass, and Kaplan (1980) published norms on these tests obtained from a population similar in age and education to the aphasics. Converting their scores to percentages, their normals scored 99.4% correct on body parts; 98.3% on word discrimination (used here as a neutral task); and 87.1% on geographical place names. This accords well with the assumption that the average adult may miss one or two map questions, but rarely a body part. Noting that anomic aphasics, of all aphasic subgroups, have minimal lexical comprehension disorder, might raise the possibility that the anomics in the Goodglass and Butters (1988) study were simply following normal expectations by scoring worse on maps than on body parts. This is one of the possibilities (effects of intrinsic test difficulty) that we attempt in this study to tease out from general auditory comprehension level and diagnosis-specific dissociations.

METHOD

Subjects

The data source for this study were the records of 167 aphasic patients who had been seen and tested at the Aphasia Research Center in Boston. Of the 167 patients, 18 were classified as having Broca's aphasia, 25 were Mixed (anterior) Nonfluent aphasics, 10 were Transcortical Motor aphasics, 31 had Wernicke's aphasia, 13 had Conduction aphasia, 14 had Anomic aphasia, 16 had Mixed (posterior) Fluent aphasia, 10 had Transcortical Sensory aphasia, and 30 had Global aphasia. All of the patients used in this study had been diagnosed as a result of confirmed lesions to the perisylvian region of the left hemisphere as determined by CT scan or MRI. The only criterion for inclusion was that subjects had scores available for all three tests of interest (Word Discrimination, Body-part Identification, and Map Orientation), and that not more than one of these showed a potential ceiling effect.

Descriptive information for the complete patient group is given in Table 1. Diagnostic classifications were determined by a consensus among staff neurologists and neuropsychologists, and by the pattern of performance on the Boston Diagnostic Aphasia Examination (BDAE) (Goodglass & Kaplan, 1983). The term 'Mixed Nonfluent' is used as defined by Goodglass and Kaplan (1983) to refer to nonfluent aphasics with impaired comprehension. The term 'Mixed Fluent' is used as a classification for patients who had features of Wernicke's, Anomic, or Conduction aphasia, but were not considered classifiable in one of those three categories.

Stimuli and Procedures

Each of the subjects was seen individually and was given each of the following tests, either in one or two testing sessions. Two of the tests (Word Discrimination and Body-part identification) were taken from the BDAE (Goodglass & Kaplan, 1983), and the remaining test (Map Orientation) was taken from the supplementary test battery routinely given to patients seen at the Aphasia Research Center.

Word Discrimination and Object Identification.   The word discrimination subtest of the BDAE consists of two cards, one card bearing six examples each of objects (chair, key, glove, feather, hammock, cactus), letters (L, H, R, T, S, G), and forms (circle, spiral, square, triangle, cone, star), and the other card with six examples each of pictures depicting actions (smoking, drinking, running,

TABLE 1
Descriptive Information for the Complete Patient Group

	(1) Wernicke's (n=31)	(2) Global (n=30)	(3) Anomic (n=14)	(4) Broca's (n=18)	(5) Mixed Nonfluent (n=25)	(6) Transcortical Motor (n=10)	(7) Conduction (n=13)	(8) Mixed Fluent (n=16)	(9) Transcortical Sensory (n=10)
Age (years)									
Mean	58.6	54.8	56.0	54.9	56.5	60.7	58.2	62.1	56.2
Range	20–82	26–71	28–66	38–66	36–70	51–71	41–80	50–78	41–78
S.D.	6.0	10.5	9.8	8.1	8.3	6.4	12.1	8.9	10.4
Education (years)									
Mean	12.7	13.0	11.2	12.5	12.1	11.8	12.0	12.0	12.0
Range	6–18	8–20	8–18	8–16	3–18	8–14	8–14	6–18	8–16
S.D.	3.0	2.8	3.2	1.9	3.5	1.7	1.5	3.2	2.1
Gender									
M/F	31/–	29/1	14/–	18/–	25/–	10/–	12/1	15/1	10/–
Time Post-onset (months)									
Mean	5.1	6.8	3.4	8.9	10.8	2.4	3.3	3.6	3.9
Range	<1–72	1–48	1–9	<1–88	1–42	1–5	<1–20	1–21	<1–20
S.D.	13.1	9.4	2.7	21.4	12.8	1.5	5.2	5.0	5.8
Etiology									
CVA/Trauma	29/2	28/2	11/3	18/–	25/–	10/–	13/–	15/1	9/1

Summary of patient information for each of the nine aphasic subgroups, showing mean, range, and standard deviation (S.D.) for age at time of testing, years of formal education, and time (in months) between stroke or injury and time of testing (time post-onset). Also indicated are the distributions of patient gender (male, female), and sources of the lesions, whether due to a cerebro-vascular accident (CVA), or penetrating head injury (trauma).

sleeping, falling, dripping), colours (blue, brown, red, pink, grey, purple), and numbers (7, 42, 700, 1936, 15, 7000).

In the administration of this test, each of the cards is presented separately and the patient is allowed to look over all the pictures on the particular card being presented. The subject is then asked to point to each picture or symbol on the card by saying, "Show me ———." Following the procedures outlined in the BDAE, correct identification was scored 2 points if the identification occurred within five seconds, 1 point otherwise, and 0 points if the object or symbol could not be identified. The maximum score on word discrimination was thus 72 (36 x 2 = 72).

Body Part Identification.   Patients were asked to point to 18 body parts on their own body as each was named aloud (ear, nose, shoulder, knee, eyelid, ankle, chest, neck, middle finger, wrist, thumb, thigh, chin, elbow, lips, eyebrow, cheek, index finger). Following the BDAE scoring procedure for this subtest, 1 point was scored if identification occurred promptly (within five seconds) and ½-point if the body part was identified correctly, but only after a long hesitation (i.e. greater than five seconds). As part of this subtest, right–left discrimination was also tested. For this test the subject was asked to point to his or her right ear, left shoulder, left knee, right ankle, right wrist, left thumb, right elbow, and left cheek. Two additional points were added to the subject's score if the subject was correct on all eight discriminations. (Credit was given so long as the right–left discrimination was correct, even if the body part itself was not indicated correctly.) The maximum score was thus 20 points (1 × 18 + 2 = 20). (Although actual body parts were used in these procedures, as indicated previously, other research has shown that similar performance is obtained whether the patient points on himself or herself, or on a picture of a human figure [Semenza & Goodglass, 1985].)

Map Orientation.   The patient was presented with an outline map of the United States and was asked to indicate by pointing on the map, or in the appropriate off-map direction, to the location of 14 geographical features or locations (Europe, Hawaii, Atlantic Ocean, Canada, New York, Pacific Ocean, Mexico, California, Miami, Maine, San Francisco, Mississippi River, Chicago, 'Rockies'). Subjects received 1 point for each. For credit the patient needed to point merely in the correct general area on the outline map; locations such as Canada, Europe, and Mexico were given credit if the patient was able to indicate the correct general direction relative to the US map by pointing. (Maximum score = 14.) Because of differences in maximum possible scores across the three tests, all scores were converted to percentages for analysis.

RESULTS

Correlations

Table 2 shows correlations among the three tests: Word Discrimination *vs* Body Part Identification (WD x BP), Word Discrimination *vs* Map Orientation (WD x MAPs), and Body Part Identification *vs* Map Orientation (BP x MAPs). The first column of figures gives the number of subjects in each of the subgroups. The symbols to the right of the correlation values give their levels of significance when this occurred.

Because all three measures of interest involve the factor of auditory comprehension, the effect of lesion severity would be expected to impose some degree of positive correlation between them. This positive correlation is apparent in the top row of Table 2, where all 167 subjects are pooled. The differences between correlations, however, are revealing. There is a substantial overall correlation ($r = 0.76$) between Body Part Identification and Word Discrimination, and this correlation is significant in seven of the nine diagnostic subgroups, dropping below the 0.05 level only for the Transcortical Motor aphasics ($r = 0.45$) and the Conduction aphasics ($r = 0.36$) where the number of subjects per group is small.

In contrast, the overall correlation of Word Discrimination with Map Orientation is only $r = 0.22$. This correlation is numerically smaller than that between Word Discrimination and Body Part Identification in all nine subgroups, and falls below the 0.05 level of significance in seven of the nine

TABLE 2
Correlations Among the Three Tests

		Product-Moment Correlations (r)		
Type	*(n)*	*WDxBP*	*WDxMAP*	*BPxMAP*
All Subjects	(167)	0.76***	0.22*	0.26**
(1) Wernicke's Aphasia	(31)	0.80***	0.39*	0.52**
(2) Global Aphasia	(30)	0.38*	0.25	0.09
(3) Anomic Aphasia	(14)	0.78***	0.43	0.11
(4) Broca's Aphasia	(18)	0.75***	0.37	0.43
(5) Mixed Nonfluent Aphasia	(25)	0.51*	-0.04	0.09
(6) Transcortical Motor Aphasia	(10)	0.45	-0.41	-0.15
(7) Conduction Aphasia	(13)	0.36	0.35	-0.01
(8) Mixed Fluent Aphasia	(16)	0.79***	-0.26	-0.15
(9) Transcortial Sensory Aphasia	(10)	0.81**	0.72*	0.64*

Product-moment correlations among scores on Word Discrimination (WD). Body Part Identification (BP), and Map Orientation (MAPs) for all subjects ($n = 167$) and for each of the nine patient subgroups. (*$P < 0.05$; **$PP < 0.01$; ***$P < 0.001$)

subgroups. The exceptions are Wernicke's aphasics ($r = 0.39$) and Transcortical Sensory aphasics ($r = 0.72$). Because there were only ten subjects within the latter group, the r-value is very unreliable. The pattern of correlations between Map Orientation and Body Part Identification follows exactly that between Word Discrimination and Map Orientation.

One account of the low correlation of Map Orientation with the other two tests is that it involves a factor of spatial geographic knowledge, which has no obvious relationship to Word Comprehension impairment.

Levels of Performance

The percentage of correct responses on each subtest is presented for the 167 subjects both pooled and by diagnostic subgroup in Table 3. Also shown in Table 3 for reference are the previously cited results from 147 normal controls, similar in age and education to the aphasics, who had been tested with these same materials (Borod, Goodglass, & Kaplan, 1980).

The patient data were analysed with 9(Patient Group) x 3(WD, BP, MAPs), 2-way Analysis of Variance (ANOVA) with percentage correct on each of the three subtests as a within-subjects factor and membership in one of the nine diagnostic subgroups as a between-subjects factor. Significant main effects were obtained for Test type, $F(2,316) = 5.36$, $P < 0.005$, because of the superior overall performance on Map Orientation, and for Patient Group, $F(8,158) = 11.83$, $P < 0.001$.

TABLE 3
Mean Percentage of Items Correct, and Data for Normal Controls

Patient Diagnostic Subgroups	(n)	Subject Accuracy Scores (%)			Mean, all tests:
		WD	BP	MAP	
(1) Wernicke's Aphasia	(31)	42.6	32.9	56.7	44.1%
(2) Global Aphasia	(30)	30.4	20.0	52.4	34.3%
(3) Anomic Aphasia	(14)	74.9	86.5	59.2	73.5%
(4) Broca's Aphasia	(18)	65.7	74.3	75.8	71.9%
(5) Mixed Nonfluent Aphasia	(25)	59.4	53.9	58.6	57.3%
(6) Transcortical Motor Aphasia	(10)	57.2	68.4	63.6	63.1%
(7) Conduction Aphasia	(13)	70.8	71.7	75.8	72.8%
(8) Mixed Fluent Aphasia	(16)	56.3	60.9	64.7	60.6%
(9) Transcortical Sensory Aphasia	(10)	29.7	33.2	54.3	39.1%
Mean, all patients:	(167)	51.7	50.5	61.0	54.4%
Normal Controls*	(147)	99.7	98.3	87.1	95.0%

Mean percentage of items correct on Word Discrimination (WD), Body Part Identification (BP), and map orientation (MAPs) tests for 167 aphasic patients, listed by diagnostic category. (*Data for normal controls taken from Borod, Goodglass, & Kaplan, 1980.)

Differences in scoring methods among the three test types are bound to weaken the interpretation of the main effect of test type. However it is noticeable that the results reverse the expectation based on the relative frequency and age of acquisition of body-part *vs* map-location names. Especially important, then, was a significant interaction between Test type and Patient Group, $F(16,316) = 3.23$, $P < 0.001$. This interaction invited us to look in detail at the Word Discrimination, Body Part Identification, and Map Orientation pattern within the individual diagnostic categories.

Wernicke's aphasics and Global aphasics displayed identical patterns: in each case, Map Orientation was superior to Word Discrimination, and Word Discrimination was, in turn, superior to Body Part Identification. Consequently both subgroups had a marked superiority of Map Orientation scores over Body Part Identification scores. (Differences cited in this discussion were confirmed by Newman-Keuls tests with a criterion for significance of at least $P < 0.05$.)

The pattern for the Anomic aphasics, however, was reversed. In this case, Body Part Identification was superior to Word Discrimination, whereas Map Orientation was worse than Word Discrimination. (Body Part Identification was consequently superior to Map Orientation.)

Transcortical Sensory aphasics had Map Orientation scores that were significantly superior to both Body Part identification and Word Discrimination scores, whereas their Word Discrimination and Body Part scores did not differ. No significant differences among any of the subtests were found for Transcortical Motor aphasics, Conduction aphasics, Mixed Fluent and Mixed Nonfluent aphasics. Broca's aphasics were superior in Body Part Identification over Word Discrimination, but no differences were found that involved Map Orientation.

Overall mean score differences can easily obscure pattern similarities or differences for individual patients. To examine this question we first tabulated the total number of subjects in each diagnostic category who showed Map Orientation scores that were either equal to Body Part Identification scores (plus or minus 5%), greater than Body Part scores, or less than Body Part scores, A 3 x 9 Chi Square analysis showed that the pattern of whether Body Part Identification was superior to Map Orientation, or vice versa, was related to the diagnostic category of the patients, $\chi^2(16) = 37.06$, $P < 0.01$. The nine diagnostic subgroups broke down into essentially the same three categories defined by the overall group mean scores in Map Orientation *vs* Body Part Identification shown in Table 3.

Most notable again were the Wernicke's aphasics and the Global aphasics, where the preponderance of subjects in both groups were better at Map Orientation than they were at Body Part identification. This might be thought surprising because of geographical place names' status as proper names. Specifically, 23 of the 31 Wernicke's aphasics, and 24 of the 30 Global aphasics showed this Map Orientation superiority. (Five of the eight remaining

Wernicke's aphasics, and five of the remaining six Global aphasics showed better Body Part scores, with the final three Wernicke's and one Global aphasic having approximately equal Map Orientation and Body Part scores.) A 2 x 4 Chi Square analysis supported the impression that the pattern of distribution of patients' scores did not differ for these two patient groups, $\chi^2(2) = 1.01$, $n.s.$ Thus, the surprising superiority of Map Orientation scores over Body Part scores observed for the Wernicke's and Global aphasic groups as a whole, held true for the great majority of the patients in these two groups as individuals.

The performance pattern of the Wernicke's and Global aphasics can be contrasted with a different pattern that was shown by the bulk of the diagnostic subgroups: the Broca's, Mixed Nonfluent, Transcortical Motor, Conduction, Mixed Fluent and Transcortical Sensory aphasics. The members of each of the six diagnostic categories were approximately equally divided between those who obtained either slightly better Map Orientation scores or slightly better or equivalent Body Part Identification scores. Again, for this group, a 6 x 3 Chi Square analysis of the pattern of this distribution across subjects did not respect diagnostic category, $\chi^2(10) = 7.67$, $n.s.$ (The comparison of group mean scores in Table 3 showed the Transcortical Sensory aphasics to partly duplicate the Map Orientation superiority shown by the Wernicke's and Global aphasics. Although Map Orientation scores were significantly higher than Body Part Identification for these subjects, this effect was determined by only five of the ten subjects.)

The final grouping was that of the Anomic aphasics, who showed a diametrically opposite effect to that of the Global and Wernicke's aphasics. As we saw in Table 3, their scores on Body Part Identification were significantly superior to their scores on Map Orientation (and also significantly superior to their performance on Word Discrimination). For this subgroup, as we saw in the previous section, Body Part Identification was superior to Map Orientation, and 11 of the 14 subjects showed this direction of difference. This was confirmed by including the Anomic aphasics in a 3 x 3 Chi Square analysis along with the Wernicke's and Global aphasics, which now produced a significant pattern change, $\chi^2(4) = 26.12$, $P < 0.01$.

One may ask whether the highly consistent finding that Anomic aphasics stand out from other diagnostic groups in their superiority on Body Part Identification as compared to Map Orientation is a dissociation that is in the reverse direction from that observed in Wernicke's and Global aphasics. One alternative is that Anomics are simply performing at a near normal level. As previously noted (see Table 3), the norms published by Borod, Goodglass and Kaplan (1980) show that normal adults obtain mean scores of 99.7% on Word Discrimination, 98.3% on Body Part Identification, and 87.1% on Map Orientation, with respect to the maximum possible scores. Thus, the Anomics were performing at only slightly below normal levels on Body Part Identification, but were impaired on Word Discrimination and Map Orientation. In fact, when converted to BDAE percentiles, their Word Discrimination percentile is 52, but their Body Part Identification percentile is 75. That is, whether taken with reference to standards for normal controls, norms for aphasics, or their own word discrimination scores, Anomic aphasics' comprehension of Body Part names appears to be more resistant to impairment than other word categories.

Broca's and Transcortical Motor aphasics also had Body Part scores that were somewhat elevated with reference to Word Discrimination (see Table 3). Percentile scores are not available for Map Orientation, but Anomics were in the midrange of the other aphasic diagnostic groups. Thus, there is some indication that comprehension of body part names is relatively well preserved in these patients and that this accounts for the reversal of their word comprehension pattern from that observed in Wernicke's and Global aphasics.

Independence vs relatedness of the dissociations

If the same subjects who had superior Map Orientation scores relative to Word Discrimination also had inferior Body Part Identification scores relative to Word Discrimination, then subjects should tend to have either both of these differences, or neither of them. If the dissociations are independent, then the proportion of subjects with superior Map Orientation scores who also have inferior Body Part Identification scores should be the same as the proportion for the entire diagnostic group.

For Wernicke's aphasics, 18 of the 31 patients (58%) had Map Orientation scores better than Word Discrimination; 19 out of 31 (61%) had Body Part Identification better than Word Discrimination. Nine of these cases (50% and 47% respectively of the two deviant groups) coincided—a rate that is close to the percentage for either of the dissociations taken independently. Performing the same inspection for the Global aphasics showed that 23 out of 30 patients (77%) had Map Orientation scores better than Word Discrimination, and 21 out of 30 (70%) had Body Part Identification better than Word Discrimination, whereas 16 (69% and 76% respectively) coincided. These results are most consistent with the hypothesis that each of the two dissociations we have observed is independent of the other, and that both are characteristic of more than half of subjects with either Global aphasia or Wernicke's aphasia.

It may be suggested that the special vulnerability of body-part comprehension to impaired auditory comprehension is due to the fact that this task is more sensitive to resource limitations affecting word comprehension than is the Map Orientation task. A milder comprehension deficit could have relatively more impact on Map Orientation than on Body Part Identification. Consistent with this argument is the fact that Anomic aphasics produce the highest percentage of correct scores overall (73.5% as seen in Table 3), whereas the Wernicke's and Global aphasics produce only averages of 44.1% and 34.3% respectively. The

Transcortical Sensory aphasics who also have an overall low score (39.1%) also show the same pattern as Wernicke's and Global aphasics. However, the Transcortical Sensory aphasics whose comprehension score was low, include eight out of ten subjects whose Body Part identification scores were superior to their Word Discrimination scores. Furthermore, differential sensitivity to resource limitations would still require that Word Discrimination would have some impact on Map Orientation scores. Five of the Global aphasics had Map Orientation scores of better than 90% correct. The mean Body Part Identification percentage for these five subjects was 24.2% correct and their mean Word Discrimination score was 37.2% correct. Thus, it seems unlikely that the dissociation between body-part comprehension and map orientation can be reduced to differential sensitivity of these two tasks to general resource limitations for auditory comprehension.

DISCUSSION

In a retrospective analysis of a new group of aphasic patients we have partially replicated the findings reported by Goodglass and Butters (1988). As in the earlier study, we found that Wernicke's aphasics and Global aphasics showed a preponderance of subjects who had selective preservation of comprehension of geographical place names in comparison with their performance on the comprehension of body-part names. Like Goodglass and Butters, we also found that anomic aphasics showed the opposite dissociation between these two comprehension tasks. Our results differ from the earlier set in that Goodglass and Butters reported that Broca's aphasics and Conduction aphasics also had superiority for map locations in comparison to body part identification, although they did not show the extreme disparities reserved for Wernicke's and Global aphasics. In the present data, no diagnostic groups except for Wernicke's and Global aphasics showed this disparity.

Goodglass and Butters suggested that the individual aphasics who had deficient comprehension of body parts were most likely to have selectively spared comprehension of geographical place names. In contrast, our analysis indicates that preservation of map location is independent of deficiency in the comprehension of body-part names, although both dissociations occur in the same two diagnostic groups. In addition to the frequent reports of deficient body-part name comprehension in aphasics, the present study, for the first time, identifies a subgroup (Anomic aphasics) for whom body part comprehension is a privileged category. (The naming of body parts is also relatively spared in a proportion of fluent aphasics—see Goodglass, Theurkauf & Wingfield, 1984.)

Although a special retrieval difficulty for proper names is a common complaint in normal aging (Cohen & Faulkner, 1984; 1986), and selective retrieval impairments for proper names have been reported in rare cases of aphasia (Lucchelli & DeRenzi, 1992; Semenza & Zettin, 1989), there are no corresponding reports of selective deficits in name comprehension. In fact, Van Lancker and Klein (1990) report normal levels in the ability to match famous faces with their spoken and written names in three global aphasics. The aphasic patients reported by Lucchelli and DeRenzi, and by Semenza and Zettin could both match spoken names of persons with their correct photographs. To our knowledge, no one has studied the comprehension of proper names in a more general sample of aphasic patients. This is an obvious question to be explored. In the absence of such information, we cannot determine whether the selective preservation that we observed is unique to the category of place names. If this proves to be the case, one may consider the role of memory for extrapersonal space in the facilitation of this task.

This study leaves two unanswered questions. First, although the selective loss of retrieval for proper nouns may be explained by damage to a system specialised for terms that have purely referential (as opposed to descriptive) value (Semenza & Zettin, 1989), the relevance of such a system for the *comprehension* of proper nouns is still undetermined. To the extent that we have found selective loss of comprehension in a category of proper nouns, the postulation of such a specialised system may be relevant to the ability to correctly identify the referent of a proper name. As it has been pointed out by Semenza and Zettin (1989), and by Warrington and Shallice (1984), such a system would be independent of other dimensions (e.g. abstract/concrete, natural/artificial) that have been suggested in prior analyses of category-specific deficits. This dimension could conceivably override other dimensions or interact with them.

A second question remaining to be answered is why the observed dissociations involving comprehension of place names and body parts are restricted to the diagnostic groups of Wernicke's, Global, and Anomic aphasics. That is, although these dissociations indicate that the brain respects the distinctions between these categories, we cannot conclude that the brain areas damaged in these patients necessarily subserve the categories themselves. It is our hope, however, that current interests in proper name anomia and comprehension may serve as an important stimulant for resolving these and other long-standing questions in cognitive neuropsychology.

Manuscript received 15 December 1992
Manuscipt accepted 1 June 1993

REFERENCES

Assal, G., & Buttet, J. (1973). Troubles du schema corporel lors des atteintes hémisphèriques gauches. *Praxis, 62*, 172–179.
Benedet, M.J., & Goodglass, H. (1989). Body image and comprehension of body part names. *Journal of Psycholinguistic Research, 18*, 485–496.
Borod, J.P., Goodglass, H., & Kaplan, E. (1980). Normative data on the Boston Diagnostic Aphasia Examination, The Parietal Lobe Battery, and the Boston Naming Test. *Journal of Clinical Neuropsychology, 2*, 209–216.

Cohen, G., & Faulkner, D. (1984). Everyday memory in the over sixties. *New Scientist*, *11*, 49–51.

Cohen, G., & Faulkner, D. (1986). Memory for proper names: Age differences in retrieval. *British Journal of Developmental Psychology*, *4*, 187–197.

Dennis, D.F. (1976). Dissociated naming and locating of body parts after left anterior temporal lobe resection: an experimental case study. *Brain and Language*, *3*, 147–163.

Goodglass, H., & Budin, C. (1988). Category- and modality-specific dissociations in word-comprehension and concurrent phonological dyslexia: A case study. *Neuropsychologia*, *26*, 67–78.

Goodglass, H., & Butters, N. (1988). Psychobiology of cognitive processes. In R. Atkinson, R. Herrnstein, D. Luce, & G. Lindzey (Eds.), *Stevens handbook of experimental psychology*. New York: Wiley-Interscience.

Goodglass, H., & Kaplan, E. (1983). *The assessment of aphasia and related disorders* (2nd Ed.) Philadelphia: Lea & Febiger.

Goodglass, H., Klein, B., Carey, P., & Jones, K. (1966). Specific semantic word categories in aphasia. *Cortex*, *2*, 74–89.

Goodglass, H., Theurkauf, J.C., & Wingfield, A. (1984). Naming latencies as evidence for two modes of lexical retrieval. *Applied Psycholinguistics*, *5*, 135–146.

Goodglass, H., Wingfield, A., Hyde, M.R., & Theurkauf, J.C. (1986). Category-specific dissociations in naming and recognition by aphasic patients. *Cortex*, *22*, 87–102.

Hart, J., Berndt, R.S., & Caramazza, A. (1985). Category-specific naming deficit following cerebral infarction. *Nature*, *316*, 439–440.

Hart, J., & Gordon, B. (1992). Neural subsystems for object knowledge. *Nature*, *359*, 60–64.

Lucchelli, F., & De Renzi, E. (1992). Proper name anomia. *Cortex*, *28*, 221–230.

McCarthy, R.A., & Warrington, E.K. (1988). Evidence for modality-specific meaning systems in the brain. *Nature*, *334*, 428–430.

McCarthy, R.A., & Warrington, E.K. (1990). The dissolution of semantics. *Nature*, *343*, 599.

McKenna, P., & Warrington, E.K. (1978). Category-specific naming preservation: a single case study. *Journal of Neurology, Neurosurgery and Psychiatry*, *41*, 571–574.

Munk, H. (1980). *Ueber die Funktionen der Grosshirnrinde*. Berlin: Hirschwald.

Newcombe, F., Oldfield, R.C., & Wingfield, A. (1965). Object-naming by dysphasic patients. *Nature*, *207*, 1217–1218.

Newcombe, F., Oldfield, R.C., Ratcliff, G., & Wingfield, A. (1971). Recognition and naming of object-drawings by men with focal brain wounds. *Journal of Neurology, Neurosurgery and Psychiatry*, *34*, 329–340.

Newcombe, F., & Ratcliff, G. (1990). Disorders of visuospatial analysis. In F. Boller & J. Grafman (Eds.) *Handbook of neuropsychology* (Vol. 2). Amsterdam: Elsevier.

Poeck, K., & Orgass, B. (1971). The concept of body schema: A critical review and some experimental results. *Cortex*, *7*, 254–277.

Semenza, C., & Goodglass, H. (1985). Localization of body parts in brain injured subjects. *Neuropsychologia*, *23*, 161–176.

Semenza, C., & Zettin, M. (1989). Evidence from aphasia for the role of proper names as pure referring expressions. *Nature*, *342*, 678–679.

Semmes, J., Weinstein, S., Ghent, L., & Teuber, H.L. (1983). Correlates of impaired orientation in personal and extrapersonal space. *Brain*, *86*, 747–772.

Stewart, F., Parkin, A.J., & Hunkin, N.M. (1992). Naming impairments following recovery from herpes simplex encephalitis: Category-specific? *Quarterly Journal of Experimental Psychology*, *44*, 261–284.

Van Lancker, D., & Klein, K. (1990). Preserved recognition of familiar personal names in global aphasia. *Brain and Language*, *39*, 511–529.

Wapner, W., & Gardner, H. (1979). A note on patterns of comprehension and recovery in global aphasia. *Journal of Speech and Hearing Research*, *29*, 765–771.

Warrington, E.K. (1975). The selective impairment of semantic memory. *Quarterly Journal of Experimental Psychology, 27,* 635–657.

Warrington, E.K., & McCarthy, R.A. (1983). Category-specific access dysphasia. *Brain, 106,* 859–878.

Warrington, E.K., & McCarthy, R.A. (1987). Categories of knowledge: Further fractionations and an attempted integration. *Brain, 110,* 1273–1296.

Warrington, E.K., & Shallice, T. (1984). Category-specific semantic impairment. *Brain, 107,* 829–853.

Wingfield, A. (1968). Effects of frequency on identification and naming of objects. *American Journal of Psychology, 81,* 226–234.

MEMORY, 1993, *1* (4), 329–349

Repetition Priming and Proper Name Processing. Do Common Names and Proper Names Prime Each Other?

Tim Valentine and Viv Moore
University of Durham, UK

Brenda M. Flude
University of Lancaster, UK

Andrew W. Young
University of Durham, UK

Andrew W. Ellis
University of York, UK

Three experiments are reported in which a repetition priming technique was used to investigate whether recognition of a person's surname which is also a known word (e.g. Baker) activates the lexical representation that mediates word recognition.

Experiment 1 showed that a familiarity decision to familiar full names produced an effect of repetition priming on subsequent lexical decision to words that were presented in the initial task as surnames. Experiment 2 demonstrated that, conversely, a lexical decision primed subsequent familiarity decision to full names involving the same word. Experiment 3 showed that repeating the same decision during the initial and test phases did not produce a larger repetition priming effect than that obtained when the task at test differed from the prime task (name familiarity decision *vs* lexical decision or vice versa). The results are interpreted as support for the view that repetition priming is due to repeated activation of representations that are accessed by both common names and proper names.

Requests for reprints should be sent to Tim Valentine, Department of Psychology, University of Durham, Science laboratories, South Road, Durham DH1 3LE, UK.

The experiments reported in this paper were presented in a symposium on 'Proper name processing' at the 5th Conference of the European Society for Cognitive Psychology, Paris, September 1992. This research was supported by grants from the Economic and Social Research Council (nos. R000 23 2836 and R000 23 3091).

INTRODUCTION

Currently influential information-processing models of face recognition have been derived from models of visual word recognition, most notably from the logogen model (Morton, 1969; 1979). For example, Bruce and Young (1986) made detailed comparisons between the processes involved in recognition and naming of faces, words, and objects. They noted that there is a common sequence of processing stages for all three classes of stimuli. First, an input or structural code is formed which activates the appropriate recognition unit, followed by access to semantic information and finally a name code. In the case of word recognition, however, it is postulated that output name codes can be accessed in parallel with semantic information direct from logogens or word recognition units (but see Hillis & Caramazza, 1991, for an alternative view).

Researchers following this approach have not made any distinction between processing of proper names and common names. Indeed, although the contrast of theoretical models has been between recognition of faces and words, experiments have often involved comparisons between faces and people's names. See for example work on face–name interference (Young, Ellis, Flude, McWeeny, & Hay, 1986a); semantic and repetition priming (e.g. Bruce & Valentine, 1985; 1986); and semantic categorisation and naming (Young, McWeeny, Ellis, & Hay, 1986b). An implicit assumption underlying the development of information-processing models of person recognition has been that there is no need to distinguish proper name recognition from word recognition. Processing of proper names and common names has been assumed to be directly analogous. Indeed, what was impressive about the work carried out during the 1980s was that the analogies held up so well: faces are processed like objects and names are processed like words.

Valentine, Brédart, Lawson, and Ward (1991) outlined an information-processing model of name processing which was based on Bruce and Young's model of face recognition and Morton's logogen model of word recognition (see Fig. 1).[1] They argued that the identification of a word as a proper name must be based on the initial processes that are involved in recognition of words. Although it seems extremely likely that proper names and common names are subjected to the same early visual analysis, people's names allow access to the identity-specific semantics about known people that can also be accessed by familiar faces. That is to say, name processing requires a link from the

---

[1] In Valentine et al.'s model, the final stage of naming familiar faces and words was labelled "phonological output codes". Brédart & Valentine (1992) presented data of face naming errors which they interpret as support for a two-stage process of lexical access, as found in models of speech production (e.g. Levelt, 1989). This issue is not central to the current study, but we have labelled the final stage as "lexical output codes" to be neutral on the issue of whether it could be further subdivided into two stages.

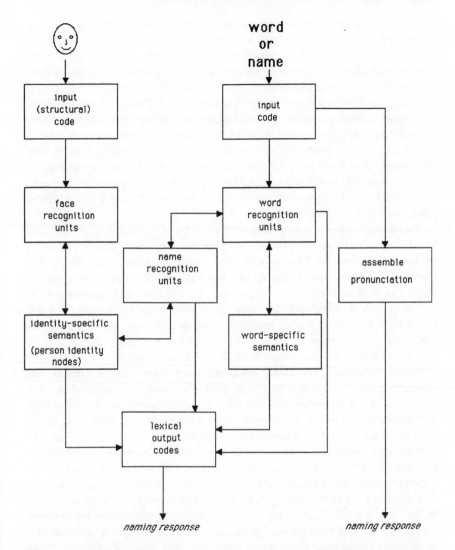

FIG. 1.   The functional model of face, name, and word recognition adapted from Valentine et al. (1991). Name recognition proceeds via name recognition units which mediate between word recognition units and identity-specific semantics.

derivation of an input code for the word recognition system to a multi-modal semantic system associated with person recognition.

Valentine et al. (1991) proposed that name recognition units, the logical equivalent of face recognition units, mediate between the word recognition system and access to identity-specific semantics about individuals. Lexical items that are used as proper names are assumed to be represented by a logogen or word recognition unit. There is one word recognition unit for each known word. By analogy there is one name recognition unit to represent the name of each familiar individual, just as there is assumed to be a face recognition unit for each familiar face. The input to a name recognition unit might commonly be the first name or surname alone, an initial and surname, or a full name. It was assumed that name recognition units can access lexical output codes directly. This connection is analogous to the direct link from visual word recognition units to lexical output codes postulated in models of word recognition and reading. It is also consistent with evidence that name output codes can be accessed in parallel to identity-specific semantics from written names but that name codes can only be accessed via identity-specific semantics from faces (Young, Ellis, & Flude, 1988; Young et al., 1986b).

The information-processing model proposed by Valentine et al. (1991) was based on a study of the effects of surname frequency which supported predictions derived from the model in a number of name processing tasks. Burton and Bruce (this issue) report a simulation of these data using an interactive activation network to implement the Valentine et al. framework.

The proposed framework for name processing begs the question of the relationship between processes involved in recognition of common names and proper names. Valentine et al.'s study of surname frequency shows that an analogy with word frequency only holds for tasks that do not require recognition of familiar individuals from their names, and is consistent with the proposal that recognition of the words comprising people's names is mediated by the recognition units or logogens of the word recognition system. An alternative architecture would be for name recognition units to receive their input direct from the input code rather than via word recognition units (see Fig. 1). Whether or not proper names and common names share representations at a lexical level, a stimulus that is both a common noun and a person's name (e.g. baker) could activate both the name recognition units and word recognition units in parallel.

The aim of the experiments reported here is to employ a repetition priming technique to provide a further empirical exploration of the relationship between common noun and proper name processing. Repetition priming refers to the facilitation in processing of a stimulus that results from a prior experience of that stimulus. If a lexical decision to stimulus words are repeated, subjects' RTs to decide that the stimuli are words in the second test are faster compared to lexical decisions to the stimuli that have not been previously seen in an initial phase (Scarborough, Cortese, & Scarborough, 1977). The effect is long-lasting and has been found after hours or days (Jacoby & Dallas, 1981; Scarborough et al., 1977). The phenomenon of repetition priming is not restricted to lexical decision tasks but is also found in other aspects of word recognition (see Monsell 1985; 1991 for reviews); recognition of familiar faces (e.g. Bruce & Valentine, 1985; Ellis, Young, & Flude, 1990); and picture naming (e.g. Wheeldon & Monsell, 1992).

The mechanisms of repetition priming are not fully understood. However, three classes of accounts have been proposed; increased availability of lexical information, retrieval of episodic traces, and learning of task-specific responses (Monsell, 1991; Wheeldon & Monsell, 1992). At this stage we shall assume that repetition priming results from increased availability of lexical knowledge following the initial processing of a word. Such increased availability might result from a change in threshold of a word recognition unit (Morton, 1969), an increase in the baseline activation level (McClelland & Rumelhart, 1981), or from an increase in the weights of links between levels of representation (Monsell, Matthews, & Miller, 1992; Vitkovitch & Humphreys, 1991; Wheeldon & Monsell, 1992). A discussion of the basis of repetition priming will be deferred until the introduction of Experiment 3, which aims to distinguish accounts based on access to lexical knowledge from an episodically mediated account of repetition priming or a transfer-appropriate processing account.

The aim of Experiment 1 was to investigate whether a name familiarity decision to the name of a celebrity whose surname also happens to be an English word would prime subsequent lexical decision to that word. Fortunately such surnames are not uncommon (e.g. Baker, Green, Wood). Repetition priming from a name recognition task to a lexical decision task alone could not in itself determine whether processing of proper names and common names is mediated by a shared representation as proposed by Valentine et al. (1991). Separate representations might be activated in parallel by an appropriate stimulus. However, empirical exploration of repetition priming between proper name and common noun processing tasks will provide further constraints on modelling of name recognition (e.g. Burton & Bruce, this issue).

EXPERIMENT 1

Method

Subjects.   24 students from the University of Lancaster acted as subjects.

Stimuli.   The stimuli for the name familiarity decision task consisted of the first names and surnames of 48 celebrities. Twenty-four of the celebrities had surnames that were also English words (e.g. Pat Cash, Max Wall, Charles Dance; see appendix for a list of these critical items). These stimuli were divided into two sets of 12 stimuli matched on the number of letters in the surname and the word frequency of the surname (Hofland & Johansson, 1982). A further 24 celebrities' names were selected as fillers, and 36 full names were created to serve as unfamiliar names. The stimuli for the lexical decision task consisted of the 24 words that were the celebrities' surnames, and 12 words (also matched on the number of letters and word frequency) to serve as fillers. Thirty-six pronounceable non-words were created, which were matched to the words for the number of letters. Eight further stimuli were selected for each task for use in practice trials. All stimuli were prepared as black and white transparencies in upper case letters.

Apparatus. The stimuli were presented by back-projecting onto a screen using an Electronic Developments projection tachistoscope. The subject responded by pressing one of two push-buttons which stopped a timer. The experimenter recorded the response and RT (in milliseconds) for correct responses after each trial.

Design. The experiment consisted of two phases; a prime phase and a test phase. During the prime task, subjects made familiarity decisions to full names. The test phase involved lexical decision to words and pronounceable non-words. The dependent variable was the latency of correct decisions made using push-buttons. There were two sets (A and B) of 12 critical items which appeared both as surnames of celebrities in the name familiarity decision task and as words in the lexical decision task (e.g. Buddy Holly & holly; Charles Dance & dance). One set of 12 critical items occurred in the prime phase (name familiarity decision task). These were set A items for half of the subjects, and set B items for the remaining subjects. All 24 critical items were included in the test phase (lexical decision task). The control (unprimed) data were collected from the 12 critical items which were not included in the prime task so that, across subjects, the same items contributed to primed and unprimed trials. Thus, the comparison between primed and unprimed items formed a within-subjects factor.

Procedure. Subjects first participated in the name familiarity decision task. They were instructed to decide as quickly and as accurately as possible whether or not each of the names to be presented was familiar to them. They were informed that half the names were of celebrities and were instructed to respond by pressing the appropriate response button. Immediately after the name familiarity decision task had been completed, the subjects participated in the lexical decision task. They were instructed to decide as quickly and as accurately as possible whether each stimulus was a word or a non-word. In both tasks, the stimuli were presented for 2.5 seconds with an inter-stimulus interval of 4 seconds.

Results

The following procedures were adopted in the analysis of all the experiments reported. The reaction times of correct responses to the critical 12 'primed' and 12 'unprimed' items in the test phase were subjected to analysis of variance. Correct responses in the test phase were excluded if the subject had not responded 'correctly' during the prime task (i.e. in this case, if they failed to recognise the name of the corresponding celebrity in the familiarity decision task). Analyses taking both subjects (F_1) and items (F_2) as the random factor are reported. No outlying reaction times were excluded, for example, by removing from the analysis reaction times over some fixed or distribution based criterion.

The error rate to critical items in the lexical decision task was extremely low (< 1%). The error rate to 'critical' unprimed items was 1.9%; there were no errors to primed items. The proportion of critical trials for which the data were missing increased to 5.5% after removal of items for which a 'correct' response was not obtained during the prime task. The mean RT to primed items was 546ms and the mean RT to unprimed items was 574ms. A one-way within-subjects ANOVA showed that RTs to primed items were significantly faster than RTs to unprimed items, $F_1(1,23) = 13.61$, $P < 0.01$; $F_2(1,23) = 9.29$, $P < 0.01$.

Discussion

The results of Experiment 1 have demonstrated that making a familiarity decision to a full name primed lexical decision to a word that was previously encountered as a surname. This finding is consistent either with activation of common pathways and/or representations, or with automatic activation of separate representations of common names and proper names. In either case, repetition priming would be obtained if the order in which the tasks were carried out was reversed, i.e. lexical decision would be expected to produce a repetition priming effect on name familiarity decision. To test this prediction Experiment 2 involved the same tasks as Experiment 1, except that lexical decision served as the prime task and name familiarity decisions were made in the test phase.

It is possible that repetition priming could have been obtained in Experiment 1 because subjects noticed repetition of words/surnames between the two tasks, and used this as a cue to make a 'yes' response in the test task. It could be argued that even in the absence of explicit recall of the prime, familiarity induced by the prime could be used as cue to respond 'yes', i.e. a specific response is associated with familiarity induced by repetition (e.g. Feustal, Shiffrin, & Salasoo, 1983). Only 12 out of 72 trials in the test task involved repetition, but each surname from the name familiarity decision task which was included in the test phase of Experiment 1 occurred as a word in the lexical decision task. One design strategy to address this problem could be to include non-words from the test phase as surnames in the prime task. The disadvantage of this strategy is that it would involve repeating a higher number of stimuli, and would therefore make episodic retrieval more likely. Therefore, in Experiment 2 the design of Experiment 1 was retained to keep the number of repeated stimuli to a minimum. However, after the experiment subjects were carefully de-briefed to ascertained whether they were aware of repetition of stimuli.

This approach was taken for the following reasons: first, the rationale of the approach is to make retrieval of episodic information as difficult as possible.

Our aim was to establish whether lexical information is more easily available after a prior encounter in different context (proper names *vs* common names). Increasing the number of repeated items, especially non-words, will mean that subjects are more likely to retrieve episodic information. In this case our experiment would not be an adequate test of the issue we aim to address. Second, there is evidence from studies of repetition priming of person recognition that cannot be accounted for by use of familiarity associated to a specific response. Ellis et al. (1990) found that repetition priming of familiar faces was independent of the decision made during the prime task. Judging the expression or sex of a face gave an effect of priming of a subsequent familiarity decision, which was equivalent to that found from a prior familiarity decision. This result is incompatible with the effect of repetition being based only on an association between a response and a representation of the stimulus.

EXPERIMENT 2

Method

Subjects.   24 students from the University of Lancaster, who had not participated in Experiment 1, acted as subjects.

Stimuli.   The stimuli were the same as those used in Experiment 1, except that 12 extra words were selected to act as fillers in the lexical decision task. Only 12 of the 24 celebrities' names which served as fillers in the name familiarity decision task in Experiment 1 were required for Experiment 2. These differences in the number of fillers between the two experiments arise because only 12 critical items are included in the prime task but all 24 critical items are required in the test phase (12 primed and 12 unprimed items).

Apparatus.   The apparatus used was the same as described for Experiment 1.

Design and Procedure.   The design was the same as Experiment 1, except that subjects carried out the lexical decision task during the prime task and the name familiarity decision task during the test phase. As in Experiment 1, there were 72 trials in each task preceded by 8 practice trials. All other aspects of the design and procedure were the same as Experiment 1, except that subjects were asked whether they had noticed repetition of stimuli between tasks after they had completed the experiment.

Results

The error rate to critical items in the name familiarity decision task was 11.8%. (12.0% for 'critical' unprimed items and 11.6% for primed items). Correct responses in the name familiarity decision task were not included if the subject had not recognised the word in the lexical decision task during the prime phase. This criterion resulted in only one RT being excluded from the analysis, as the number of incorrect responses was greater in the name familiarity decision task than in the lexical decision task. The mean reaction time of correct responses to the 12 'primed' items in the test phase was 684ms and mean reaction time to 'unprimed' items was 705ms. A one-way within-subjects ANOVA showed that RTs to primed items were significantly faster than RTs to unprimed items, $F_1(1,23) = 6.20$ $P < 0.025$, but the effect of priming in the analysis of means by item was not significant, $F_2(1,23) = 1.70$, ns. When asked whether they had noticed that some words from the initial task had occurred as surnames in the name familiarity decision task, 69% of subjects reported not having been aware of any repetition at all.

The results of Experiments 1 and 2 were also subjected to a two-way split-plot ANOVA, with priming as a within-subjects or within-items factor and the nature of the prime and test task (i.e. Experiment 1 *vs* Experiment 2) as a between-subjects or between-items factor. There was a significant main effect of task, $F_1(1,46) = 21.70$, $P < 0.001$; $F_2(1,46) = 65.16$, $P < 0.001$. RTs of name familiarity decisions were slower than RTs of lexical decisions. The main effect of priming was significant, $F_1(1,46) = 18.52$, $P < 0.001$; $F_2(1,46) = 5.65$, $P < 0.025$. RTs to primed items were faster than RTs to unprimed items. The interaction term was not significant ($F_1 < 1$; $F_2 < 1$).

Discussion

Experiment 2 has demonstrated that making a lexical decision to a word prior to making a familiarity decision to a celebrity's name, which includes the same word as the surname, produces a repetition priming effect on the latency to decide that the name is familiar. Experiment 1 showed that, conversely, a name familiarity decision primes subsequent lexical decision to a word that has been seen as the surname of a familiar name. The combined analysis of both experiments demonstrated equivalent degrees of repetition priming from proper names to common names, and from common names to proper names. This analysis also revealed that lexical decisions were faster than name familiarity decisions. This result would be expected if only because name familiarity decisions require two words to be read, but lexical decisions are based on a single word.

The majority of subjects did not report having noticed any repetition of stimuli between the two tasks. Although their self-report can not be used to exclude all possibility of the subjects using some familiarity induced by their encounter with the stimulus in the first task (*cf* Jacoby, Kelley, Brown, & Jasechko, 1989), the reports suggest that most subjects are not consciously recalling prior episodes when making their response. Given the changed context of common names and proper names between the prime and test task, any theoretical account of repetition priming which assumes that subjects are able to base their decisions on familiarity arising from the prior encounter with the stimulus, for which they do not have an explicit episodic memory, must also assume that processing of proper names and common names activates the same pathways or representations.

EXPERIMENT 3

An information-processing model, such as that proposed by Valentine et al. (1991) postulates that repetition priming reflects easier access to stored knowledge about proper names or common names, a likely mechanism being that an increase in the weight of links leads to faster and/or higher activation of recognition units or nodes. (A discussion of the possible loci of repetition effects will follow.) The aim of Experiment 3 was to distinguish between this activation-based account of repetition priming and an account based on mediation by retrieval of episodic traces (Jacoby & Dallas, 1981; Jacoby, 1983).

Episodic accounts of repetition priming assume that an episodic trace of the stimulus and its processing is stored during the prime task. Subsequent decisions to the stimuli can then be made by retrieval of the episodic trace of the earlier processing of the stimulus, rather than repeating the same processing again. In an episodic account, repetition priming therefore reflects the degree to which retrieval of the episodic trace is faster than repeating the processing required. Wheeldon and Monsell (1992) suggest the analogy of multiplying 53 by 17. If, a few minutes after having solved the problem, you are asked to perform the same calculation again, you can either calculate the product again or retrieve an episodic trace of what the answer was when the problem was solved previously. Wheeldon and Monsell (1992) point out that repetition priming is more likely to be episodically mediated if the processing required of the stimulus is slow and episodic retrieval is easy. Therefore, the tasks can be designed in order to make it unlikely that any effect of repetition found is mediated by episodic retrieval.

The design of Experiments 1 and 2 makes it seem unlikely that the effect of repetition observed could be explained by an episodic account. First, the task required was relatively fast and the error rate was relatively low. Name familiarity decisions were not as fast as lexical decisions, but the mean RTs were still under a second even in the unprimed conditions. Second, subjects were not led to expect repetitions and the number of repeated items was small (12 out of 72 trials). Subjects were led to believe they were taking part in two unrelated experiments, and most subjects did not notice any repetition of stimuli. Third, there were many intervening items. Therefore, subjects would have had to store many stimuli which would have interfered with recall of the critical episodes. Finally, the items were repeated in different contexts (i.e. as words or names) which is also likely to impair episodic memory. For all these reasons it is unlikely that subjects would have been motivated to base their responses on trying to remember the stimuli.

A related theoretical account of the effect of repetition is that based on transfer-appropriate processing (Blaxton, 1989; Kolers & Roediger, 1984; Srinivas & Roediger, 1990). According to this framework, the degree of facilitation due to prior processing of a stimulus on a subsequent decision to the stimulus will be determined by the extent to which processing at study and test overlap. Notwithstanding the reasons given earlier as to why episodic mediation might have been unlikely in Experiments 1 and 2, the aim of Experiment 3 was to explicitly contrast the prediction of an activation-based account of repetition priming against an episodic or transfer-appropriate processing account.

Aside from the aspects of the present experiments which suggest that episodic retrieval is unlikely to mediate the effect of repetition reported here, there is evidence that is inconsistent with episodic retrieval as a sufficient explanation of repetition priming. Repetition priming of word recognition tasks has been found to be relatively unaffected by a number of factors known to affect episodic memory; for example, the task at study, delay, context and visual characteristics of the stimuli. (See Monsell, 1987, 1991; Wheeldon & Monsell, 1992, for reviews.) Ellis et al. (1990) have also found that repetition priming of recognition of familiar faces is unaffected by the task that subjects carried out during the prime task of their experiments. This latter result is inconsistent with both transfer-appropriate processing and episodic mediation as accounts of repetition priming. Both theories would predict a greater effect of repetition when prime and test tasks are the same, as the similarity between the prime and test episodes will be greatest under these conditions.

The design of Experiment 3 was equivalent to that used by Ellis et al. (1990). The aim was to distinguish an activation-based account from an episodically mediated or transfer-appropriate processing account of the repetition priming effects found in Experiments 1 and 2. Episodic mediation and transfer-appropriate processing imply that the degree of facilitation observed will be related to the similarity between the stimulus *and its processing* in the prime and test phases of an experiment. The task demands and the response made will form part of the episodic trace.

In Experiment 3, subjects either carried out the same task in both phases of the experiment (either lexical decision or name familiarity decision) or they carried out two different asks (as in Experiments 1 and 2). If repetition priming is mediated by episodic memory or transfer-appropriate processing, greater facilitation should be found when the task in the test phase is the same as in the prime task. In this case the subject repeats the decision to the same stimulus, and so the stimulus is subjected to the same processing on both occasions. However, if repetition priming reflects easier access to stored representations, the effect would be no greater when the same task is repeated, provided that the relevant representations and/or pathways are either shared by the decision required in the prime and test task, or separate representations and/or pathways are automatically activated by the prime task. According to an activation-based account, as long as the representation of the stimulus required for processing at test is activated during the prime task, repetition priming would be independent of processing during the prime task.

Method

Subjects.   48 students from the University of Manchester acted as subjects. 27 were female, 21 were male.

Stimuli.   The stimuli were those used in Experiments 1 and 2, except for extra celebrities' names (for use as fillers), unfamiliar full names, words (for use as fillers), and non-words selected using the criteria described for Experiment 1. The extra items were required to allow different filler items, unfamiliar names, and non-words to be used in two versions of each task in the prime and test phases when required.

Apparatus.   An Apple Macintosh Plus was used to present the stimuli. Subjects' responses and reaction times (in milliseconds) were recorded by the microcomputer.

Design.   A three factor split-plot factorial design was used. There were two between-subject factors; prime task and test task. The tasks were either lexical decision or name familiarity decision. The comparison between primed and unprimed items formed a within-subjects factor. Twelve subjects participated in each combination of prime and test tasks. The same sets of 'critical' items as used in the previous experiments served as stimuli, and were rotated through the primed and unprimed conditions as described previously. When the same task was used in the prime and the test phase, different filler items (for both positive and negative trials) were used, so that only the 12 primed items appeared in both tasks. As before there were 72 trials in each task, of which 36 were words or famous names, and 36 were pronounceable non-words or unfamiliar names.

Procedure.   During the experiment there was a white rectangle in the centre of a grey Macintosh screen. At the beginning of each trial a fixation spot appeared in the centre of the rectangle. After 750ms the spot was replaced by a stimulus (word or full name) in upper case letters. The subject responded by pressing either a key on the keyboard labelled 'yes' (the command key) or a key labelled 'No' (0 on the keypad). The subject's response terminated the display of the stimulus.

Each subject was assigned to one combination of prime and test task according to the experimental design. Half of the subjects in each condition saw the set A items during both prime and test (primed items) and set B at test only (unprimed items—see Appendix). For the remaining subjects, set B stimuli served as the primed items and set A as the control. The nature of the task was explained to subjects and they were instructed to respond as quickly and as accurately as possible. Subjects were recruited to take part in two short experiments "one on word recognition and one on recognising people's names". Therefore subjects were not led to expect any repetition of stimuli in both 'experiments'.

Results

The error rate was 3.5% across all conditions. The error rates as function of experimental condition and repetition are shown in Table 1. After exclusion of data for trials in which an error was made during the prime task, there were missing data from 4.3% of trials. No further analysis of error rate was carried out.

The mean RT of correct responses to the critical stimuli in the primed and unprimed condition of the test phase are shown in Fig. 2. Correct responses were only included if the subject had responded positively to the corresponding stimulus during the prime task.

The data were subjected to three-way ANOVAs. There was a significant main effect of test task, $F_1(1,44)=14.02$, $P<0.001;F_2(1,46)=26.01$, $P<0.001$. Lexical decisions were made more quickly than name familiarity decisions (623ms vs 776ms). The main effect of prime task was significant in the analysis by items, but just failed to reach the conventional level of significance in the analysis by subjects, $F_1 1,44)=3.53$, $P<0.07$: $F_2(1,46)=12.73$, $P<0.001$. Subjects who carried out name familiarity decisions in the prime task tended to be faster at test than subjects who carried out lexical decision during the prime phase, regardless of the task at test. (661ms vs 776ms). The main effect of prime task needs to be interpreted in the context of a task x prime task interaction which

TABLE 1
Mean Error Rates, Experiment 3

Prime Task	Test Task	Primed	Unprimed
LDT	LDT	0	0.79
NFD	LDT	0.35	0
LDT	NFD	4.86	9.37
NFD	NFD	4.86	7.98

Mean error rates (%) to critical items in the test phase of Experiment 3 as a function of prime task, test task, and priming. LDT = lexical decision task; NFD = name familiarity decision.

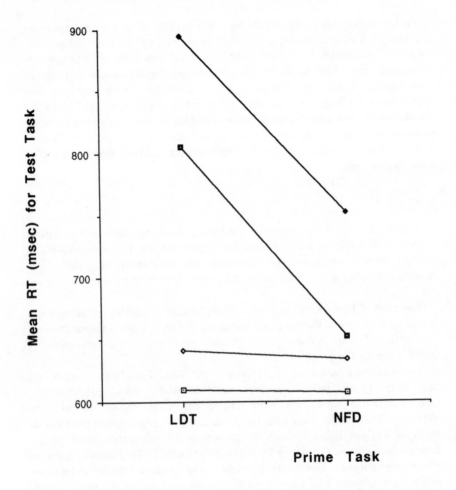

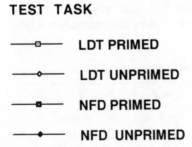

TEST TASK

———□——— **LDT PRIMED**

———◇——— **LDT UNPRIMED**

———■——— **NFD PRIMED**

———◆——— **NFD UNPRIMED**

FIG. 2. Mean reaction time (msec) of correct responses to critical items in the test phase of Experiment 3 as a function of prime task, test task, and priming. LDT = lexical decision task; NFD = name familiarity decision.

342

also approached statistical significance in the analysis by subject and was significant in the analysis by item, $F_1(1,44) = 3.09$, $P < 0.09$; $F_2(1,46) = 9.95$, $P < 0.005$. When the test task is lexical decision, RT is independent of the nature of the prime task. When the test task is name familiarity decision RTs are faster if the prime task was also name familiarity decision than if the prime task was lexical decision. This is true for both primed and unprimed items; that is, the effects depend on repetition of the task rather than the items. Thus, the effects of prime task and the prime task x test task interaction appear to reflect a task-specific practice effect for name familiarity decision, but not for lexical decision.

There was a main effect of priming, $F_1(1,44) = 11.47$, $P < 0.005$; $F_2(1,46) = 11.13$, $P < 0.005$. RTs to primed items were faster than RTs to unprimed items (669ms vs 731ms). The interaction between priming and test task approached statistical significance in analyses by subject and by item, $F_1(1,44) = 3.17$, $P < 0.09$, $F_2(1,46) = 2.99$, $P < 0.10$. This interaction appears to reflect a trend for the mean effect of repetition priming to be greater when the test task involved name familiarity decisions than it was for lexical decisions (94ms vs 29ms). All other F ratios were less than 1. It should be noted that the effect of priming was additive with the task-specific practice effect discussed earlier.

Discussion

A transfer-appropriate processing account or episodic mediation of repetition priming would predict a greater effect of repetition when the same stimulus and task are repeated during prime and test. In the present experiment, such an effect would be revealed as a three-way interaction between prime task, test task, and priming. The results show no evidence of this effect. Therefore, Experiment 3 provides no support for episodic-mediation of repetition priming, or for an account in terms of transfer-appropriate processing. However, the results are broadly consistent with an account of repetition priming based on facilitation of access to lexical representations.

The effect of repetition priming, found in the previous experiments, was replicated. Lexical decisions were made more quickly than name familiarity decisions, as was found in the combined analysis of Experiments 1 and 2. However, in Experiment 3 there was a trend for repetition priming to have a greater effect on name familiarity decision than it did on lexical decisions. The effect of repetition priming (21ms) on name familiarity decision obtained in Experiment 2 was similar in magnitude of the effect on lexical decision found in Experiment 1 (27ms). The trend for a greater effect of repetition priming on name familiarity decision found in Experiment 3 could be explicable, at least in part, by the difference in processing speed for lexical and name familiarity decisions (i.e. name familiarity decisions are slower and so have more scope to be speeded by priming).

The main effect of prime task and the marginal interaction between prime and test task appear to reflect a task-specific practice effect for the name familiarity decision task. Reaction times to make name familiarity decisions are longer than lexical decisions and appear to decrease after practice at the task. Subjects who had made name familiarity decisions during the prime task were faster to make name familiarity decisions again at test than were subjects who had made lexical decisions during the prime task. Lexical decisions were made more quickly and did not show an effect of task-specific practice. The practice effect found for name familiarity decisions is an example of transfer-appropriate training, but it is important to note that the effect was independent of repetition of the *stimuli*. Therefore, it appears to be an effect of repetition of the task, and does *not* provide an account of repetition priming of stimuli.

GENERAL DISCUSSION

The experiments reported here demonstrate clearly that common names and proper names can prime each other. A familiarity decision to a familiar full name primed a subsequent lexical decision to a word that had previously been seen as a celebrity's surname. A lexical decision also primed a subsequent name familiarity decision to a famous name. Moreover, it was shown that the effect of repetition priming between proper names and common names was as substantial as that obtained when the same task and stimulus was repeated in both the prime and test phases. The latter result is not consistent with an account of repetition priming based on episodic retrieval, in which the entire episode of stimulus, task, and response is retrieved, or with transfer-appropriate training. However, the results are consistent with increased availability of lexical representations which are activated by perception of a familiar letter string regardless of whether it is encountered in the context of a common or a proper name.

The possibility that subjects were able to make use of familiarity induced by repetition to bias responses in the test task in favour of a 'yes' response, and so speed responses to repeated items cannot be excluded. However, it would have to be necessary to assume that the induced familiarity is unaffected by a change in task between prime and test. This assumption seems a little unlikely, especially in the case of name familiarity decisions being made on both occasions. This condition involves repetition of full names rather than surnames only but does not show any greater effect of repetition. It would also be necessary to assume that subjects can distinguish familiarity due to recent repetition from variations in 'baseline' familiarity of the names of different celebrities. Even if subjects were able to use familiarity induced by the prime to facilitate repetition of the response, the account is based on activation of common representations. If processing resulted in access to or storage of separate representations for proper names and common names which are not activated by the same word encountered in the different context (e.g. baker–

Baker), no familiarity with result from an encounter with the stimulus in the different prime task.

The results reported here are broadly consistent with the model of name processing proposed by Valentine et al. (1991). Repetition priming could be attributed either to changes in the word recognition units or to changes in the weights of links connecting one level of representation to another. Changes to the recognition units could be either a reduction in the threshold activation required for the unit to achieve 'recognition', or an increase in the resting level of activation. Simulations of repetition priming of face recognition using interactive activation networks suggest that residual activation of nodes could not produce effects that are as long lasting as the effects of repetition priming observed in experiments (Burton, Bruce, & Johnston, 1990). Although a different threshold could be dynamically set for each lexical node to provide a mechanism for repetition priming, a preferred solution is to conceptualise the effect of repetition as increasing the strength of the links connecting pools of units at different levels of representation (Burton et al., 1990). Monsell et al. (1992) present evidence that the locus of repetition priming in picture naming is in changes to the weights of links mapping a semantic representation to a phonological representation in speech production.

If repetition priming is believed to affect the weights of links, the repetition priming effect observed in the experiments reported here could have several possible loci in the model shown in Fig. 1. Repetition priming could be the result of an increase in the weight of the links between the representations of the input code and word recognition units. This pathway is common to the processing requirements of both name familiarity decisions and lexical decisions. Therefore an increase in the weight of these links alone could account for the transfer of repetition effects between tasks. The analogous link was excluded from Burton et al.'s (1990) simulation of repetition priming of face recognition, because the input to the network consisted of simply activating a face recognition unit node directly. However, it seems reasonable to suppose that an increase in the weight of links between all levels are potential loci of repetition priming.

Burton et al. (1990) have argued that familiarity decisions for faces are taken on the basis of the activity of person identity nodes, and locate the locus of repetition priming as increases in the weights of the links between face recognition units and person identity nodes. By analogy, the effects of repetition priming would be located at the links between word recognition units and word-specific semantics for lexical decisions; and between name recognition units and person identity nodes for name familiarity decisions. In the case of name processing an additional possible locus is at the links between word recognition units and name recognition units.

These links can only account for the present data if it is assumed that the 'alternative meanings' of lexical items that serve as both common names and proper names are automatically activated whenever the stimulus is encountered.

That is, the links as far as person identity nodes are automatically activated whenever a common name that is also a proper name is encountered; and conversely, the links up to word-specific semantics are activated whenever a proper name that is also a common name is encountered. However, this assumption would be entirely consistent with work on the resolution of lexical ambiguity of homographs. It is well-established that both meanings of a homograph can be available simultaneously, although the activations of meanings can have a different time course and are subject to effects of frequency and context (e.g. Onifer & Swinney, 1981; Seidenberg, Tanenhaus, Leiman, & Bienkowski, 1982; Simpson & Krueger, 1991; Tanenhaus, Leiman, & Seidenberg, 1979).

Equally the results obtained are consistent with a model in which common names and proper names have separate lexical representations, but both representations are automatically activated by an encounter with the stimulus. The issue of separate *vs* shared lexical representations for common names and proper names appears analogous to a similar debate concerning language-specific representations in bilinguals. Christoffani, Kirsner, and Milech (1986) found that repetition priming in bilingual subjects is obtained for lexical decision to visually presented cognates in Spanish–English bilinguals (e.g. 'Obediencia' primed 'obedience'). No effect of repetition is found for non-cognate forms at equivalent delays (Kirsner et al., 1980; Kirsner et al., 1984; Scarborough, Gerard, & Cortese, 1984). Christoffani et al. argue that a common language-independent representation is accessed for cognates, but concede that their data do not exclude the possibility that separate language-specific representations are automatically activated by cognates.

It is not possible to unambiguously identify the locus or loci of repetition priming, or distinguish between activation of a shared lexical representation for common names and proper names from automatic activation of separate representations, on the basis of the experiments reported here. However, what our study does serve to do is to rule out accounts based exclusively on episodic records or transfer-appropriate processing. It is unlikely that there is a single locus of repetition priming or even a single mechanism. Undoubtedly repetition priming can be mediated by episodic retrieval under some circumstances (Wheeldon & Monsell, 1992; Monsell, 1991). Further research would be required to provide a more specific locus of the effect of repetition priming between proper names and common names. The contrast to homographs could provide a methodology for research into the time course and effects of context on the activation of representations of words and proper names.

Manuscript received 16 November 1992
Manuscript accepted 1 May 1993

REFERENCES

Blaxton, T.A. (1989). Investigating dissociations among memory measures: Support for a transfer-appropriate processing framework. *Journal of Experimental Psychology: Learning, Memory and Cognition, 15,* 657–668.

Brédart, S., & Valentine, T. (1992). From Monroe to Moreau. An analysis of face naming errors. *Cognition, 45,* 187–223.

Bruce, V., & Valentine, T. (1985). Identity priming in the recognition of familiar faces. *British Journal of Psychology, 76,* 363–383.

Bruce, V., & Valentine, T. (1986). Semantic priming of familiar faces. *Quarterly Journal of Experimental Psychology, 38A,* 125–150.

Bruce, V., & Young, A. (1986). Understanding face recognition. *British Journal of Psychology, 77,* 305–327.

Burton, A.M., Bruce, V., & Johnston, R.A. (1990). Understanding face recognition with an interactive activation model. *British Journal of Psychology, 81,* 361–380.

Burton, A.M., & Bruce, V. (1993). (this issue.) Naming faces and naming names: exploring an interactive activation model of person recognition. *Memory.*

Christoffanini, P., Kirsner, K., & Milech, D. (1986). Bilingual lexical representation: The status of Spanish–English cognates. *Quarterly Journal of Experimental Psychology, 38A,* 367–393.

Ellis, A.W., Young, A.W., & Flude, B.M. (1990). Repetition priming and face processing: priming occurs within the system that responds to the identity of a face. *Quarterly Journal of Experimental Psychology, 42A,* 495–512.

Feustel, T.C., Shiffrin, R.M., & Salasoo, A. (1983). Episodic and lexical contributions to the repetition effect in word identification. *Journal of Experimental Psychology: General, 112,* 309–346.

Hillis, A.E., & Caramazza, A. (1991). Mechanisms for accessing lexical representations for output: Evidence from a category-specific semantic deficit. *Brain and Language, 40,* 106–144.

Hofland, K., & Johansson, S. (1982). *Word frequencies in British and American English.* Bergen: Longman.

Jacoby, L.L. (1983). Perceptual enhancement: persistent effects of an experience. *Journal of Experimental Psychology: Learning, Memory and Cognition, 9,* 21–38.

Jacoby, L.L., & Dallas, M. (1981). On the relationship between autobiographical memory and perceptual learning. *Journal of Experimental Psychology: General, 110,* 306–340.

Jacoby, L.L., Kelley, C., Brown, J., & Jasechko, J. (1989). Becoming famous overnight: Limits on the ability to avoid unconscious influences of the past. *Journal of Personality and Social Psychology, 56,* 326–338.

Kirsner, K., Brown, H.L., Abrol, S., Chaddha, N.N., & Sharma, N.K. (1980). Bilingualism and lexical representation. *Quarterly Journal of Experimental Psychology, 32,* 585–594.

Kirsner, K., Smith, M.C., Lockhart, R.S., King, M.-L., & Jain, M. (1984). The bilingual lexicon: Language-specific units in an integrated network. *Journal of Verbal Learning and Verbal Behavior, 23,* 519–539.

Kolers, P.A., & Roediger, H.L. (1984). Procedures of mind. *Journal of Verbal Learning and Learning Behavior, 23,* 425–449.

Levelt, W.J.M. (1989). *Speaking: From intention to articulation.* Cambridge, MA: MIT Press.

McClelland, J.L., & Rumelhart, D.L. (1981). An interactive activation model of context effects in letter perception: Part 1. An account of basic findings. *Psychological Review, 88,* 375–407.

Monsell, S. (1985). Repetition and the lexicon. In A.W. Ellis (Ed.), *Progress in the psychology of language.* London: Lawrence Erlbaum Associates Ltd.

Monsell, S. (1987). Nonvisual orthographic processing and the orthographic input lexicon. In M. Coltheart (Ed.), *Attention and performance XII. The psychology of reading.* Hove: Lawrence Erlbaum Associates Ltd.

Monsell, S. (1991). The nature and locus of word frequency effects in reading. In D. Besner & G.W. Humphreys (Eds.), *Basic processes in reading: visual word recognition* (pp. 148–197). Hillsdale, NJ: Lawrence Erlbaum Associates Inc.

Monsell, S., Matthews, G.H., & Miller, D.C. (1992). Repetition of lexicalization across languages: a further test of the locus of priming. *Quarterly Journal of Experimental Psychology, 44A*, 763–783.

Morton, J. (1969). Interaction of information in word recognition. *Psychological Review, 76*, 165–178.

Morton, J. (1979). Facilitation in word recognition: experiments causing change in the logogen model. In P.A. Kolers, M. Wrolstad, & H. Bouma (Eds.), *Processing of visible language, 1* (pp. 259–268). New York: Plenum.

Onifer, W., & Swinney, D.A. (1981). Accessing lexical ambiguities during sentence comprehension: Effects of frequency of meaning and contextual bias. *Memory & Cognition, 9*, 225–236.

Scarborough, D.L., Cortese, C., & Scarborough, H.S. (1977). Frequency and repetition effects in lexical memory. *Journal of Experimental Psychology: Human Perception and Performance, 3*, 1–17.

Scarborough, D.L., Gerard, L., & Cortese, C. (1984). Independence of lexical access in bilingual word recognition. *Journal of Verbal Learning and Verbal Behavior, 23*, 519–539.

Seidenberg, M.K., Tanenhaus, M.K., Leiman, J.M., & Bienkowski, M. (1982). Automatic access of the meanings of ambiguous words in context: Some limitations of Knowledge-based processing. *Cognitive Psychology, 14*, 489–537.

Simpson, G.B., & Krueger, M.A. (1991). Selective access of homograph meanings in sentence context. *Journal of Memory and Language, 30*, 627–643.

Srinivas, K., & Roediger, H.L. (1990). Classifying implicit memory tasks: Category association and anagram solution. *Journal of Memory and Language, 29*, 389–412.

Tanenhaus, M.K., Leiman, J.M., & Seidenberg, M.K. (1979). Evidence for multiple stages in the processing of ambiguous words in syntactic contexts. *Journal of Verbal Learning and Verbal Behavior, 18*, 427–440.

Valentine, T., Brédart, S., Lawson, R., & Ward, G. (1991). What's in a name? Access to information from people's names. *European Journal of Cognitive Psychology, 3*, 147–176.

Vitkovitch, M., & Humphreys, G.W. (1991). Perseverant responding in speeded naming to pictures: It's in the links. *Journal of Experimental Psychology: Learning, Memory, and Cognition, 8*, 336–341.

Wheeldon, L.R., & Monsell, S. (1992). The locus of repetition priming of spoken word production. *Quarterly Journal of Experimental Psychology, 44A*, 723–761.

Young, A.W., Ellis, A.W., & Flude, B.M. (1988). Accessing stored information about familiar people. *Psychological Research, 50*, 111–115.

Young, A.W., Ellis, A.W., Flude, B.M., McWeeny, K.H., & Hay, D.C. (1986a). Face–name interference. *Journal of Experimental Psychology: Human Perception and Performance, 12*, 466–475.

Young, A.W., McWeeny, K.H., Ellis, A.W., & Hay, D.C. (1986b). Naming and categorising faces and written names. *Quarterly Journal of Experimental Psychology, 38A*, 297–318.

APPENDIX

Critical items used in Experiments 1–3

SET A	*SET B*
VICTORIA WOOD	VICTORIA PRINCIPAL
RUBY WAX	KATE BUSH
ANN DIAMOND	ANNEKA RICE
TOM KING	MICHAEL FOOT
CHARLES DANCE	BOBBIE BALL
MAX WALL	MICHAEL FISH
DAVID STEEL	JIMMY HILL
EDWARD FOX	TED HEATH
JOHN PEEL	PAT CASH
JOHN PARROT	DAVID FROST
BUDDY HOLLY	BRYAN FERRY
GARY GLITTER	DAVID VINE

MEMORY, 1993, *1* (4), 351–366

Retrieval Failures in Face Naming

Serge Brédart

University of Liège, Belgium

Several authors have reported that the incidence of retrieval failures is higher for people's names than for object names. The first aim of the paper was to evaluate the role of one factor that might contribute to making face naming difficult. Face naming usually requires the retrieval of one specific label: the name of the seen individual. Object naming is less restricting. First, object names may have synonyms. Second, labels available from different levels of categorisation of an object may be appropriate to name that object (e.g. trousers, jeans, Levis). Such a degree of freedom does not exist in naming faces. The hypothesis that face naming is made difficult by the simple fact that people have only one name was tested by studying faces having the exceptional property of bearing two names: faces of actors playing nameable characters (e.g. Harrison Ford playing Indiana Jones). Consistent with the hypothesis, data from two experiments showed that when bypassing a block is possible by producing another name that is known for a face, the incidence of blocks falls dramatically.

The other aim of the paper was to test the reversed frequency effect in person naming reported previously in several diary studies, in an experimental setting. A direct frequency effect rather than a reversed frequency effect was obtained in the present study.

INTRODUCTION

Putting names to faces is difficult. This opinion is widely held by cognitive psychologists working in the field of face recognition, and the statement refers to two distinct difficulties: first, access to a person's name is more difficult than access to biographical information defining the identity of that person, and second, the retrieval of people's names is more difficult than the retrieval of common nouns. The present paper deals with the latter difficulty. The objective

Requests for reprints should be sent to Serge Brédart, Department of Psychology (B-32), University of Liège, B-4000 Liège 1, Belgium.

A part of this paper was presented at the 5th Conference of the European Society for Cognitive Psychology, Paris, September 1992. Work reported in the present paper was carried out while the author was at the University of Louvain.

Thanks to Tim Brennen for his comments on an earlier version of the paper. The author is a research associate of the Belgian National Fund for Scientific Research.

was to evaluate the role of one factor that might contribute to making face naming difficult: naming a face usually requires the retrieval of one label from one particular level of categorisation, that of the individual, whereas naming an object allows for more degrees of freedom, by resorting to the use of synonyms or by using a label from a different level of categorisation of the object.

In Search of the Specificity of Persons' Names Retrieval

Although Bruce and Young's original (1986) model of face processing, and its more recent revisions in terms of serial frameworks (Brédart & Valentine, 1992) or interactive activation frameworks (Burton & Bruce, 1992) can explain why names are more difficult to retrieve than is biographical information about people, none of these models has provided an account for the fact that persons' names are harder to recall than common nouns. These models did not provide an explanation for the repeatedly reported fact that persons' names are more vulnerable to the tip of the tongue (TOT) phenomenon than common nouns (Burke, MacKay, Worthley, & Wade, 1991; Cohen & Faulkner, 1986; see also Brown, 1991).

Low frequency of use and low imageability have been suggested as factors that could explain why proper names are harder to recall than common nouns. The exact role of these factors is not very well known but McWeeny, Young, Hay, and Ellis' data (1987) suggest that this role is not a crucial one. Indeed, they showed that the same label is harder to retrieve as a proper name than it is as the name of an occupation: learning that somebody's name is "Mr Baker" is harder than learning that somebody is a baker.

Meaninglessness and arbitrariness are other features of proper names that are often cited to explain why access to names is relatively difficult (Cohen, 1990a; McWeeny et al., 1987). Properties of meaninglessness and arbitrariness are not really differentiated in these works. The basic notion is that proper names are detached from the semantic network representing conceptual knowledge (Cohen, 1990a; Burke et al., 1991). McWeeny et al. (1987) argued that names are arbitrary labels because the label "Baker" says nothing about the identity of Mr Baker. As a matter of fact, if you meet somebody for the first time and you are told that this person is a baker, you automatically derive a number of properties of that person. Being a member of the "baker" category, this person presumably bakes bread, gets up early, and so on. By contrast if you meet somebody in the same conditions and you are told that this person is called "Baker", you do not have the possibility of deriving relevant information about the identity of that person (apart from some trivial information like "He has an Anglo-saxon name", "He has the same name as my worst enemy" and so on).

The fact that a proper name conveys no information about the entity it names seems to be a consequence of the fact that proper names typically denote individuals and not categories in which exemplars inherit properties defining the category. Denoting a category to refer to one exemplar (this guy is a baker) allows inheritance of properties from the denoted category to the referred exemplar. Such inheritance of property is not possible if a proper name is used. Indeed the name "Baker" is not a label for a category within which exemplars (for instance, James Baker, Norma Jean Baker, Ginger Baker, or Samuel Baker) share a number of properties specific to people called "Baker". Apart from some very general properties like "is a human being" or "probably belonging to the anglo-saxon culture", properties you know about one person called "Baker" are not shared by other people called "Baker", whereas most of the properties of, for example, your car are shared by the other objects named "car".

Other authors have adopted a very similar view. For Semenza and Zettin the function of proper names is simply to refer to the objects so-named, and not to describe them by any property: names are pure referring expressions (Semenza & Zettin, 1988; 1989). More recently, Lucchelli and De Renzi (1992) expressed a similar idea: they see proper names as tags that permit identification of their bearers but that, on their own, express nothing about the properties of these bearers. In short, all these explanations stress the same characteristic of proper names: a proper name conveys almost no information about the entity it names.

People Have Only One Name

Another factor that might contribute to making face naming difficult lies in the fact that face naming requires the retrieval of one specific label: the name of the seen person. Such a constraint does not seem to hold as much for object naming. First, it is not infrequent for common nouns to have synonyms. Dictionaries of synonyms comprise thousands of entries. This is not the case for people's names; people generally only have one name. This point was stressed by Cohen and Faulkner (1986, p. 187): "It is probable that retrieval failures for object names are less noticeable since synonyms ... can be substituted and effectively mask the lapse". Of course people generally have a first name and a surname, but what will be called a name is a full-name in this paper. However, there are some exceptions to the rule that people have only one name—in particular, artists often have a pseudonym. The two names "Norma Jean Baker" and "Marilyn Monroe" can be used to refer to the same person. However, artists represent only a small proportion of the people we know. Moreover, artists' real names are often not known to people. If many people know that the real name of Marilyn Monroe is "Norma Jean Baker", fewer people know that Michael Caine's real name is "Maurice Mickelwhite", and who knows that Kirk Douglas' name is 'Yssur Danielovitch Demsky''?

A second important difference between naming objects and naming persons is the fact that in most conversational contexts, labels from different levels of categorisation of an object may be relevant to refer to that object. To name a self-propelled vehicle passing in the street, a speaker may use the word "car", but the word "Volkswagen" from a hyponymous level of categorisation, or the yet more precise word "Golf" would also be correct. This is, of course, not only true for cars. You can use labels such as "trousers", "jeans", or "Levis" to name an article of clothing. Such a degree of freedom does not exist in naming persons. Naming a face or more generally naming a person requires the retrieval of a label bound to one particular level of categorisation: the level of individuals. Saying "the nuclear physicist' can refer to Albert Einstein but is obviously not an act of naming Albert Einstein.

One aim of the present paper is to provide a first empirical test of the following hypothesis: the simple fact that naming a person requires the retrieval of one particular label contributes to making face naming difficult. The hypothesis will be tested through the study of exceptions to the previous statement that naming a face requires the retrieval of one particular label. There is indeed one type of face that can be named by using two different labels—the faces of actors playing a well-known and nameable character. For instance, imagine you are looking at the film "Raiders of the Lost Ark" and you see a man wearing a hat and holding a whip. You may name this man's face by giving the name of the actor (Harrison Ford) or by giving the name of the character he is playing (Indiana Jones). From the hypothesis, it was predicted that the occurrence of blocks[1] (unresolved within a given period of time) would be less frequent in naming faces that can be referred to either by giving the actor's name or by giving the character's name, than in naming faces of actors playing characters whose names are not known to subjects (Experiment 1), or in naming characters played by actors whose names are not commonly known (Experiment 2).

The second point investigated in the present study is the puzzling 'reverse frequency effect' in name retrieval. On the basis of Cohen and Faulkner's (1986) and Reason and Lucas' (1984) results, Cohen (1990b) concluded that retrieval failures are reported much more often for very familiar names than for names that are less well-known. But both Cohen and Faulkner's research and Reason and Lucas's research were diary studies. The present study offered an opportunity to test this reverse frequency effect in an experimental setting.

EXPERIMENT 1

The main aim of the first experiment was to evaluate whether the fact that naming a person usually requires the retrieval of one specific label contributes to making face naming difficult. To evaluate this hypothesis, the occurrence of blocks in naming faces for which subjects knew the actor's name as well as the character's name was compared to the occurrence of blocks in naming faces for

---

[1] In this paper, the word 'block' will simply refer to a retrieval failure for a known name. The use of that word must be seen as absolutely neutral with regards to the current theoretical debate about the cause of retrieval failures (i.e. inhibition *vs* insufficient activation).

which only the actor's name is known. In the 'actor/character' condition, the subjects' task was to name faces by using *either* the actor's name *or* the character's name, whereas in the 'actor only' condition the task was to give the actor's name exclusively. It was predicted that in the first condition the occurrence of blocks should be lower when naming faces for which two names are known than in naming faces for which only the actor's name is known. Two different patterns of results were possible for the second condition which required the production of the actors' names. The first possibility is that the retrieval of a character's name (e.g. Indiana Jones) has no influence on the retrieval of an actor's name (e.g. Harrison Ford) and vice versa. In this case, the occurrence of blocks should not be different across the two sets of faces—that is, those with two names and those with only one name—in the second condition. A second possibility is that different labels known for a given face compete, and that retrieving the character's name might interfere on some occasions with the retrieval of the actor's name. If this second possibility is correct, the occurrence of blocks should be higher in naming faces for which subjects know both the characters' names and actors' names, than in naming faces for which subjects know the actors' names but not the characters' names.

Method

Subjects.   Eighty students and employees from the University of Liège and the University of Louvain-la-Neuve participated. All of them were native French speakers and were aged between 17 and 34 (mean age = 22.4). There were 40 female and 40 male subjects. Forty subjects were randomly assigned to each condition.

Stimuli.   Two sets of items were constructed: a set of pictures showing famous actors playing characters whose names were known to subjects (faces with two names), and a set of pictures showing famous actors playing characters whose names were not known to subjects (*faces with one name*). The two final sets of stimuli were constructed from the results of two pilot studies during which subjects rated names for familiarity on a 7-point scale. The first pilot study involved 20 subjects who did not participate in the main experiment. These subjects' task was to rate the names of 32 actors. Twenty other subjects rated the names of 52 characters. Two sets of 12 pictures were selected from these pilot studies. Both sets of items included pictures of actors whose names were rated as unknown by a maximum of 3 out of the 20 subjects included in the first pilot study. Mean rated familiarity of actors' names was 5.321 (sd = 0.782) for the first set, and 5.421 (sd = 0.628) for the second set. Moreover, the first set (*faces with two names*) included only pictures of actors playing characters whose names were rated as unknown by a maximum of 3 out of the 20 subjects involved in the second pilot study. Mean rated familiarity of characters' names was 5.614 (sd = 0.469). These items were Harrison Ford/Indiana Jones; Sean Connery/James Bond; Julie Andrews/Mary Poppins; Tom Selleck/Thomas Magnum; Peter Falk/Colombo; Jean Richard/Maigret; Gérard Depardieu/Cyrano de Bergerac; Jacques Dutronc/Vincent Van Gogh; Sylvester Stallone/Rambo; Romy Schneider/Sissi; Christopher Lambert/Tarzan; and Elisabeth Taylor/ Cleopatra.

The second set of items (*faces with one name*) included pictures of actors playing characters whose names were rated as unknown by a minimum of 14 out of the 20 subjects involved in the second pilot study. Mean rated familiarity of these characters' names was 1.271 (sd = 0.319) for this set. These items were Julia Roberts/Vivian Ward; Richard Gere/Zack Mayo; Dustin Hoffman/ Raymond Babbitt; Emmanuelle Béart/Marie Volange; Eddie Murphy/Axel Foley; Carole Bouquet/Florence Barthélemy; Lino Ventura/Dalla Chiesa; Vanessa Paradis/Mathilde Tessier; Daniel Auteuil/Ugolin; Philippe Noiret/ Dellaplane; Gérard Jugnot/Bernard; and Woody Allen/Kleinman.

Black and white pictures showing the face and about a quarter of the bust were used. Clothing was deliberately not concealed in order to facilitate the identification of the relevant characters. The same stimuli were used in both experimental conditions.

Procedure.   Subjects were tested individually. They were told that they would be shown famous faces with various degrees of fame so that some of these faces might be unknown to them. Stimuli were presented in a booklet of which pages were arranged so that each subject received the stimuli in a different random order.

The condition (actor/character or actor only) was a between-subjects variable, and the set of items (faces with one *vs* two names) was a within-subjects variable. In the 'actor/character' condition, subjects were instructed that their task was to name famous faces by giving either the name of the actor or the name of the character played by the actor. As an example, they were shown a picture of Charlton Heston as Moses in the film *The Ten Commandments*, and were told that this face might be named either as "Charlton Heston" or as "Moses" (these two names were cited in the reverse order for half the subjects). Subjects were then presented with the 24 experimental items.

In the 'actor only' condition, subjects were told that their task was to name actors by seeing their faces. They were also shown Charlton Heston's face and instructed that the expected response to this face was to give the name "Charlton Heston".

For each stimulus, subjects were asked to say whether the face was familiar to them or not. In the case of a "no" response, the next stimulus was presented. In the case of a "yes" response, subjects had to name the presented person. Three possibilities might occur at this time:

- when subjects produced the correct name within a period of 20 seconds, the next item was presented;
- when subjects produced an erroneous name, they were asked to give some biographical details about the person in such a way that somebody could identify this person simply by hearing this definition. They were encouraged to mention titles of movies or TV series in these definitions. This was done to discriminate between a misidentification of a face and the selection of an erroneous lexical item;
- subjects who remained unable to name the presented face within the period of 20 seconds were asked whether they thought they knew the name of the person so that they could retrieve it if they had a little more time to think about it (hereafter this question will be referred to as the 'TOT question'), and then whether another name came persistently to their mind instead of the name they were searching for. They were then invited to give some biographical details about the person (as before). Finally, subjects who responded "yes" to the TOT question were presented with a card including four names (the target name and three names of actors of the same sex and generation as the target person) and asked whether the name they were searching for was on the card; if they responded "yes" they were asked to produce it.

RESULTS

As expected, in the 'actor/character' condition, subjects produced *characters'* names much more often in naming faces with two names than in naming faces with one name. In the former set of faces, out of 386 successful naming trials and blocks resolved after the 20-second period, subjects produced actors' names in 168 cases (43.5%); characters' names in 158 cases (40.9%); and both names in the remaining 60 cases (15.5%). In the latter set of faces, out of 319 relevant trials, subjects produced actors' names in 314 cases (98.4%); a character's name in 1 case (0.3%); and both names in 4 cases (1.3%).

Recorded incidents fell into four main categories: 1 *Unfamiliar face:* incidents where the subject judged the present face unfamiliar. 2 *Name not known:* incidents where the subject found the face familiar but responded that the name of the presented person was not known to them. This category also included incidents where a subject responded "no" to the TOT question. 3 *Errors:* the subject produced a name which was not that of the presented face and did not correct themself. 4 *Blocking states:* the subject judged the presented face familiar, was unable to produce the name within the 20 seconds allowed and responded "yes" to the TOT question. Over 181 recorded blocks, 29 were resolved during the lapse of time from the TOT question to the recognition test. One hundred and thirty-five blocks were associated with both a correct recall of the title of a movie or a TV series in which the presented person acted, and a correct choice at the recognition test. For 11 other cases of blocks, subjects chose the correct name at the recognition test, were unable to recall the title of a movie but were able to give other specific information about the target person (e.g. "He is an American actor and director, his wife is Mia Farrow" for Woody Allen; "She currently acts in a commercial for Chanel, her father is also an actor" for Carole Bouquet). The remaining six cases of blocks were false TOTs and were excluded from the following analyses.

The first dependent measure was the number of correct naming responses. A two-way 2 ('actor/character condition' vs 'actor only condition') × 2 (set of items: 'faces with two names' vs 'faces with one name') ANOVA was performed on the numbers of correct naming responses, using the sets of items as a within-subject variable and the response conditions as a between-subjects variable. Mean numbers of correct naming responses and retrieval incidents are presented in Table 1.

The ANOVA revealed a significant main effect of the set $F(1,78) = 20.032$; $P < 0.0001$; a significant 'condition × set' interaction effect, $F(1,78) = 19.005$, $P < 0.0001$; but no main effect of the condition ($F < 1$). An analysis of the interaction effect revealed that faces with two names were more often correctly named in the 'actor/character' condition than in the 'actor only' condition (Newman-Keuls, $P < 0.01$), whereas there was no effect of the condition for faces with one name. Moreover faces with two names were correctly named more often than faces with one name in the 'actor/character' condition ($P < 0.01$), but not in the 'actor only' condition. A control ANOVA taking the items as the random factor showed no effect of the set, $F(1,22) = 3.622$; $P = 0.07$, and no effect of the condition ($F < 1$), but revealed a significant interaction effect, $F(1,22) = 6.179$; $P < 0.05$. Post-hoc tests ($P < 0.05$) showed the same pattern of interaction as for the analysis on subjects.

The second dependent measure was the block rate, which was calculated for each subject using the following formula:

$$n \text{ blocks}/(n \text{ naming trials} - n \text{ UF} - n \text{ UN} - n \text{ E} - n \text{ FT})$$

where UF = unfamiliar face incidents, UN = name not known incidents, E = errors, and FT = false TOTs. The same ANOVA as that performed on correct naming trials was carried out on block rates using the sets of items as a within-subject variable and the conditions as a between-subjects variable.

The ANOVA showed a main effect of the set, $F(1,78) = 12.962$, $P < 0.001$; a significant 'condition × set' interaction effect, $F(1,78) = 20.401$, $P < 0.0001$; but no main effect of the condition, $F(1,78) = 2.753$, $P > 0.10$. An analysis of the interaction effect indicated that blocks to faces with one name occurred significantly more often than blocks to faces with two names in the 'actor/character' condition (Newman-Keuls, $P < 0.01$), but not in the 'actor only' condition where there was no significant difference across sets. Moreover there was no significant effect of condition on the occurrence of blocks to faces with

TABLE 1
Experiment 1

Condition:	Actor only		Actor/Character	
Set:	1 name	2 names	1 name	2 names
Correct naming	8.250	8.275	7.750	9.650
Block	1.225	1.350	1.500	0.300
Block rate	0.130	0.144	0.159	0.031
Error	0.300	0.275	0.350	0.275
Unfamiliar face	1.625	1.250	1.800	1.400
Name not known	0.575	0.850	0.525	0.325
False TOT	0.025	0.000	0.075	0.050

Mean absolute numbers of correct naming trials and of other responses, and mean block rates (n blocks/n correct naming + n blocks) as a function of the condition and of the set of items (Experiment 1).

one name, whereas blocks to faces with two names occurred more often in the 'actor only' condition than in the 'actor/character' condition ($P<0.01$). Descriptive data are presented in Table 1.

A control ANOVA taking the items as the random factor confirmed this interaction. For this analysis, the dependent measure calculated for each item was:

$$n\ S\ block/(40 - n\ SUF - n\ SUN - n\ SE - n\ SFT)$$

where S block = subjects who experienced a block while being able to provide relevant biographical information and to recognise the name, SUF = subjects who found the presented face unfamiliar, SUN = subjects who did not know a name for the presented face, SE = subjects who produced an erroneous name, and SFT = subjects who experienced a false TOT. The analysis showed a main effect of the set of items, $F(1,22)=6.545$, $P<0.02$; a main effect of the condition, $F(1,22)=7.638$, $P<0.02$; and a significant interaction effect, $F(1,22)=19.437$, $P<0.001$. Post-hoc tests ($P<0.05$) revealed the same pattern of interaction as for the analysis on subjects.

In order to test the reverse frequency effect, it was checked whether blocks rates (from the 'actor only' condition) were positively correlated to scores of name familiarity. A Spearman rank correlation test revealed a tendency to a negative correlation (rho = -0.334, $P<0.10$, one tailed test). Names rated as more familiar tended to elicit fewer blocks than names rated as less familiar.

Another way to evaluate the frequency with which the name of an actor had been encountered by subjects was to calculate the number of times each target actor appeared on TV screens during a given period. This procedure was applied to evening programmes from six French-speaking channels available in the Belgian French-speaking Community, for a period of 20 randomly chosen weeks during 1992. A Spearman test showed a significant negative correlation between frequencies of occurrence on TV screens and blocks (rho $= -0.556$, $P < 0.01$, one tailed test). Thus, present data show a direct frequency effect rather than a reverse frequency effect.

Discussion

Data from Experiment 1 are consistent with Cohen and Faulkner's (1986) idea that the constraint consisting of retrieving one particular label makes face naming difficult. From this hypothesis, the occurrence of blocks was expected to be lower in naming faces for which two names (the actor's name and the character's name) were known to subjects, than in naming faces for which the actor's name alone was known—at least when the naming task allowed subjects to produce either actors' names or characters' names. Indeed, knowing two relevant names by which to refer to a face was presumably helpful only with such instructions: if one of these names cannot be retrieved, the subject may still produce the other known name.

The prediction was confirmed in Experiment 1. When subjects were presented with faces for which they knew two names, the occurrence of blocks dropped significantly and dramatically. The consequence (if any) of knowing two names for a given face in a task that required the retrieval of actors names exclusively was also investigated. In particular, it was checked whether knowing character's names might interfere with the retrieval of actors' names. Data from Experiment 1 showed no evidence for such interference.

The results from Experiment 1 might be due to the fact that characters' names were easier to retrieve than actors' names. Experiment 2 was designed to examine this possibility. In the second experiment, the occurrence of blocks in naming faces with two names was compared to the occurrence of blocks in naming faces of famous characters played by actors whose names were not known to subjects. This comparison was made in an 'actor/character' condition and in a 'character only' condition that required subjects to produce characters' names alone.

The second point addressed in Experiment 1 was to test the reversed frequency effect in an experimental setting. Data showed a direct frequency effect rather than a reversed frequency effect: the names of the more frequently-encountered persons elicited fewer retrieval blocks than the names of the less frequently-encountered persons. Experiment 2 provided an opportunity for a further test of this effect.

EXPERIMENT 2

Method

Subjects. Forty-four students from the University of Liège and the University of Louvain-la-Neuve participated. They were all native speakers of French and were aged between 19 and 28 (mean age = 21.7). There were 20 male and 24 female subjects. Twenty-two subjects were randomly assigned to each experimental condition.

Stimuli. The set of faces with two names was the same as that used in Experiment 1. The second set of items (faces with one name) included pictures of famous characters whose names were rated as unknown by a maximum of 5 out of the 20 subjects who participated in the second pilot study (see Experiment 1). These characters were played by actors whose names were rated as unknown by a minimum of 14 out of the 20 subjects involved in the first pilot study. Mean rated familiarity of characters' names was 5.433 (sd = 0.496), and mean rated familiarity of actors' names was 1.288 (sd = 0.229). These items were Duncan Regehr/Zorro; Lindsay Wagner/Super Jaimie; Lou Ferrigno/Hulk; Fred Dryer/Ric Hunter; Paul Hogan/Mick Dundee; Leonard Nimoy/Spock; Richard Anderson/McGyver; Jean Bouise/Haddock; Michael Glaser/Starsky; Stefanie Powers/Jennifer Hart; Telly Savalas/Kojak; and Félix Fernandez/Tournesol. As in Experiment 1, black and white pictures showing about a quarter of the bust as well as the face were used. The same stimuli were used in both conditions.

Procedure. In the 'actor/character' condition, the instructions to subjects were the same as those given in the corresponding condition of Experiment 1. In the 'character only' condition, subjects were instructed that their task was to name famous characters from movies or TV serials from their faces. They were shown Charlton Heston's picture from *The Ten Commandments* and were told that the expected response to that face was to give the name "Moses". The remainder of the procedure was the same as Experiment 1.

Results

In the 'actor/character' condition, subjects more often produced actors' names in naming faces with two names than in naming faces with one name. In the former set of faces, out of 216 successful naming trials and blocks resolved after 20 seconds, subjects produced characters' names in 97 cases (44.9%); actors' names in 67 cases (31%); and both names in 52 cases (24.1%). In the other set of items, out of 177 relevant naming trials, subjects produced characters' names in 168 cases (94.9%); actors' names in 2 cases (1.1%); and both names in the remaining 7 cases (4%).

Out of 78 recorded blocks, 27 were resolved during the lapse of time from the TOT question to the recognition test. Forty-five blocks were associated with both correct recall of relevant biographical details and a correct choice at the recognition test. The remaining six blocks (four false TOTs and two blocks for which the subject remained unable to provide correct biographical details) were excluded from the following analyses.

A two-way 2 ('actor/character' condition vs 'character only' condition) × 2 (set of items) ANOVA was carried out on the numbers of correct naming responses. The set of items was a within-subjects factor and the condition was a between-subjects factor. The analysis revealed no effect of condition ($F < 1$) but both an effect of the set, $F(1,42) = 13.136$; $P < 0.02$, and an interaction effect $F(1,42) = 5.668$; $P < 0.05$. Further analyses showed that faces with two names were correctly named more often in the 'actor/character' condition than in the 'character only' condition (Newman-Keuls, $P < 0.05$) and there was no effect of condition for faces with one name. Moreover faces with two names were more often correctly named than faces with one name in the 'actor/character' condition ($P < 0.01$) whereas there was no significant difference across sets in the 'character only' condition. Descriptive data are presented in Table 2.

A control ANOVA taking the items as the random factor showed no main effect of the set ($F < 1$), no main effect of the condition ($F < 1$). The interaction just failed to reach significance, $F(1,22) = 3.657$; $P=0.06$.

The same ANOVAs were carried out on block rates. The analysis taking the subjects as the random factor showed a main effect of the set of items, $F(1,42) = 8.162$; $P <;0.01$; a 'condition × set' interaction effect, $F(1,42) = 5.969$, $P < 0.02$; but no main effect of the condition, $F(1,42) = 1.165$, $P>0.10$. An analysis of the interaction effect showed that the block rates were higher for faces with one name than for faces with two names in the 'actor/character' condition (Newman-Keuls, $P < 0.01$) but not in the 'character only' condition.

TABLE 2
Experiment 2

Condition:	Character only		Actor/Character	
Set:	1 name	2 names	1 name	2 names
Correct naming	8.909	8.955	8.364	9.864
Block	1.000	0.863	1.136	0.273
Block rate	0.103	0.095	0.125	0.028
Error	0.273	0.273	0.409	0.364
Unfamiliar face	1.455	1.636	1.364	1.000
Name not known	0.318	0.182	0.636	0.454
False TOT	0.045	0.091	0.091	0.045

Mean absolute numbers of correct naming trials and of other responses, and mean block rates as a function of the condition and of the set of items (Experiment 2).

Blocks to faces with two names occurred more frequently in the 'character only' condition than in the 'actor/character' condition ($P < 0.05$), whereas no significant difference across conditions appeared for faces with one name. The control ANOVA taking the items as the random factor showed no main effect of the condition, $F(1,22) < 1$, a main effect of the set of items, $F(1,22) = 4.643$, $P < 0.05$, and a significant interaction effect, $F(1,22) = 4.927$, $P < 0.05$. Post-hoc test ($P < 0.05$) revealed the same pattern of interaction as for the analysis on subjects.

Measures of the characters' occurrence on TV screens were not used to test the reversed frequency effect in this experiment. Indeed, although the appearances of actors during 20 randomly selected weeks seems to be a good estimate of their appearances during a longer period, it is not the case for characters, especially for characters in serials who can be seen every day for weeks and then disappear for months or years. However, it was possible to correlate block rates (from the character only condition) to the characters' familiarity rating scores. A significant negative correlations was obtained (Spearman rho = 0.653, $P < 0.01$, one tailed test): the more familiar a character was rated, the fewer retrieval blocks his or her face elicited.

Discussion

Data from the second experiment are quite consistent with those of Experiment 1. First, as expected, blocks to faces with two names were significantly less frequent than blocks to faces with one name in the condition that allowed for the production of either actors' names or characters' names. This result indicates that the pattern of data reported in Experiment 1 was not due to the fact that retrieving characters' names would have been easier for subjects than retrieving actors' names.

Second, block rates were not significantly different across the two sets of faces in the condition that required the production of characters' names. Thus, as in Experiment 1, no evidence for interference between two names known for a face has been found.

Third, a direct frequency effect rather than a reversed frequency effect was again obtained; block rates correlated negatively with familiarity scores.

GENERAL DISCUSSION

Several possible explanations of why face naming is particularly prone to retrieval difficulties have been proposed during the last few years. The fact that people generally have only one name, and consequently that face naming requires the retrieval of one particular label, has been considered as one factor contributing to making face naming difficult (Cohen & Faulkner, 1986). Evaluating this hypothesis was one aim of the present paper. If this hypotheses is correct then blocks to faces with the exceptional property of bearing at least two names would occur less frequently than blocks to faces that bear one name only. Indeed, bypassing a block is possible only if you have another relevant name available to give the seen face. To test this hypothesis, we compared the occurrence of blocks that remained unresolved after an arbitrary period of 20 seconds in naming faces of famous actors playing characters whose names were known to subjects and in naming faces of famous actors playing characters whose names were not known to subjects. As predicted, in a naming context that allowed the subject to produce either actors' names or characters' names, blocks were significantly less frequent for faces with two names than for faces with one name. In the second experiment, the task was to name faces with two names, and faces of famous characters played by actors whose names were not known to subjects. Consistent with the data of Experiment 1, the rate of blocks was lower in naming faces with two names than in naming faces for which characters' names only were known.

These results show that when bypassing a block is possible by producing another name, the number of blocks in face naming drops dramatically almost to zero. It is also possible that blocks have been masked because the retrieval of one name occurred before any conscious experience that the alternative name was not available. Whatever it is, results support the idea that face naming is difficult because of the simple fact that it requires the retrieval of one particular label, whereas object naming may allow for the use of synonyms or labels from other relevant levels of categorisation of the object. In some sense, this hypothesis simply applies to a naming situation the principle that a task is presumably easier when several correct responses are available than when a single correct response is available.

This suggests that object naming (or more generally common names retrieval) would be as difficult as person naming in a context where resorting to different labels is not relevant or not possible. This is the case, for instance, when subjects have to find a word from a precise definition if the target word has no synonym. Burke et al. (1991) compared person naming with object naming and non-object noun retrieval. Most of the words included in this study had no synonym. This point was verified by using Webster's *Dictionary of synonyms* (1984). Three cases of possible synonyms were found over the 40 target nouns, but in two cases these were more like the quasi-synonyms that Burke et al. had in fact used as foils. Interestingly enough, the occurrence of TOTs was not higher in person naming than in object nouns and non-object nouns retrieval in young subjects (i.e. a sample of subjects comparable to ours). Note that familiarity ratings did not differ for names and nouns for these subjects. In fact, the rate of TOTs was even lower, but not significantly, in person naming.

Further comparison of person naming and object naming would be useful. However the reason why such a comparison has not been undertaken in the present study is that we have no means to match proper names and common nouns on frequency (a crucial variable). Word frequency is an estimate of the relative number of times a word has been encountered. According to Valentine, Brédart, Lawson, and Ward (1991), the number of times a person's name has been encountered depends both on what they called the frequency of this name (the frequency of a name 'X' being an estimate of the number of persons named 'X' who are known to the subjects) and on the familiarity of that name (an estimate of the familiarity of the person named 'X'). One completely unsolved problem arises when a comparison between nouns and proper names is needed: how can name frequency and name familiarity be combined to obtain a word-frequency-like measure?

In the present study a face with two names is a visual entity that can be named by using two different labels. However each of these labels designates a different individual. For instance Indiana Jones is not Harrison Ford. The former is an unmarried adventurous archaeologist who hates snakes, while the latter is a famous actor, Melissa Mathison's husband and the father of three sons and a daughter. An interesting follow-up to the present study would be to evaluate whether results can be replicated using individuals (and not merely faces) with two names like Marilyn Monroe/Norma Jean Baker. Such an experiment has not been carried out here, simply because finding a sufficient number of persons whose two names were known to subjects turned out to be an insurmountable obstacle.

The fact that face naming requires the retrieval of one specific label is not the only reason why face naming is particularly prone to retrieval blocks. This factor is seen as one relevant item among a bundle of factors making face naming difficult; including the fact that proper names are pure referring expressions (Semenza & Zettin, 1988; 1989) or relatively meaningless (Cohen, 1990a).

The second aim of this study was to test, in the laboratory, the reversed frequency effect reported earlier in diary studies of memory for names. Cohen (1990b, p.195) summarised this effect as follows: "well known names are blocked more often than little known ones". From this reversed frequency effect, a positive correlation between the block rates and measures of familiarity was expected. Data from the present experiments contradicted the reversed frequency effect. In both experiments, block rates correlated negatively with familiarity measures. There is a plausible explanation for this discrepancy: the reversed frequency effect might simply reflect the relative frequency of recall attempts. Indeed, names of frequently encountered persons are likely to be recalled more often than names of infrequently encountered persons. Then, if all other factors were equal, the absolute number of blocks to very familiar persons' names should be higher than the absolute number of blocks to less familiar persons. Of course, the relevant measure for testing the reversed frequency effect is not the absolute number of blocks but their occurrences relative to the number of retrieval attempts. Unfortunately, it is not possible to control the number of recall attempts in diary studies, so that it is impossible to estimate the ratio of number of blocks to number of recall attempts. In the present study, the number of recall attempts was controlled, and a direct frequency effect rather than a reversed frequency effect was obtained. Present results favour the idea that the reversed frequency effect reported in diary studies is an artefact.

Manuscript accepted 6 June 1993

REFERENCES

Brédart, S., & Valentine, T. (1992). From Monroe to Moreau. An analysis of face naming errors. *Cognition*, *45*, 187–223.

Brown, A.S. (1991). A review of the Tip of the Tongue experience. *Psychological Bulletin*, *109*, 204–223.

Bruce, V., & Young, A. (1986). Understanding face recognition. *British Journal of Psychology*, *77*, 305–327.

Burke, D.M., Mackay, D.G., Worthley, J.S., & Wade, E. (1991). On the tip of the tongue: What causes word finding failures in young and older adults? *Journal of Memory and Language*, *30*, 542–579.

Burton, A.M., & Bruce, V. (1992). I recognize your face but I can't remember your name: a simple explanation? *British Journal of Psychology*, *83*, 45–60.

Cohen, G. (1990a). Why is it difficult to put names to faces? *British Journal of Psychology*, *81*, 287–297.

Cohen, G. (1990b). Recognition and retrieval of proper names: Age differences in the Fan effect. *European Journal of Cognitive Psychology*, *2*, 193–204.

Cohen, G., & Faulkner, D. (1986). Memory for proper names: Age differences in retrieval. *British Journal of Developmental Psychology*, *4*, 187–197.

Lucchelli, F., & De Renzi, E. (1992). Proper name anomia. *Cortex*, *28*, 221–230.

McWeeny, K.H., Young, A.W., Hay, D.C., & Ellis, A.W. (1987). Putting names to faces. *British Journal of Psychology*, *78*, 143–149.

Reason, J.T., & Lucas, D. (1984). Using cognitive diaries to investigate naturally occurring memory blocks. In J.E. Harris & P. Morris (Eds.), *Everyday memory, actions and absent-mindedness* (pp. 53–70). London: Academic Press.

Semenza, C., & Zettin, M. (1988). Generating proper names: A case of selective inability. *Cognitive Neuropsychology*, *5*, 711–721.

Semenza, C., & Zettin, M. (1989). Evidence from aphasia for the role of proper names as pure referring expressions, *Nature*, *342*, 678–679.

Valentine, T. Brédart, S., Lawson, R., & Ward, G. (1991). What's in a name? Access to information from people's names. *European Journal of Cognitive Psychology*, *3*, 147–176.

MEMORY, 1993, *1* (4), 367–391

Access to Visual Information from a Name is Contingent on Access to Identity-specific Semantic Information

Mark Craigie and J. Richard Hanley

University of Liverpool, UK

In this study, we investigated subjects' ability to retrieve information about a familiar person's facial appearance in response to seeing their name. Each famous name was associated with one of four occupations (sport, music, politics, and acting) and one of four distinctive facial features (beard, long hair, glasses, baldness). Subjects were asked to state which occupation, and which facial feature was associated with each name. The most important finding was that subjects were generally only able to recall the distinctive facial feature that a person possessed if they were also able to recall their occupation. Recall of the person's occupation, by contrast, was not contingent on remembering the person's facial appearance. These results suggest that there are no direct links between the representation of a person's name in memory and visual information about their facial appearance. The link appears to be indirect, and to be mediated by non-visual semantic information about the person, such as their occupation. This conclusion was also supported by an examination of the effects of biographical cues on subjects' ability to recall facial information that they had previously failed to recall. In a second experiment, subjects were presented with biographical details about famous people, and were asked to retrieve information about their face and name. Retrieval of facial information did not appear to be contingent on recall of the name, nor did recall of the name appear to be contingent on retrieval of facial information. On the basis of the results, an hierarchical model of name recognition is presented which is analogous to current models of face recognition (e.g. Bruce & Young, 1986).

Requests for reprints should be sent to Dr J.R. Hanley, Department of Psychology, University of Liverpool, Eleanor Rathbone Building, PO Box 147, Liverpool L69 3BX, UK.

The authors would like to thank Gillian Cohen, Nicola Stanhope, and an anonymous reviewer for their constructive criticisms of a previous draft. Our thanks also go to Clare Crofton, Diane Dutton, Clare Forster, Catherine Ryder, and Ann Toole for help with a pilot study on which Experiment 1 was based.

INTRODUCTION

An hierarchical model of person identification was first put forward by Hay and Young (1982). Since then, there have been several developments to the original model; part of the framework put forward by Bruce and Young (1986) is shown in Fig. 1. This model claims that the face identification system is made up of a series of sub-components that are connected hierarchically. Face recognition units (FRUs), which are in some ways analogous to logogens for words (Morton, 1969; 1979), represent a structural description of a particular face which is view-

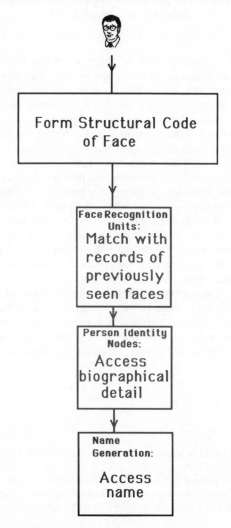

FIG. 1. The Bruce & Young (1986) framework for retrieval of names.

independent. An FRU 'fires' when a structural description from visual processing matches the structural description represented by the FRU. Person identity nodes (PINs) access identity-specific semantic information (such as a person's occupation or where they are regularly encountered) upon activation by the appropriate FRU. Activation from the PINs feeds into the name code generation system which produces the name of the person identified.

Over recent years, a considerable body of evidence has accumulated in support of Bruce and Young's (1986) model. A major prediction from the model is that accessing a name from a face should be contingent on accessing semantic information about the person. Young, Hay, and Ellis (1985), using a diary study, reported that normal subjects can frequently recall semantic information about a person without recalling their name. However, there were no reported cases where the name was recalled in the absence of any biographical detail, a finding that has been replicated in laboratory studies (Hanley & Cowell, 1988; Hay, Young, & Ellis, 1991). Further evidence for the model comes from reaction time studies showing that it takes significantly longer to retrieve information about a person's name from a face than it does to retrieve biographical information about them such as their occupation (Johnston & Bruce, 1991; Young, Ellis, & Flude, 1988; Young, McWeeny, Ellis, & Hay, 1986a; Young, McWeeny, Hay, & Ellis, 1986). Names have also been found to be more difficult to learn than occupations, even when the same words are used in both tasks, eg. *Mr. Baker* versus *a baker* (Cohen, 1990; Mcweeny, Young, Hay, & Ellis, 1987).

Pathologies of person recognition also provide evidence for the hierarchical model of name retrieval. Patients have been reported who experience extreme difficulty in retrieving names when presented with faces of people familiar to them, despite being able to recall biographical detail about those people (Flude, Ellis, & Kay, 1989; Semenza & Zettin, 1988). Furthermore, even though there have been reports of patients with impairments at the level of face recognition units (e.g. de Haan, Young, & Newcombe, 1987; McNeil & Warrington, 1991), and reports of patients who have problems in retrieving biographical detail about familiar people (de Haan, Young, & Newcombe, 1991; Ellis, Young, & Critchley, 1989; Hanley, Young, & Pearson, 1989), there has never been a report of a patient who could recall names but found it difficult to recall other types of information about them.

Evidence for an hierarchical model of name retrieval also comes from studies using cueing paradigms, which show that it is when a cue acts at the point in the model at which a subject's retrieval attempt has faltered that it will be most likely to help the subject recall a name. Hanley and Cowell (1988) gave subjects photographs of famous people and asked the subjects to make a face familiarity decision, and recall the occupation and name of each famous face presented. On those trials where the name was not recalled by the subjects, a cue was presented. Results showed that a second photograph of the person was most useful in enabling subjects to access the name on trials where the face was originally not found familiar. Biographical cues were most useful in cases where the face had been recognised but no other information had originally been retrieved. The initials of the name were most effective as a cue when the subjects were in a tip-of-the-tongue (TOT) state (*cf* Brown & McNeill, 1966; Yarmey, 1973). Similar results were achieved by Brennen, Baguley, Bright, and Bruce (1990) who gave subjects biographies of famous people and asked the subjects to recall the name of the person. In those subjects who experienced a TOT state for a name, neither a photograph, nor repetition of the biography were effective in helping subjects to retrieve the name, whereas the initials of the name significantly aided its recall.

In addition to FRUs, the Bruce and Young (1986) model also postulates the existence of other recognition units that are involved in person identification, all of which feed information into the PIN. One hypothesised set of units are name recognition units (NRUs). Valentine, Bredart, Lawson, and Ward (1991) have provided evidence for the existence of these units as mediators between ordinary word recognition units and the semantic system. There is also evidence to suggest that names are at least as effective as faces in allowing access to the rest of the person recognition system. Names are recognised more accurately than faces (Borges & Vaughn, 1977; Clarke, 1934; Yarmey, 1970) and more quickly than faces (Bruce, 1979). Recall of facial information from names is significantly higher than recall of names from faces (Read & Wilbur, 1975), and recall of occupations from names (in a learning task) is significantly higher than recall of names from occupations (Cohen & Faulkner, 1986). In addition, processing of names appears to be similar to processing of faces, in that both types of stimuli show a negatively accelerated search function relating response latency to set size in a visual search task (Bruce, 1979).

The main issue that we investigate in this paper is subjects' ability to retrieve information about a familiar person's facial appearance and their occupation in response to seeing their name. Figure 2 contains a framework for the processing of familiar names that is similar to the model proposed by Valentine et al. (1991). NRUs fire when the word recognition units making up the name represented in the NRU are activated. This allows subjects to recognise the name presented as that of a familiar person. After recognition has taken place, identity-specific semantics can be accessed from the PIN. Finally, a representation of a face can be activated by the face code generation system. In the following experiments, subjects were given either names or biographies of famous people. When a name was presented (Experiments 1 and 2), subjects were requested to provide the occupation and information about the face of that famous person. When a biography was presented (Experiment 2 only), subjects were requested to supply information about the face and the name.

Our prediction was that subjects' retrieval could falter at any part of the model represented in Fig. 2. Hence, when shown a famous name, it should be possible for subjects to fail to recognise the name, or to recognise the name but

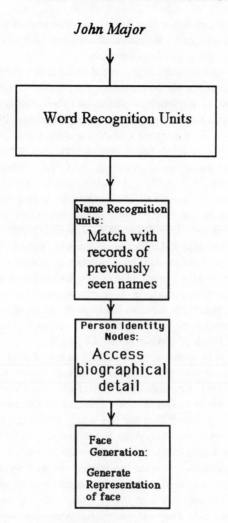

FIG. 2. A model for person identification from names.

fail to access any other information about the person. It should also be possible for subjects to recognise the name and access identity-specific semantics, but fail to recall visual information concerning the face of the familiar person. According to our model, however, when subjects are presented with a name, it should be impossible for them to recall that person's face without first recognising their name and accessing identity-specific semantic information about them. In Experiment 1, therefore, in which *names* of famous people were presented, the prediction was that subjects should be able to recall the occupation associated with a familiar name more often than they could recall information about that person's face. However, most important of all, a subject should never be able to recall information about a person's face from their name if they did not know the person's occupation.

In contrast, when a biography is presented to subjects rather than a name (as in Experiment 2), there should be no contingency between the subjects' ability to retrieve the name of a particular person and their ability to access visual information concerning that person's face. Because the PIN has a direct connection to both the face generation system and the name generation system, subjects should be able to recall facial information without recalling the name, and be able to recall the name without recalling facial information.

The model shown in Fig. 2 also makes specific predictions as to the effectiveness of cues for the recall of information in response to a name. In Experiment 1, all trials on which subjects did not recall facial information correctly from a name were repeated in Phase 2, with presentation of one of two types of cue (either biographical information about the person, or else their name once again). There will, of course, be a number of occasions when a subject simply does not know what a particular person looks like, whether they know that person's occupation or not. Under these circumstances, presenting a cue will be of no use. However, there are also likely to be occasions when the subject *does* know the appropriate piece of information but is unable to recall it due to a temporary retrieval block at some point in the system.

When a subject is in such a state, an effective cue should act at the precise point in the system at which a subject is finding difficulty in recalling the required information (*cf* Brennen et al., 1990; Hanley & Cowell, 1988). It was therefore expected that there would be a significant interaction between the state of knowledge of the subject before the cue was given, and the effectiveness of the two different types of cue. According to our model, a biographical cue might prove helpful in enabling a subject to recall visual information about a face on a number of those occasions where the subject previously found the name familiar, but could not access any other information about the person concerned. This is because a biographical cue might bridge the gap between the name recognition unit (where the retrieval process has become stalled) and the person identity node. Should this occur, then retrieval of the appropriate piece of facial information might become possible. Biography cues should not be effective in the case where a subject has already successfully recalled semantic information about the person concerned, because the cues will then merely provide information to which the subject already has access.

In addition, half of the subjects were simply presented with the name again in Phase 2. The re-presentation of the name serves as a baseline against which to measure the effectiveness of the biography cues. This is because some previously unrecalled information is likely to be retrieved in the presence of a biographical cue, simply because the subject is being given a second opportunity to recall it (Brennen et al., 1990; Hanley & Cowell, 1988).

The recall tasks in both Experiment 1 and Experiment 2 involved the subject choosing one out of four categories according to the nature of the information requested. All of the famous people that were used as stimuli had one, and only one, of four distinctive facial features. These were a balding head, a beard, a pair of glasses, and long hair. Subjects were considered to have accessed information about the person's face if they successfully indicated which of these four features were associated with the famous person in question. Recall of biographical information was operationally defined by a choice from four occupation categories (actor, musician, politician, and sportsman). For recall of names (Experiment 2), subjects were presented with four categories corresponding to approximately equal-sized sections of the alphabet and were requested to choose the category containing the initial letter of the last word in the name they had recalled. It was considered necessary to equate the task requirements of all three types of recall in this way because it is possible that the number of categories may in itself affect recall performance (cf Hanley, Pearson, & Howard, 1990; Young, Ellis, & Flude, 1988).

EXPERIMENT 1

Method

Subjects.   40 males and 40 females of age range 18–50 were recruited at random from various sites at the University of Liverpool. All but two were students at the University: one of these was a student at a different University, and the other subject was a resident of Liverpool.

Materials.   In total, subjects were shown 96 index cards on which a name had been typed. Sixty four of the names were of famous personalities from each of the four occupational categories used (16 actors, 16 politicians, 16 musicians, and 16 sportsmen). Table 1 provides details of some of the famous people that were used. In each occupational category, four personalities were drawn from each of the facial categories used (balding, beard, glasses, and long hair). All fitted into a single category at the time when subjects were tested, although several have since changed their appearance. In this way, a completely balanced design was set up, with four personalities for each pairwise combination of the two recall categories. On the reverse of these cards was a short typed biography of that famous person, consisting of their occupation and three other items of identity-specific semantic information that was nonvisual in nature (e.g. ethnicity was not used). In some cases, giving an occupation provided two items of semantic information—the general occupational category, and the more specific job that the person does (e.g. a singer automatically fits into the musician category). All the biographies used as cues in the second phase of the experiment therefore contained an equal amount of semantic information. For

TABLE 1
Some Examples of the Names of Famous People That Were Used in Experiment 1.

	Actors	Musicians	Politicians	Sportsmen
Beards	Brian Blessed Timothy Busfield	James Galway George Michael	Fidel Castro David Blunkett	Mike Gatting Miroslav Mecir
Glasses	Michael Caine Peter Sellers	Roy Orbison Craig Read	Douglas Hurd Tom King	Tom Kite Clive Lloyd
Balding	Bob Hoskins Brian Glover	Mark King Yehudi Menuhin	Norman Tebbit François Mitterand	Willie Thorne Duncan Goodhew
Long Hair	Michael Praed Richard Harris	Simon Rattle Marc Bolan	Michael Heseltine Carlos Menem	Ruud Gullitt Kirk Stevens

example, the biographical cue for Yehudi Menuhin read "Classical violinist and conductor, famous for his international peace efforts."

On the other 32 cards, distractor names were typed. These were produced in one of four ways: a famous name was altered by changing a phoneme or a syllable in the name; the forename and surname of two famous people from the same category were mixed; or a name was chosen which was unrelated to any famous person, but which allowed control over distinctiveness of the target and distractor names.

Famous names were chosen according to two criteria. First, each famous person was selected so as to fit as exclusively as possible into only one occupational and one facial category. Second, all the stimuli were male: this was necessary to prevent different facial categories being used for male and female stimulus names (a balding head and a beard are not attributes associated with female faces!). Two other index cards were used in the experiment, one showing the four occupational categories and one showing the four facial categories (the category cards). These were visible throughout the experiment.

Procedure.   All subjects were tested individually. The procedure consisted of two phases. In the first phase, subjects were shown the names on each card and were initially required to make a name-familiarity decision. For names that they found familiar, they were then asked to recall occupation and facial information by selecting one category from the category cards. This was not a forced choice procedure: subjects were instructed not to guess and were therefore allowed to respond by saying they did not know into which occupation and/or facial category a name fitted, even though they had found the name familiar. Names were shown one at a time, in a pre-determined random order. The order of the names was reversed for every other subject to prevent order effects. Subjects were given as long as they needed to make a response. In some situations, subjects said that they thought a name fitted into more than one category from a particular category card. In these cases, the subjects were required to choose the category that they thought was most representative of the person whose name they had been shown.

All the famous names for which the subjects had failed to give correct responses on all three tasks (familiarity decision, occupation, and facial categorisation) went forward into Phase 2. In this phase, subjects were given the names in the same order as in Phase 1. No feedback was given to the subjects as to why these names were being repeated—they were not told that their responses had been incorrect. For half the subjects, the procedure was identical to Phase 1 except that subjects were not required to make a familiarity decision. For the other subjects, the names were presented, and then the card was turned over to reveal the biographical cue. Subjects were then requested to give the appropriate facial information category. All subjects were thoroughly debriefed at the end of the experiment. This debriefing included a discussion of certain names that they had not correctly identified, especially if their responses had not been consistent across both phases of the experiment.

Results

Familiarity Decisions. The false alarm rate in Phase 1 of the experiment (i.e. responses of "familiar" to distractor names) was low, with no subject producing more than five false alarms. The false alarms that did occur were all to distractors which provided a particularly difficult familiarity decision (e.g. Vladimir Stalin). Mean hit rate for the famous names was 46/64.

Recall of Occupation and Facial Information. The mean number of occupations correctly recalled per subject in Phase I of the experiment was 66% (42.5/64). On 2% of trials the subject gave an incorrect occupation, and on 32% of trials the subject said that they did not know the correct occupation. The mean number of items of facial information that were correctly recalled in Phase 1 was 48% (31/64). On 6% of trials, the subject gave an incorrect piece of facial

TABLE 2
Pooled Contingency Table, Experiment 1

Facial Feature Recalled?	Occupation Recalled?	
	Yes	No
Yes	2480	15
No	927	1698

The number of responses in the total data set in Experiment 1 falling into each cell of a pooled contingency table.

information, and on 46% of trials the subject said that they did not know the correct facial information. A repeated-measures t-test showed that the mean number of occupations recalled was significantly higher than the mean number of items of facial information recalled [$t(71)$=23.4 ($P < 0.0001$)].

To test whether recall of facial information might be contingent on recall of occupation, data from Phase 1 of the experiment were collated into 2×2 contingency tables for occupation and facial recall for *each individual subject*. A pooled contingency table for all subjects is shown in Table 2. It can be seen that the number of trials on which a subject recalled the appropriate facial feature without recalling the correct occupation is extremely small. Fisher exact probability tests for each individual subject were calculated; all of these were highly significant ($P < 0.001$). Visual inspection of each contingency table showed a consistent pattern: namely, the cell corresponding to correct facial recall without occupation recall was consistently zero or near to zero. This pattern of data supports the hypothesis that recalling facial information from a name is contingent on prior recall of the occupation. There were only 23 occasions in the experiment (15 in Phase 1 and 8 in Phase 2) when correct recall of facial information occurred without correct recall of occupation. This figure represents less than 0.4% of the total data set. Because these trials are critical for the success of our model, they will be discussed in some detail.

On 13 of these occasions, the problem seemed to have occurred because the subject gave the wrong occupation as a result of accessing the PIN for a different person. The person whose PIN was activated happened to share the same distinctive facial feature as the target person, but had a different occupation (e.g. a few subjects described *Richard Baker* when presented with the name of *Kenneth Baker*—both wear glasses, but the latter is a politician, whereas the former is a broadcaster). On two occasions, subjects appeared to have activated the correct PIN, but accessed information from the PIN which led them to categorise the person differently from the experimenters (e.g. *Brian Blessed*, the actor, was placed in the musician category by one subject because he has appeared in several musicals). On two further occasions, subjects appeared to have made careless errors by saying one occupational category when they meant to say another, or by misreading the name on the card. These became apparent in the debriefing session, when the subjects were amazed to hear what their original response had been. On five of the remaining six trials, a wrong occupation appeared to have been recalled because the subject seemed to have incorrect biographical detail stored at the PIN—e.g. *Roy Orbison* (Music, Glasses) was classified by one subject as a politician with glasses. None of these 22 instances appear to be incompatible with our model.

The situation which the model cannot explain would be where a subject knew the facial information but claimed *not to know* the occupation. This occurred only once in the entire experiment in response to the name of *Abraham Lincoln* (politics/beard). The subject said "beard" but was unwilling to give an occupation. This was, however, a subject whose motivation became suspect during the experiment, and who started saying "sportsman" to every name. Consequently, the significance of this one instance for our model is probably negligible.

Effects of Cues.   Although 80 subjects were run in total, only 72 were put forward into the analysis of variance of the Phase 2 cueing data. Two subjects were dropped because analysis of their responses suggested that they were guessing on a substantial number of trials. A further three subjects were dropped because they failed to reach an *a priori* criterion of five or more names in Phase 2 for each level of previous knowledge from Phase 1.

It had been anticipated that the data would be analysed using three levels of previous knowledge as a factor (i.e. unfamiliar name; familiar name; familiar name plus correct occupation category). However, when these three levels were used, 63 subjects failed to reach the criterion value of five responses per level. Hence, the three levels were collapsed into two levels (occupation unknown and occupation known). The final three subjects were dropped to equalise group sizes, and these were the three subjects from the relevant groups who made the highest number of errors in any one category.

The proportion of previously unrecalled facial information that was recalled in Phase 2 was analysed using a 2×2 mixed ANOVA, with previous knowledge of occupation as the repeated measures factor, and type of cue (i.e. name again or biography) as the between-subjects factor. A significant main effect for both type of cue and previous knowledge of occupation was found. A biography was found to lead to significantly more facial information being recalled than did repetition of the name (30.4% compared to 13.0% of previously unrecalled information) $[F(1,70) = 40.4 (P < 0.0001)]$. Subjects who knew the biography in Phase 1 recalled significantly more previously unrecalled facial information in Phase 2 than those who did not have prior knowledge of the biography (26.7% compared with 16.8%) $[F(1,70) = 28.0 (P < 0.0001)]$. The interaction between the two factors was also found to be significant $[F(1,70) = 11.02 (P < 0.005)]$.

The nature of this interaction (see Fig. 3) was further investigated by tests of simple main effects. These showed that when subjects had not previously recalled the occupation from the name, a biographical cue was significantly more effective than repetition of the name in helping the subjects to recall facial information that they had not been able to retrieve previously $[F(1,70) = 91.1 (P < 0.0001)]$. Although the effect is clearly much smaller, the biographical cue also led to significantly better recall of the visual information than the repeated name when subjects had recalled the occupation in Phase 1 $[F(1,70) = 7.97 (P < 0.01)]$. Subjects who were given the name again in Phase 2 were significantly more likely to recall previously unretrieved facial information if they had recalled the occupation in Phase 1 than if they had been unable to retrieve an

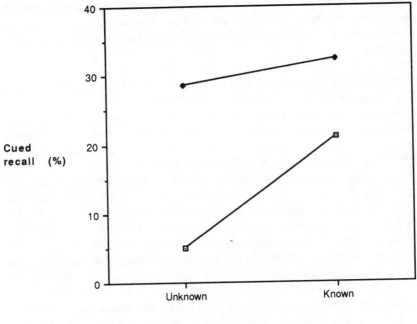

FIG. 3. Subjects' ability to recall previously unrecalled visual information in response to cues in Phase 2 of Experiment 1.

occupation $(F(1,70) = 37.1$ $(P < 0.0001)]$. However, there was no significant difference in the Phase 2 recall performance of subjects who were given a biographical cue between those who had previously recalled the occupation correctly, and those who had not $[F(1,70) = 1.95$ $(P > 0.10)]$.

A comparison of the two subject groups was made in order to discover whether the recall differences in Phase 2 might have been caused by differences in Phase 1 performance. This revealed no apparent differences. For familiarity decisions, false alarms were consistently low across the two groups, whereas hits did not differ significantly (hit rate for name-again group = 45/64; hit rate for biographical cue group = 47/64). The two subject groups also showed similar levels of performance in terms of number of occupations and amount of facial information incorrectly recalled in Phase 1 (see Table 3 for details).

Incorrect responses in Phase 2 were also compared to examine the possibility of criterion differences in facial judgments for the two groups. This revealed that 7.9% of facial categorisations were incorrect in the name-again group, compared

TABLE 3
Nature of Responses, Experiment 1

	Occupation Wrong	Occupation Unknown	Facial Info Wrong	Facial Info Unknown
Name again group	1.9%	34.2%	5.8%	49.7%
Biographical Cue group	2.2%	29.8%	5.3%	43.0%
All subjects	2.0%	32.0%	5.5%	45.6%

The nature of the responses that subjects made when they were unable to provide correct occupation or facial information about a famous person in Phase 1 of Experiment 1.

with 11.0% of facial categories in the biographical cue group. The corresponding figures for Phase 1 were 5.8% and 5.3% respectively. It is possible that subjects did show a slightly higher tendency to guess in Phase 2 of the experiment, therefore, but it is unlikely that this had a major effect on the results. In addition, the vast majority of responses in Phase 2 remained identical to the response made in Phase 1 (over 80% in the name-again condition and over 60% in the biographical cue condition).

Discussion

The results of Experiment 1 provide strong evidence that recall of visual information in response to a name is dependent on prior retrieval of the person's occupation. Occupation was recalled significantly more often than the distinctive feature of a famous person's face, and, crucially, information concerning a face was in general not recalled without the subject recalling the famous person's occupation. There was a small number of trials on which the correct visual information was given when the biographical information was not recalled correctly. Nevertheless, virtually all of them could be explained in terms of the hierarchical model.

It must be emphasised that the results do not simply show that facial information is very difficult to recall, or that facial information is difficult to recall relative to a person's occupation. In fact the percentage of all trials in Phase 1 on which the visual information was correctly retrieved was as high as 49%. The percentage of trials where occupation was correct in which visual information was correct was 73%. Recall of facial information is only very difficult (perhaps impossible) where the subject does not know the occupation.

It must also be emphasised that it is not simply the case that recall of the visual information is *logically* contingent on recall of the occupation. Logically, it would be reasonable to suppose that recalling that a man is, for instance, a pianist is contingent on recalling that he is a musician. However, there is no logical reason why recall of visual detail about his face should be contingent on recalling he is a musician.

It is important to consider the extent to which the results of Experiment 1 might reflect an asymmetry of knowledge acquisition rather than an asymmetry of access to information stored in memory. That is, it might reasonably be argued that names and occupations co-occur much more frequently in everyday life than do names and faces in the absence of biographical information. It would follow from this that subjects might be more likely to recall an occupation than a piece of facial information from a name. It does not follow from this account, however, that subjects should *never* be able to recall what a person looks like unless they can recall that person's occupation. It is therefore difficult to believe that an asymmetry of knowledge acquisition could be the sole explanation for the pattern of results that is displayed in Table 2. One way of investigating this issue further would be to conduct a learning study along the lines of McWeeny et al. (1987), in which subjects are required to associate an occupation and a piece of facial information with a previously unfamiliar name.

The effects of a biographical cue in the second phase of the experiment are also consistent with our model. A biographical cue was shown to be most effective in helping subjects recall facial information (relative to the name-again condition) when they had not previously recalled the occupation of the person concerned. If the subject does in fact know the facial information but was unable to recall it because the PIN could not be accessed in Phase 1, then the biography may allow the subject to activate the previously inaccessible PIN, and then recall the appropriate visual information about the person concerned, which becomes available for recall once the PIN is activated.

However, a biographical cue also gave rise to a significant improvement in recall of previously unretrieved facial information (relative to the name-again group) when presented to subjects who had already been able to recall the occupation. This was a result that was not anticipated. We had assumed that subjects who had correctly categorised a name in terms of its occupation would have already accessed the correct PIN, and so should have biographical information available to them already. Consequently, a biographical cue should have been redundant. There are at least two possible explanations of this result.

The first of these is that activation of a PIN is not all-or-none (Burton, Bruce, & Johnston, 1990). On some occasions, it may be that the PIN is only partially activated, and can only provide access to a person's occupation. There are other results that also favour the view that a person's occupation might be the first piece of information that is accessed about them (Cohen, 1990). As Cohen argues (page 295) "Occupation is clearly the key feature in person recognition, defining the person's identity and providing the access point for further information." It may then be that subsequent presentation of the biographical information as a cue raises the activation level of the PIN to a point at which it can allow other information about the person to be retrieved.

There is a more mundane alternative, however, which is that subjects sometimes recalled the correct occupation but actually had the wrong person in mind. The biographical information which they received in Phase 2 may have made this obvious to the subjects, who were then able to recall the appropriate visual information. As we did not question subjects about the reasons why the biography sometimes helped them when they already knew the occupation, we do not know which of these alternatives is correct. Nevertheless, this is an issue that we would hope to explore in future experiments.

Finally, the finding that subjects were more likely to recall the visual information when given the name again in Phase 2 (the control condition) if they had correctly recalled the occupation in Phase 1 can be explained in a straightforward fashion. Because we believe that a subject must recall the occupation before they can recall the visual information, subjects who recalled the occupation in Phase 1 have only one piece of information to recall rather than two. They need only recall the visual information; the other subjects must first recall the occupation.

EXPERIMENT 2

The results of Experiment 1 suggest that access to information about a person from a name does appear to be sequential, with access to facial information being contingent on access of identity-specific semantics such as the occupation of the person. This is the mirror image of the processes involved in the recall of a person's name from seeing their face, which also seems to be contingent on recall of the person's occupation (Hanley & Cowell, 1988; Hay et al., 1991; McWeeny et al., 1987; Young et al., 1985). In Experiment 2, we investigated subjects' ability to recall information about a person's face and name when they are presented with *biographical detail* about the person. Our model enables us to make no predictions regarding which of the two types of information is likely to be recalled more readily. However, if our model is correct, then it should be the case that recalling the name is not dependent on recalling information about the face, and recalling information about the face should not be dependent on recalling the person's name. This is because both the face and the name code generation systems have direct connections with the PIN.

In Experiment 2, we also attempted to replicate the results from Experiment 1, and compare them with those obtained when subjects are presented with biographical detail. Consequently, half of the subjects were presented with biographical information about a set of people, and half of the subjects were presented with their names. Subjects who were presented with names were asked to recall the famous person's occupation and facial feature (as in Experiment 1). Subjects who were presented with biographies were asked to recall information about the face and the name.

Method

Subjects. The 42 subjects comprised 15 males and 27 females aged between 18–50, who were recruited from the University of Liverpool, and from among acquaintances of one of the experimenters.

Materials.   Many of the famous people were those used in Experiment 1. We removed anyone over whom there had been any ambiguity about which occupation category best fitted them in Experiment 1. In addition, the criteria for selection needed to be rather more stringent in Experiment 2. This is because it was necessary to ensure that the initial letters of the famous people's surnames were equally distributed across four approximately equal sized sections of the alphabet. The sections of the alphabet selected as name categories were A–F; G–L; M–R; S–Z. This meant that 16 of the 64 famous people had surnames that started with the letters A–F, 16 had surnames that started with the letters G–L, 16 had surnames that started with the letters M–R, and 16 had surnames that started with the letters S–Z. Full details of the famous people used in Experiment 2 can be found in the Appendix.

Thirty two fake biographies were also produced, eight for each occupational category. All biographies, fake and real, were equated on the basis of amount of semantic information they contained, as for the biography cues used in Experiment 1. For example, the biography for Kristian Schmid read "Australian actor, who plays Todd Landers in Neighbours." In total, 96 items were presented to the subjects. One further category card was produced which contained the four designated sections of the alphabet. This, together with the face category card, was present throughout the experiment for subjects in the biography condition.

Procedure.   Subjects were split into two groups. Half of the subjects received names as stimuli, the others received biographies. In both groups, the procedure was essentially the same as in Phase 1 of Experiment 1: subjects were shown the stimuli in a pre-determined random order, one at a time, and were required to make a familiarity decision. After this, two recall-categorisation responses were requested from the subjects for the familiar stimuli. Subjects receiving the names as stimuli were requested to select the occupation and facial information that they associated with that name, as in Experiment 1. Subjects who received the biographies as stimuli were requested to recall facial information in the same way. They were also asked to indicate the section of the alphabet from which the celebrity's name came. Once again, we did not use a forced-choice procedure. Subjects were instructed not to guess and were therefore allowed to respond by saying they did not know into which category a name or biography fitted.

Two subjects, one in each condition, were dropped from the analysis of the results because they did not follow the instructions correctly. One of these told the experimenter that she had made familiarity decisions on the basis of whether or not she could recall the name of the famous person; the other was suspected of guessing, as she responded "familiar" to a high proportion of the distractor names.

Results

Familiarity decisions.   As in Experiment 1, false alarms were consistently low (less than five per subject) and did not differ across conditions. Mean hit rate for subjects presented with a name was 42/64; for subjects presented with a biography, mean hit rate was considerably lower at 33/64 items.

Recall of Faces, Names, and Occupations.   Figure 4 displays the mean amount of information recalled by the two groups of subjects in Experiment 2. Subjects who received the name as a stimulus recalled significantly more information than those who received a biography [$F(1,38 = 9.57$ ($P < 0.005$)]. For subjects presented with a name, retrieval of occupation was significantly higher than retrieval of facial information [$F(1,38) = 74.3$ ($P < 0.0001$)], consistent with the results of Experiment 1. Conversely, for subjects who were presented with a biography, retrieval of facial information was significantly higher than retrieval of name information [$F(1,38) = 5.80$, ($P < 0.05$)].

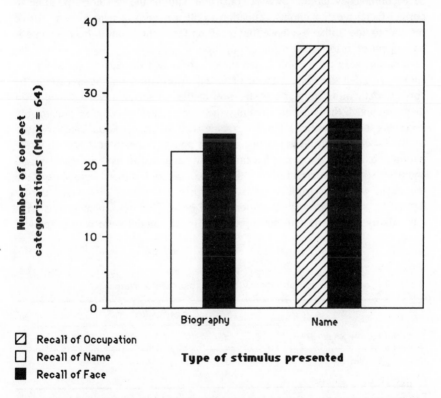

FIG. 4. Recall of name and facial information by subjects presented with biographies, and recall of occupation and facial information by subjects presented with names in Experiment 2.

For subjects in the biography condition, 2.1% of name categorisations were incorrect, and on 64% of trials subjects could not give a name category. For facial recall, 5.0% of categorisations were incorrect, and on 57% of trials subjects could not make a facial categorisation. For subjects in the name condition, 3.7% of occupation categorisations were incorrect and on 39% of trials subjects said that they did not know the correct occupational category. For facial recall, 4.5% of categorisations were incorrect and on 54% of trials subjects said that they did not know the correct facial categorisation.

To test whether recall of facial information might be contingent on recall of occupation for subjects in the name condition, the data were collated into 2 × 2 contingency tables for occupation and facial recall for *each individual subject* as in Experiment 1. A pooled contingency table for all subjects is shown in Table 4. It can be seen that, as in Experiment 1, the number of trials on which a subject recalled the appropriate facial feature without recalling the correct occupation is extremely small. Fisher exact probability tests for each individual subject were calculated; all of these were highly significant ($P < 0.001$). Visual inspection of each contingency table showed a consistent pattern: the cell corresponding to correct facial recall without occupation recall was zero or near to zero. These results provide further evidence that recalling facial information from a name is contingent on prior recall of the occupation.

It can be seen from Table 4 that there were only 13 occasions on which the subject recalled the correct piece of visual information without recalling the correct occupation. Further investigation of these 13 trials revealed that 10 of them involved the subject recalling the correct person (hence presumably accessing the correct PIN), but disagreeing with the occupational category used by the experimenters. Another one of them involved the subject accessing the wrong person from the name, but this person happened to have the same visual characteristic as the correct person. The remaining two of them were slips of the tongue in which the subject expressed surprise when they discovered during debriefing what their original response had been. Therefore, response patterns not initially consistent with those predicted by our model were very infrequent

TABLE 4
Pooled Contingency Table, Experiment 2; Names

	Occupation Recalled?	
Facial Feature Recalled?	Yes	No
Yes	517	13
No	217	533

The number of responses in the total data set in Experiment 2 falling into each cell of a pooled contingency table for subjects presented with a name.

(1.0% of total data set), and all of these responses subsequently turned out to be easily explicable in terms of the hierarchical model.

However, a quite different pattern emerged on the 217 trials in which the subject got the occupation correct but not the facial information. In as many as 166 of these, the subject said that they did not know which of the four facial features the person possessed. It is therefore a common occurrence for a subject to know an occupation but not know the facial features of that person's face when they see a name. It does not appear to be possible, however, for a subject to know the facial features associated with a name while stating that they do not know the person's occupation.

Performance by the subjects in the biography condition broken down in a similar way is shown in Table 5. Fisher exact probability tests for each individual subject were all significant ($P < 0.005$), though the significance levels were in general much lower than for the data shown in Table 4. However, the significance of these tests reflects a completely different pattern of results from those for subjects presented with a name. It can be seen that there was a substantial number of trials (70) on which subjects recalled the name without recalling the facial feature, and a large number of trials (127) on which subjects recalled the facial information without recalling the famous person's name. It appears that the significance of the Fisher exact probability tests is due to the large number of occasions (715) on which subjects were unable to give either item of information. Overall, these results suggest that recall of visual information from a biography is not contingent on recall of the name, and that recall of a name is not contingent on recall of facial information.

Perhaps the most direct and most revealing comparison of the biography and name conditions in this experiment is between recall of facial information from a biography, and recall of facial information from a name. Table 5 shows that there were a substantial number of trials (127, 9.9% of the total) on which subjects recalled facial information about a person without recalling that famous person's name. The pattern is therefore unlike that shown in Table 4, in which there were only 13 trials (1.0% of the total) when the facial information was recalled without the occupation. This difference is particularly striking when one

TABLE 5
Pooled Contingency Table, Experiment 2; Biographies

Facial Feature Recalled?	Name Recalled?	
	Yes	No
Yes	368	127
No	70	715

The number of responses in the total data set in Experiment 2 falling into each cell of a pooled contingency table for subjects presented with a biography.

bears in mind the fact that the overall amount of facial information correctly recalled by the two groups is very similar (see Fig. 4).

The nature of the 127 errors that subjects made in the biography condition when they got the facial information correct is also interesting. It will be recalled that the overwhelming majority of the corresponding errors when subjects were given names were trials on which the subject seemed to have the *wrong person* in mind, or had the correct person in mind, but disagreed with the experimenters about which occupation fitted them best. There was only one trial in Experiment 1, and no trials in Experiment 2 in which a subject got the facial information correct but responded that they *did not know* what the person's occupation was. The corresponding 127 trials when subjects received biographies, however, break down into 117 trials where the subject knew the facial information but said that they *did not know* the name, and 10 trials where the *incorrect name* was given. This contrast is perhaps the most critical piece of data in this study supporting the view that recall of facial information is contingent on recall of a person's occupation in response to seeing their name.

Just as recall of facial information does not seem to be dependent on recall of the name, so recall of the name does not appear to be contingent on recall of facial information from the biography. Of the 70 occasions on which the name was recalled without the facial information, there were 35 in which the subject said that they did not know the facial information, and 35 in which the subject gave incorrect facial information. It is therefore clearly possible for a subject to recall the name when they don't know the face, consistent with the view that recall of the name is not contingent on recall of the face.

It is also clear from Table 5 that there were approximately double the number of trials where subjects recalled both pieces of information about a person rather than just one. Retrieval of just one piece of information does reliably occur, but not as often as one might have expected. It seems unlikely that this result is telling us anything important about the person-recognition system; it probably means that most often we either know a lot about a person, or else we know nothing about them.

Discussion

The results of Experiment 2 were again consistent with the model presented in Fig. 2. When the subjects were presented with names, the critical finding was that no trials were observed where the subject knew the facial information but said they did not know the occupation. This strongly suggests that recall of visual information from a person's name is not possible without recall of the person's occupation. In the biography condition, by contrast, subjects quite frequently said that they did not know the name when they recalled the correct facial feature. They also often said that they did not know the facial feature when they correctly recalled the person's name. The evidence therefore indicated that recall of a name is not contingent on being able to recall a face, and recall of a face is not contingent on recall of a name. This finding is consistent with the results of Brennen et al. (1990) who showed that when a subject could not recall a name in response to a biography, then a photograph of that person was of no help in enabling the subject to retrieve the person's name. If recall of the name was contingent on recall of the face then providing a picture of the famous person should have proved extremely valuable.

The findings are also consistent with those reported by May and Clayton (1973), who read a series of definitions of uncommon objects (e.g. *gondola*, *mongoose*) to subjects, and asked them both to name and draw a picture of each one. Their results showed that subjects could sometimes form an image and draw a picture of an object even when they could not recall its name. There were also trials where the subject recalled the name but did not know what the object looked like. In other words, May and Clayton showed that retrieval of visual information could occur without retrieval of the name, and vice-versa. The similarity between their results and our results provides further evidence that objects and faces are represented in memory in similar ways (*cf* Ellis, Young, & Hay, 1987; Young, McWeeny, Ellis, & Hay, 1986b).

Figure 4 also shows that subjects in the biography condition had particular difficulties in recalling names. First, they recalled significantly fewer names than pieces of facial information, even though it would appear that the face and name generation systems are both directly linked to the PIN. In addition, the subjects who were given names recalled more occupations than the subjects who were given a biography were able to recall name information. In other words, it was easier for subjects to recall an occupation from a name than it was to recall a name from an occupation. The same pattern of performance was also reported by Cohen and Faulkner (1986) in their study, which involved learning of novel information about previously unfamiliar people. This shows that names are particularly difficult to recall even when one takes into account the sequence of processing stages that occur in person identification, as shown in Fig. 1.

It is also interesting to note that both groups recalled a similar amount of facial information even though it is assumed that recall of facial information involves two stages for the name group but only one stage for the biography group. We believe that this result suggests that the biographical condition was more difficult than the name condition. The higher hit rate for familiarity decisions in the name condition also shows that the biographical condition was more difficult. A name probably specifies a particular person more precisely, and thus activates a PIN more reliably, than do a few biographical facts about a person. In future experiments, the two conditions could be equated for difficulty by providing more extensive biographies and by collecting normative data from non-experimental subjects.

It must be acknowledged that the hierarchical model of name recognition that is represented in Fig. 2 does not explain *why* visual information about a famous person cannot be accessed without recall of their occupation. In order to answer this question, one might turn to current models of name retrieval, which attempt to explain why names are difficult to recall relative to occupations. According to the interactive activation and competition model proposed by Burton et al. (1990), and extended by Burton and Bruce (1992), names are difficult to retrieve because they are *unique* items of semantic information, not because they are stored separately from other items of semantic information. It would be unwise to speculate as to how the Burton and Bruce (1992) model would cope with retrieving visual information *from* names, as an implementation of this process has not been set up. However, it seems unlikely that the relative difficulty of retrieving facial information from a name could be explained in terms of the uniqueness of individual facial features.

Cohen (1990) has argued instead that names differ from occupations in that names are generally treated as meaningless. An occupation, in contrast, enables us to infer a lot of additional semantic information about a person. In other words, knowing that someone is called *Mr Baker* tells us much less about a person than knowing their occupation is that of *a baker*. Cohen argues that as a consequence of not being processed semantically, names are stored at the periphery of the semantic network in which other types of biographical detail are registered. It also seems quite reasonable to assume that much less can be inferred about a person from knowing that they have, for instance, a beard, than from knowing their occupation. As a consequence, facial features and names (perhaps voices also) may all lie at the edge of the semantic network in which more meaningful facts about people are stored. Such an account is consistent with Cohen's claim that the occupation is the key feature in defining the identity of most people that we meet, and would also explain why the occupation seems to be the access point for the recall of additional information about a person.

Theorists have frequently asked the question "What is unusual about names that makes them so difficult to recall from faces?" (Burton, 1992). We believe that the more interesting question is "What is so special about occupations that makes them so crucial for access of other types of information about people?". Of course, for people who are personally known to us the crucial item of information is likely to be different from their occupation, (e.g. kin relation for relatives). It may be that all categories of physical information by which people can be identified lie at the boundary of the semantic network and are likely to be difficult to recall relative to such central information as occupation or kin relationship.

Manuscript received 8 February 1993
Manuscript accepted 25 May 1993

REFERENCES

Borges, M.A., & Vaughn, L.S. (1977). Cognitive differences between the sexes in memory for names and faces. *Perceptual and Motor Skills*, 45, 317–318.

Brennen, T., Baguley, T., Bright, J., & Bruce, V. (1990). Resolving semantically induced tip-of-the-tongue states for proper nouns. *Memory and Cognition*, 18, 339–347.

Brown, R., & McNeill, D. (1966). The 'tip of the tongue' phenomenon. *Journal of Verbal Learning and Verbal Behavior*, 5, 325–337.

Bruce, V. (1979). Searching for politicians: An information-processing approach to face recognition. *Quarterly Journal of Experimental Psychology*, 31, 373–396.

Bruce, V., & Young, A.W. (1986). Understanding face recognition. *British Journal of Psychology*, 77, 305–327.

Burton, A.M. (1992). Good morning, Mr...er. *New Scientist, 1st February*, 39–41.

Burton, A.M., & Bruce, V. (1992). I recognize your face but I can't remember your name: A simple explanation. *British Journal of Psychology*, 81, 361–380.

Burton, A.M., Bruce, V., & Johnston, R.A. (1990). Understanding face recognition with an interactive activation model. *British Journal of Psychology*, 81, 361–380.

Clarke, H.M. (1934). Recall and recognition for faces and names. *Journal of Applied Psychology*, 18, 757–763.

Cohen, G. (1990). Why is it difficult to put names to faces? *British Journal of Psychology*, 81, 287–297.

Cohen, G., & Faulkner, D. (1986). Memory for proper names: Age differences in retrieval. *British Journal of Developmental Psychology*, 4, 187–197.

de Haan, E.H.F., Young, A., & Newcombe, F. (1987). Face recognition without awareness. *Cognitive Neuropsychology*, 4, 385–415.

de Haan, E.H.F., Young, A., & Newcombe, F. (1991). A dissociation between the sense of familiarity and access to semantic information concerning familiar people. *European Journal of Cognitive Psychology*, 3, 51–67.

Ellis, A.W., Young, A.W., & Critchley, E.M.R. (1989). Loss of memory for people following temporal lobe damage. *Brain*, 112, 1469–1483.

Ellis, A.W., Young, A.W., & Hay, D.C. (1987). Modelling the recognition of faces and words. In P.E. Morris (Ed.), *Modelling cognition*. Chichester: John Wiley.

Flude, B.M., Ellis, A.W., & Kay, J. (1989). Face processing and name retrieval in an anomic aphasic. *Brain and Cognition*, 11, 60–72.

Hanley, J.R., & Cowell, E.S. (1988). The effects of different types of retrieval cues on the recall of names of famous faces. *Memory and Cognition*, 16, 545–555.

Hanley, J.R., Pearson, N.A., & Howard, L.A. (1990). The effects of different types of encoding task on memory for famous faces and names. *Quarterly Journal of Experimental Psychology*, 42A, 741–762.

Hanley, J.R., Young, A.W., & Pearson, N.A. (1989). Defective recognition of familiar people. *Cognitive Neuropsychology*, 6, 179–210.

Hay, D.C., & Young, A.W. (1982). The human face. In A.W. Ellis (Ed.), *Normality and pathology in cognitive functions*. London: Academic Press.

Hay, D.C., Young, A.W., & Ellis, A.W. (1991). Routes through the face recognition system. *Quarterly Journal of Experimental Psychology*, 43A, 761–791.

Johnston, R.A., & Bruce, V. (1991). Lost properties? Retrieval differences between name codes and semantic codes for familiar people. *Psychological Research*, 52, 62–67.

May, J.M., & Clayton, K.M. (1973). Imaginal processes during the attempt to recall names. *Journal of Verbal Learning and Verbal Behavior*, 12, 683–688.

McNeil, J.E., & Warrington, E.K. (1991. Prosopagnosia: A reclassification. *Quarterly Journal of Experimental Psychology*, 43A, 267–287.

McWeeny, K.H., Young, A.W., Hay, D.C., & Ellis, A.W. (1987). Putting names to faces. *British Journal of Psychology, 78*, 143–151.

Morton, J. (1969). Interaction of information in word recognition. *Psychological Review, 76*, 165–178.

Morton, J. (1979). Facilitation in word recognition: Experiments causing change in the logogen model. In P.A. Kolers, M. Wrolstad, & H. Bouma (Eds.), *Processing of visible language*. New York: Plenum Press.

Read, J.D., & Wilbur, R.G. (1975). Availability of names and faces in recall. *Perceptual and Motor Skills, 41*, 263–270.

Semenza, C., & Zettin, M. (1988). Generating proper names: A case of selective inability. *Cognitive Neuropsychology, 5*, 711–721.

Valentine, T., Brédart, S., Lawson, R., & Ward, G. (1991). What's in a name? Access to information from people's names. *European Journal of Cognitive Psychology, 3*, 147–176.

Yarmey, A.D. (1970). The effect of mnemonic instructions on paired associate memory for names or faces. *Canadian Journal of Behavioral Science, 2*, 181–199.

Yarmey, A.D. (1973). I recognize your face but I can't remember your name: Further evidence on the tip-of-the-tongue phenomenon. *Memory and Cognition, 1*, 287–290.

Young, A.W., Ellis, A.W., & Flude, B.M. (1988). Accessing stored information about familiar people. *Psychological Research, 50*, 111–115.

Young, A.W., Hay, D.C., & Ellis, A.W. (1985). The faces that launched a thousand slips: Everyday difficulties and errors in recognising people. *Quarterly Journal of Experimental Psychology, 38A*, 297–318.

Young, A.W., McWeeny, K.H., Ellis, A.W., & Hay, D.C. (1986a). Naming and categorisation latencies for faces and written names. *Quarterly Journal of Experimental Psychology, 38A*, 297–318.

Young, A.W., McWeeny, K.H., Ellis, A.W., & Hay, D.C. (1986b). Getting semantic information from familiar faces. In H.D. Ellis, M.A. Jeeves, F. Newcombe, & A.W. Young (Eds.), *Aspects of face processing*. Dordrecht: Martinus Nijhoff Publishers.

Young, A.W., McWeeny, K.H., Hay, D.C., & Ellis, A.W. (1986). Access to identity-specific semantic codes from familiar faces. *Quarterly Journal of Experimental Psychology, 38A*, 271–295.

APPENDIX

The famous people used in Experiment 2

	MUSICIAN	POLITICIAN	SPORTSMAN	ACTOR
Balding				
A–F	Errol Brown	Rhodes Boyson	Bobby Charlton	Yul Brynner
G–L	Mark Knopfler	Neil Kinnock	Duncan Goodhew	Brian Glover
M–R	Yehudi Menuhin	Chris Mullin	Steve Ovett	Patrick Malahide
S–Z	Jimmy Somerville	Cyril Smith	Willie Thorne	Telly Savalas
Beard				
A–F	Acker Bilk	Fidel Castro	Geoff Capes	Brian Blessed
G–L	James Galway	Abraham Lincoln	Mike Gatting	James Robertson Justice
M–R	Luciano Pavarotti	Dave Nellist	Malcolm Marshall	David Puttnam
S–Z	Richard Stilgoe	Terry Waite	John Virgo	Orson Welles
Glasses				
A–F	Elvis Costello	Kenneth Baker	David Bryant	Michael Caine
G–L	Buddy Holly	Tom King	Clive Lloyd	Harold Lloyd
M–R	Hank Marvin	Michael Meacher	Doug Mountjoy	Rick Moranis
S–Z	John Williams	Jack Straw	David Vine	Tom Watt
Long Hair				
A–F	Marc Bolan	Oliver Cromwell	Pat Cash	Gerard Depardieu
G–L	Mick Hucknell	Michael Heseltine	Ruud Gullitt	Don Johnson
M–R	Simon Rattle	Carlos Menem	Ilie Nastase	Jimmy Nail
S–Z	John Tavener	David Sutch	Kirk Stevens	Kristian Schmid

MEMORY, 1993, *1* (4), 393–407

Spontaneous Mnemonic Strategies Used by Older and Younger Adults to Remember Proper Names

John O. Brooks III
Stanford University School of Medicine, USA

Leah Friedman
Stanford University School of Medicine, USA

Janet M. Gibson
Grinnell College, USA

Jerome A. Yesavage
Palo Alto Veteran Affairs Medical Center, USA.
Stanford University School of Medicine, USA

Little attention has been focused on the spontaneous mnemonic strategies that people use to remember proper names. In the experiment reported here, groups of younger (< 25 years old) and older subjects ($\geqslant$ 55 years old) were shown a series of 12 name–face pairs and instructed to remember them. In a subsequent test, they were shown the same faces and asked to recall the corresponding names. After the recall task, subjects completed a questionnaire about the mnemonic strategies they used. Our analyses revealed not only that the younger subjects recalled more names than did the older subjects, but also that older and younger subjects reported using certain strategies more frequently than other strategies. Moreover, regression analyses indicated that use of certain mnemonic strategies accounted for a significant proportion of recall performance beyond that accounted for by age alone. Older-old subjects ($\geqslant$ 70 years old) recalled fewer names than did younger-old subjects ($\geqslant$ 55 and < 70 years old), but they did not differ in the extent to which they used specific mnemonic strategies. Our results suggest that the use of spontaneous mnemonic strategies may play a role in the difference in proper name recall between younger and older adults.

Requests for reprints should be sent to John Brooks, PhD, Department of Psychiatry and Behavioral Sciences (TD-114), Stanford University School of Medicine, Stanford, CA 94305-5490, USA. E-mail: hf.meg.forsythe@stanford.edu

This work was supported in part by National Institute of Mental Health grant MH35182 and by a grant from Grinnell College. The authors would like to thank Christine Gray for her help in testing subjects and Delilah Farris for scoring data.

INTRODUCTION

Many people have trouble remembering proper names. On the one hand, it is difficult to understand why this happens, because remembering proper names is important in person-to-person interactions, and much in our lives depends on these interactions. Thus, recalling people's names is generally advantageous and proper names should presumably be well-remembered. Proper names, however, are often virtually meaningless words that label people. For example, the name "Marion Williams" is not descriptive of the person it refers to and conveys little information about her. In this regard, learning new names is akin to increasing one's vocabulary with little or no means of semantic organisation.

Interestingly, there are findings that other information about people is often easier to recall than their names. McWeeny, Young, Hay, and Ellis (1987) found that not only were persons' occupations recalled better than their names, but that when names and occupations were presented simultaneously, recall of the occupation was essentially prerequisite for recalling the name, whereas the reverse was not true. Cohen (1990b) replicated McWeeny et al.'s finding and found that when meaningful names or meaningful occupations were paired with meaningless counterparts (e.g. Mr. Baker was a ryman vs Mr. Ryman was a baker) names and occupations were recalled equally well. However, when meaningful names and meaningful occupations occurred together, occupations were better recalled than were names.

In keeping with observed verbal memory decrements in older adults (e.g. Taylor, Miller, & Tinklenberg, 1992), memory for proper names is especially problematic. Cohen and Faulkner (1986) found that subjects aged 60–70 years recalled fewer names than younger subjects, and subjects who were older than 70 years recalled even fewer names. Cohen and Faulkner also found that older subjects reporting experiencing 'name blocks' (inability to recall a name) twice as frequently as did younger subjects. In fact, a recent survey of older adults (average age = 73.3 years) revealed that almost half the respondents noted that memory for proper names was the memory skill that they most wanted to improve (Leirer, Morrow, Sheikh, & Pariante, 1990). These findings were echoed in a study by Bolla, Lindgren, Bonaccorsy, and Bleecker (1991) in which older subjects reported that forgetting names was the memory problem they most frequently experienced.

Why do older adults experience difficulty remembering proper names? Of course, one reason may be that younger and older adults differ on dimensions other than age that may affect their performance. For example, changes in societal and educational demands may differ for younger and older adults. It may also be that there is a general decline in memorial abilities with age (cf. Kausler, 1991; Salthouse, 1991). Such reasons are likely to be true to some extent, but there are other possibilities as well. One is that, in general, older adults may adopt less effective mnemonic strategies (Craik, 1986) or fail to use any strategy at all. Failure to use strategies could reflect a 'giving up' response on the part of older adults, because of the difficulty they experience in using effective, and sometimes complex, strategies (Craik, 1977; Craik & Rabinowitz, 1984). However, there is evidence that older subjects are capable of generating mnemonic strategies for words (e.g. Camp, Markley, & Kramer, 1983b; Hill, Allen, & Gregory, 1990), but perhaps they tend to choose relatively ineffective ones.

Because the difficulty older adults experience with remembering proper names appears to be prevalent and bothersome, information related to its occurrence could enhance both our understandings of the nature of memory for proper names as well as how memory for proper names relates to the aging process. There has been little exploration of this area—however, Finley and Rothberg (1990) conducted a questionnaire study and found that younger and older adults reported using similar memory strategies, but that the younger adults used them more frequently. The focus of the present study is on whether differences between younger and older adults in recall of proper names are related to the use of different mnemonic strategies. Or, put another way, does strategy use explain differences in recall beyond that explained by age?

In the present experiment, both younger and older adults were presented with a series of name and face pairs. (We used both first and last names to approximate more closely the challenges involved in everyday memory for proper names. And, because last names generally lend themselves more readily to the use of mnemonic strategies than do first names, it may be that the efficacy of strategy use will differ for first and last names.) Subsequently, subjects were again shown the faces and asked to recall the names that were originally paired with them. After recalling the names, subjects were asked to indicate how frequently (if at all) they had used selected mnemonic strategies to remember the names and the faces. We examined both the differences between the reported strategies of older and younger adults as well as the relations between frequency of strategy use and the number of names correctly recalled.

METHOD

Subjects

The 96 older subjects were recruited for participation in a memory training course by means of advertisements in local newspapers and talks at senior centres. None of the subjects had previously participated in a memory training course. The average age of the subjects was 68.69 (SD = 6.49) years. Subjects reported having an average of 15.27 (SD = 2.75) years of education and their average score on Form 1 of the Quick Vocabulary test (Borgotta & Corsini, 1964) was 83.62 (SD = 11.57). On the Mini-Mental State Examination (Folstein, Folstein, & McHugh, 1975) subjects received an average score of 28.32

(SD = 1.32). To be eligible for participation, the older subjects had to have an MMSE score of 27 or greater, no indications of clinically significant depression, and not currently be taking any medication that could affect their memory.

The 64 younger subjects were undergraduates at Grinnell College and participated in the experiment for pay or course credit. The average age of the younger subjects was 19.64 (SD = 1.30) years. They received an average score of 78.54 (SD = 12.07) on Form 1 of the Quick Vocabulary test.

Materials

Forty-eight black and white slides of faces from a 1968 high school yearbook were paired with 48 names, each of which comprised both a first and last name. The last names were drawn from the collection of names provided by Lorayne and Lucas (1974) (e.g. Scott Fisher, Richard Horner, Walter Mason, Wendy Russell). The slides and names were divided into four sets of 12; each subject saw only one set of stimuli.

A 10-item questionnaire was used to assess the strategies subjects used for remembering faces and names. The questionnaire was divided into three parts. In the first part, subjects were asked to circle a number on the accompanying scales to indicate the extent to which they used each of three strategies to remember the faces they had seen. The extent of use was measured with a 7-point scale on which "1" was labelled "Never used", "4" was labelled "Made some use of", and "7" was labelled "Used a great deal". The three strategies listed for faces were: "Just looked very hard at the faces", "Tried to notice some distinctive features of the face", and "Tried to notice a resemblance to someone you know".

The second part of the questionnaire pertained to strategies for remembering the names. Five strategies were listed for names and were accompanied by the same 7-point scales described for the face strategies. They were: "Just listened attentively to the names", "Repeated names to yourself over and over", "Tried to remember the first letters of the names", "Tried to find a rhyme with the name", and "Tried to give meaning to the name". Subjects were again instructed to circle the number that indicated the extent to which they used each of the strategies. For both the face strategies and name strategies, subjects were also asked to describe any other strategy they used and rate the frequency of use on a 7-point scale.

In the third part of the questionnaire, subjects were asked to describe how they "remembered that a specific name went with a specific face".

Design

The present experiment was conducted in conjunction with an unrelated experiment that involved studying words; only the results of the proper name experiment will be reported here. Because subjects participated in both experiments, half the subjects were given the name experiment first and half were given the word experiment first. Each slide was yoked with a first and last name and a given subject saw only one set of 12 slides and names. Each of the four sets of names and faces was used an equal number of times across subjects. The order of the slides in the presentation phase and the test phase was randomised separately, but within each phase the same random order was used for all subjects.

Procedure

Subjects were tested in groups of up to 21 at a time. Subjects were handed a booklet that contained the rating scales and pages on which to write their answers. They were told that they would be presented with a series of names and slides of faces, and that their task would be to try to remember the name (both first and last names) that went with each face. The slides were projected on the screen at the rate of one every minute. When a slide appeared on the screen, the experimenter held up a card with a name printed on it in Times 120-point type and read the name aloud once. After one minute had elapsed, a new slide appeared on the screen and the experimenter held up and read out a different name card.

After the last slide was presented, subjects were told to turn to the page in their booklets with 12 lines on it so that they could write the names during the forthcoming test. For the test, subjects were told that they would be presented with the same set of faces they had just seen and would be asked to recall both the first and last name associated with each face. They were also told that if they could not remember both the first and last name, they should write whatever they could remember. The slides were presented again at the rate of approximately one every minute and subjects were told to write their answers on the answer sheet.

After the recall test, subjects were told that people often have their own strategies to help them remember things. They were told to turn to the page that contained questions about the strategies that they may have used to help them remember the names and faces. They were asked to circle the number that reflected how much they used each strategy. Subjects were allowed to take as long as they needed to complete the questionnaire and they usually required about 4–6 minutes.

RESULTS

The results will be divided into four sections; the first deals with the extent to which the different strategies were used by younger and older adults; the second with the relations between reported strategy use and recall; the third with an analysis of younger and older subjects' recall errors; and the fourth with a comparison of younger-old and older-old subjects recall and strategy use.

TABLE 1
Average Ratings of Strategy Use for Older and
Younger Subjects

Strategy	Group	
	Older	Younger
Look at face	5.42 (1.67)	4.61 (1.56)
Distinctive feature	6.05 (1.26)	5.59 (1.24)
Notice resemblance	4.70 (2.35)	4.23 (2.04)
Other strategy for faces	2.34 (2.25)	2.41 (2.41)
Listen to names	4.95 (1.86)	3.52 (1.73)
Repeat names	4.94 (1.83)	5.03 (1.71)
Remember first letters	2.49 (2.01)	2.03 (1.77)
Find a rhyme	2.16 (1.87)	2.14 (1.82)
Give meaning	3.64 (2.23)	4.56 (2.23)
Other strategy for names	1.87 (1.88)	2.75 (2.53)

Standard deviations are in parentheses. Full descriptions of the strategies are provided in the text. Ratings were on a 1 ("never used") to 7 ("used a great deal") scale.

Strategy Use

The average frequency that the subjects reported for using each strategy is reported in Table 1. The ratings for "Other strategy" were not included in the following analyses because of the variability of the strategies reported. All subjects, both younger and older, reported relying on at least one strategy to at least some extent, and no subject reported exclusively "looking very hard" at faces or "listening attentively" to names. MANOVAs indicated that the two groups significantly differed with respect to the frequency of use of the strategies, for face strategies: $\Lambda = 0.92$, $F(3, 156) = 4.80$, $P = 0.01$; for name strategies: $\Lambda = 0.82$, $F(5, 154) = 6.85$, $P = 0.01$. The two age groups reported relying on different strategies. Specifically, older subjects reported that they just looked at the faces, $t(158) = 3.41$, $P = 0.01$; tried to notice some distinctive features of the face, $t(158) = 2.27$, $P = 0.02$; and just listened attentively to the names, $t(158) = 4.92$, $P = 0.01$ more often than did the younger subjects. The younger subjects, on the other hand, reported trying to give meaning to a name more frequently than did the older subjects, $t(158) = 2.57$, $P = 0.01$.

Strategies and Name Recall

Subjects' responses were scored according to whether they correctly recalled only the first name, only the last name, or both names. In each case, one point was given for a correct response, which meant that for the scoring of both "names" a point was given only if both names were correctly recalled. Because

TABLE 2
Average Number of Names Recalled by Older and
Younger Subjects

Group	First name	Last name	Both names
Older	3.68 (2.83)	3.26 (2.64)	2.21 (2.42)
Younger	8.72 (2.80)	8.53 (2.93)	7.56 (3.24)

Standard deviations are in parentheses.

different strategies may have varying degrees of usefulness for first or last names, we performed separate analyses for first names correctly recalled, last names correctly recalled, and both names correctly recalled. These three measures are not entirely independent of one another, but we present all the analyses to provide information relevant to everyday occurrences. Because mnemonic strategies are probably more easily applied to last names, our findings with last names are of primary interest.

The average number of names that were recalled correctly is provided in Table 2. In each instance, the younger subjects recalled significantly more names than did the older subjects, all $ts(158) \geq 11.09$, $Ps = 0.01$. This age difference is rather striking in that the younger subjects recalled two to three times as many names as did the older subjects.

To evaluate the relations between name recall and strategy use, and to determine which strategies were most strongly associated with recall, the frequencies of use of the strategies were regressed on recall along with age (which was dummy coded such that younger subjects were assigned a "0" and older subjects a "1"). The results of the regression analyses are provided in Table 3. Only those strategies that accounted for a statistically significant unique proportion of variance are presented. For all three measures, not only did age alone account for a statistically significant proportion of the variance of recall, but the frequency of use of the strategies themselves accounted for a significant proportion of the variance. For first names, noticing a resemblance to a familiar person and giving meaning to names were significant correlates of recall. For last names, remembering the first letters of the names related negatively to recall, whereas giving meaning related positively. Finally, for remembering both names together, noticing a resemblance and giving meaning to the names were significant correlates of recall.

Finally, we should consider the additional strategies that subjects reported using. Because these strategies were generated by the subjects, we categorised them according to their similarities. No clear pattern of alternative strategies emerged, though 9.4% of the younger subjects and 13% of the older subjects reported associating the presented name with the name of someone familiar. No other strategy was reported with as high a frequency.

TABLE 3
Results of Multiple Regression Analyses of Name Recall with
Younger and Older Subjects

	Regression coefficient	t
First names		
Age	−4.58	9.92
Notice resemblance	0.30	3.01
Give meaning	0.45	4.38
Last names		
Age	−4.68	10.41
Remember first letters	−0.23	2.14
Give meaning	0.49	5.01
Both names		
Age	−4.77	10.45
Notice resemblance	0.22	2.27
Give meaning	0.46	4.54

For all ts, $P < 0.05$; $n = 160$.

In the final part of the questionnaire, subjects were asked how they remembered which name went with each face. For the older subjects, 19% reported that they made an association between the name and a facial feature, and 9% reported trying to associate the name and face with someone familiar. Only 3% reported just repeating the name and "trying to memorise" the face. For the younger subjects, 31% reported that they attempted to associate the name with a facial feature, and 8% reported attempting associations with someone familiar. Thus, a larger percentage of younger subjects reported making associations between names and faces than did the older subjects.

Recall Errors

The subjects' responses were also scored with respect to the number and type of errors that they committed in recalling last names. Only subjects who committed errors were used in this analysis, which was based on 55 younger subjects and 95 older ones. Errors were classified according to whether they were errors of omission (no name was written); commission (a nonpresented name was written); or confusion (a presented name was written in response to the wrong face). Then, for each subject, the number of errors of each type was divided by that subject's total number of errors to yield the proportions of different errors. The average proportions of errors for younger and older adults are presented in Table 4. The older subjects made a significantly greater percentage of errors of omission, $t(148) = 3.68$, $P = 0.01$, but the younger subjects made a significantly greater percentage of commission errors, $t(148) = 3.42$, $P = 0.01$. The two

TABLE 4
Average Proportion of Recall Errors for Younger and
Older Subjects

Group	Type of error		
	Omission	Commission	Confusion
Older	0.82 (0.16)	0.06 (0.12)	0.12 (0.13)
Younger	0.67 (0.35)	0.18 (0.31)	0.16 (0.22)

Standard deviations are in parentheses.

groups did not differ with respect to the percentage of errors of confusion, $t(148) = 1.23$, $P > 0.10$.

Analyses of Younger-old and Older-old subjects

To evaluate further the relation between age and strategy use in proper name memory, we divided our older subjects into two groups: older-old subjects who were at least 70 years old, and younger-old subjects who were at least 55 but less than 70 years old. We chose 70 years of age as the point of division because previous studies have made this distinction (e.g. Cohen & Faulkner, 1986; Yesavage, Sheikh, Friedman, & Tanke, 1990). The average age of the older-old group was 74.48 years (SD = 4.34; range: 70–88), and the average age of the younger-old group was 64.19 years (SD = 3.71; range: 55–69). There were 42 older-old subjects and 54 younger-old subjects. The average recall scores for the two groups are provided in Table 5. The number of last names correctly recalled did not differ significantly between the two groups, $t(94) = 1.57$, $P > 0.10$, but the younger-old correctly recalled more first names, $t(94) = 2.74$, $P = 0.01$, and both names together, $t(94) = 2.15$, $P = 0.03$.

TABLE 5
Average Number of Names Recalled for Older-old and
Younger-old Subjects

Group	First name	Last name	Both names
Older-old	2.81 (2.22)	2.79 (2.17)	1.62 (1.61)
Younger-old	4.35 (3.08)	3.63 (2.92)	2.67 (2.83)

Standard deviations are in parentheses.

The average extent to which the younger-old and older-old subjects reported using the different strategies is provided in Table 6. Interestingly, MANOVAs

TABLE 6
Average Ratings of Strategy Use for Older-old and
Younger-old Subjects

	Group	
Strategy	*Older-old*	*Younger-old*
Look at face	5.64 (1.69)	5.24 (1.64)
Distinctive feature	6.02 (1.33)	6.07 (1.47)
Notice resemblance	4.24 (2.37)	5.06 (2.30)
Listen to names	5.00 (1.99)	4.91 (1.76)
Repeat names	5.10 (1.86)	4.82 (1.81)
Remember first letters	2.52 (2.04)	2.46 (2.01)
Find a rhyme	1.81 (1.64)	2.43 (2.01)
Give meaning	3.62 (2.23)	3.65 (2.26)

Standard deviations are in parentheses. Ratings were on a 1 ("never used") to 7 ("used a great deal") scale.

indicated that there were *no* statistically significant differences between the two groups for the frequency of use of the strategies; for faces; $\Lambda = 0.95$, $F(3, 92) = 1.47$, $P > 0.10$; for names: $\Lambda = 0.96$, $F(5,90) < 1$. That is, both groups reported using the strategies to approximately the same extent.

To evaluate which strategies were significant correlates of recall performance among the younger-old and older-old subjects, we performed regressions in which age was dummy coded and regressed, along with the ratings of the eight strategies, on name recall. The results of the regression are provided in Table 7. For first names, several strategies were related to recall independently of age: looking at the face and finding a rhyme were negatively associated with recall, whereas giving meaning to names was positively associated with recall. For last names, age did not account for a significant proportion of the variance of recall scores. However, the strategies of repeating names and giving meaning to names were significantly related to recall. For both names, age, listening to names, and finding a rhyme were all negatively associated with recall.

DISCUSSION

Our purpose in the present study was to explore differences in the strategies that older and younger subjects used spontaneously to remember proper names, and to determine how these differences related to performance. As expected, younger subjects recalled more names than did older subjects. We also found that although both older and younger subjects reported using mnemonic strategies to help them remember proper names, there were differences between the two groups with respect to the extent to which they used specific strategies. Finally, older-old subjects recalled fewer names than did younger-old subjects,

TABLE 7
Results of Multiple Regression Analyses of Name Recall with
Younger-old and Older-old Subjects

	Regression coefficient	t
First names		
Age	-3.36	6.16
Look at face	-0.34	2.21
Find a rhyme	-0.31	2.18
Give meaning	0.64	5.58
Last names		
Age	-0.65	1.22
Repeat names	-0.31	1.95
Give meaning	0.40	3.09
Both names		
Age	-3.06	5.43
Listen to names	-0.29	1.87
Find a rhyme	-0.28	1.93

For all ts, $\geqslant$ 1.93, $P < 0.05$; $n = 96$.

but the extent to which they reported relying on the different strategies did not differ significantly.

In two word-recall studies that involved younger and older subjects, Camp, Markley, and Kramer (1983a; 1983b) stressed that subjects sometimes employ rather elaborate strategies spontaneously. It takes little imagination to extrapolate this to include subjects' efforts to remember proper names. Indeed, the present data support the contention that both younger and older subjects use mnemonic strategies to remember proper names. We found that younger subjects reported using a presumably effective strategy, giving meaning to names, to a greater extent than did older subjects. Giving meaning to names was also the strategy that was the strongest correlate of recall. The strategy that older subjects reported using to a greater extent than younger subjects was ''just listening to the names''—a strategy that was presumably less beneficial. These findings suggest that older adults tend not to adopt effective strategies to the same extent as younger subjects.

The difference in relations between recall performance and strategy in the two age groups may also reflect the quality of the older subjects' meaningful associations, and perhaps their ability to engage in such a strategy at all. Although we have no direct evidence, it is possible that if the 'quality' of the older subjects' associations was not equivalent to that of the younger subjects, it is likely that such associations would be less helpful when the older subjects attempted to recall the names. We should caution that even though such an explanation may seem plausible, it is unclear whether older adults are actually deficient in dealing with semantic information (*cf.* Kausler, 1991; Light, 1992).

Our study also provided a preliminary examination of a neglected area of proper name research. We asked subjects to describe any strategies they may have used in establishing an association between the names and accompanying faces. This information is important because not only does the need to associate names with faces arise in real life, but most studies of proper name memory present faces and names together; good performance depends on making a link between names and faces. This aspect of proper name memory might provide an additional burden for older adults (*cf.* Cohen, 1990a) if they were either unable to generate spontaneously complex memorial strategies or unable to execute them effectively. We found that the most commonly reported strategy for associating names and faces was the same for younger and older adults: they attempted to find a distinctive feature of the face and relate it in some way to a meaningful elaboration of the name. However, a smaller percentage of older adults than younger adults reported using this strategy. This difference may contribute to younger adults' superior performance and, to be sure, this area warrants more in-depth research.

In the present experiment, older subjects reported using the visual strategy of noticing a distinctive facial feature more frequently than did the younger subjects. However, the frequency of noticing a distinctive facial feature was not a significant predictor of recall performance. Camp et al. (1983b) found that older subjects did not report using strategies that involved mental imagery when learning lists of words. Perhaps because of a lack of practice and consequent lack of comfort or lack of skill in forming visual images, older subjects do not use visual strategies for word recall, but because of the visual nature of faces they attempt to use them, albeit with varying degrees of success, when studying faces and names. That is, the older adults may not have been able to visualise the distinctive feature very well, or may not have been able to remember the feature after visualisation.

Our analyses of younger-old and older-old subjects' performance revealed that the younger-old recalled more first names and both names correctly, but that the two groups did not differ in the extent to which they reported using specific strategies. Thus, we were able to elaborate on Cohen and Faulkner's (1986) finding that middle-aged (40–59 years old) subjects recalled more proper names than older subjects (60–80 years old). For the older adults, recall performance for last names was positively associated with the strategy of giving meaning to the name, and negatively associated with repeating the name. It may be that the abilities to use the strategies contributed to performance differences because the frequency of strategy use did not differ between younger-old and older-old subjects.

The lack of differences in strategy use within the older age group makes it all the more puzzling as to why younger subjects and older subjects differed in their strategy choices. There are at least two possible explanations: although older adults may not have decreased their reliance on mnemonic strategies, they may have shifted their strategy choice at some point in their lives to less effective strategies, or, if no strategy shift occurred, they may have continued using less effective strategies they had developed in their youth. The error analysis suggested that older subjects seemed to have more difficulty recalling a name than did the younger subjects (because the older adults had a greater proportion of omission errors), whereas the younger subjects apparently were more likely to guess and thus respond with nonpresented names (because the younger adults had a greater proportion of commission errors). These findings are consistent with, but do not confirm, the notion that the older subjects have proportionally more difficulty with recalling the correct names associated with the faces.

As an aside, we might note that our findings are relevant to the field of mnemonic training in older adults (*cf* Finley & Sharp, 1989; McEvoy & Moon, 1988; Verhaeghen, Marcoen, & Goossens, 1992). Older adults' spontaneous strategy choices may moderate the beneficial effects of mnemonic training. Because the amount of mnemonic training can alter the relations among problems older adults experience in using mnemonics (Brooks, Friedman, & Yesavage, 1993), it may be that taking into account both training time and pre-training strategy choice can enhance the efficacy of mnemonic training. These issues require further investigation.

As we interpret our results, we should note that they may, at least in part, reflect cohort effects rather than specific effects of age *per se*. As with any cross-sectional study involving the comparison of age groups, observed differences may reflect confounded variables rather than differences associated with aging. It is conceivable that differences in subjects' strategy choices were in part influenced by differences in the nature of their education, which occurred under different societal conditions. For example, many people in older cohorts may have lived much of their lives in cohesive groups with enduring daily contacts that placed limited demand on learning novel names. Similarly, the number of years that have elapsed since subjects were last in school or have been tested may have influenced their strategy choice. That is, the education that many older people received may have provided little exposure to the types of audio-visual material that make use of visualisation—the core of a number of effective mnemonic strategies. Yet another possibility is that older adults experience a type of proactive interference because of the greater number of names they have encountered throughout their lives. If this is the case, then the older adults may be adopting a more adaptive strategy, in that they do not exert as much effort to learn new names. Disentangling these and other possibilities would, of course, require a longitudinal study, perhaps focusing on why older adults adopt the strategies they do.

Manuscript received 15 January 1993
Manuscript accepted 12 July 1993

REFERENCES

Bolla, K.I., Lindgren, K.N., Bonaccorsy, C., & Bleecker, M.L. (1991). Memory complaints in older adults: Fact or fiction? *Archives of Neurology, 48*, 61–64.

Borgotta, E.F., & Corsini, R.J. (1964). *Quick word test manual.* New York: Harcourt, Brace, & World.

Brooks, J.O. III, Friedman, L., & Yesavage, J.A. (1993). A study of the problems older adults encounter in using a mnemonic technique. *International Psychogeriatrics, 5*, 57–65.

Camp, C.J., Markley, R.P., & Kramer, J.J. (1983a). Naive mnemonics: What the "do-nothing" control group does. *American Journal of Psychology, 96*, 503–511.

Camp, C.J., Markley, R.P., & Kramer, J.J. (1983b). Spontaneous use of mnemonics by elderly individuals. *Educational Gerontology, 9*, 57–71.

Cohen, G. (1990a). Recognition and retrieval of proper names: Age differences in the fan effect. *European Journal of Cognitive Psychology, 2*, 193–204.

Cohen, G. (1990b). Why is it difficult to put names to faces? *British Journal of Psychology, 81*, 287–297.

Cohen, G., & Faulkner, D. (1986). Memory for proper names: Age differences in retrieval. *British Journal of Developmental Psychology, 4*, 187–197.

Craik, F.I.M. (1977). Age differences in human memory. In J.E. Birren & K.W. Schaie (Eds.), *Handbook of the psychology of aging* (pp. 384–420). New York: Van Nostrand Reinhold.

Craik, F.I.M. (1986). A functional account of age differences in memory. In F. Klix & H. Hagendorf (Eds.), *Human memory and cognitive capabilities: Mechanisms and performances* (pp. 403–422). Amsterdam: Elsevier Science.

Craik, F.I.M., & Rabinowitz, J.C. (1984). Age differences in the acquisition and use of verbal information. In H. Bouma & D.G. Bouwhuis (Eds.), *Attention and performance X: Control of language process.* Hillsdale, NJ: Lawrence Erlbaum Associates Inc.

Finley, G.E., & Rothberg, S. (1990). Retrieval strategies of older and younger adults for recalling names and misplaced objects. *Interamerican Journal of Psychology, 24*, 99–100.

Finley, G.E., & Sharp. T. (1989). Name retrieval by the elderly in the tip-of-the-tongue paradigm: Demonstrable success in overcoming initial failure. *Educational Gerontology, 15*, 259–265.

Folstein, M.F., Folstein, S.E., & McHugh, P.H. (1975). Mini-mental state: A practical method for grading the cognitive state of patients for the clinician. *Journal of Psychiatric Research, 12*, 189–198.

Hill, R.D., Allen, C., & Gregory, K. (1990). Self-generated mnemonics for enhancing free recall performance in older learners. *Experimental Aging Research, 16*, 141–145.

Kausler, D.H. (1991). *Experimental psychology, cognition, and human aging.* NY: Springer-Verlag.

Leirer, V.O., Morrow, D.G., Sheikh, J.I., & Pariante, G.M. (1990). Memory skills elders want to improve. *Experimental Aging Research, 16*, 155–158.

Light, L.L. (1992). The organization of memory in old age. In F.I.M. Craik, & T.A. Salthouse (Eds.), *The handbook of aging and cognition* (pp. 111–166). Hillsdale, NJ: Lawrence Erlbaum Associates Inc.

Lorayne, H., & Lucas, J. (1974). *The memory book.* Briarcliff Manor, NY: Stein & Day.

McEvoy, C.L., & Moon, J.R. (1988). Assessment and treatment of everyday memory problems in the elderly. In M.M. Gruneberg, P.E. Morris, & R.N. Sykes (Eds.), *Practical aspects of memory: Current research and issues* (Vol. 2) (pp. 155–160). NY: John Wiley & Sons.

McWeeny, K.H., Young, A.W., Hay, D.C., & Ellis, A.W. (1987). Putting names to faces. *British Journal of Psychology, 78*, 143–149.

Salthouse, T.A. (1991). *Theoretical perspectives on cognitive aging.* Hillsdale, NJ: Lawrence Erlbaum Associates Inc.

Taylor, J.L., Miller, T.P., & Tinklenberg, J.R. (1992). Correlates of memory decline: A 4-year longitudinal study of older adults with memory complaints. *Psychology and Aging, 7*, 185–193.

Verhaeghen, P., Marcoen, A., & Goossens, L. (1992). Improving memory performance in the aged through mnemonic training: A meta-analytic study. *Psychology and Aging*, *7*, 242–251.

Yesavage, J.A., Sheikh, J.I., Friedman, L., & Tanke, E. (1990). Learning mnemonics: Roles of aging and subtle cognitive impairment. *Psychology and Aging*, *5* 133–137.

MEMORY, 1993, *1* (4), 409–431

The Difficulty with Recalling People's Names: The Plausible Phonology Hypothesis

Tim Brennen

University of Oslo, Norway

Recalling the name of a person is a simple, but often a problematic, everyday task. There are various explanations of this phenomenon, but here it is argued that the explanations offered so far, by failing to consider *learning* of names, have overlooked a simple account of name recall difficulty. The starting observation for this viewpoint is that names of people are often non-words, in that they have never been encountered before. This is not true of, say, names of professions. Not only does the relatively high rate of new exemplars mean that people's names are likely to be underlearned, but furthermore, even for equal degrees of learning, a person's name is at a disadvantage because of the high plausibility of most phonologies: "dreaner" is much more readily accepted as the name of a person than as the name of their profession. So specifying the phonology of people's names is inherently a more demanding task, compared to the phonology of other names. The implications of this view are explored with regard to explanations of empirically established name recall phenomena in normal subjects, the patterns of performance of anomic patients and the difficulty of name recall in different word domains. It is shown that these arguments, derived from a real world fact, account in a simple way for existing data and make predictions in different areas of research.

INTRODUCTION

Recalling people's names is a common everyday task, and one that gives us difficulty from time to time. This observation has long interested philosophers, and in the past ten years it has become a particular focus of attention for some cognitive psychologists. Evidence from a wide range of paradigms has converged on the conclusion that a person's name is harder to recall than other facts one knows about them, and several box-and-arrow models of face processing have modelled this by a functional separation of names from the

Requests for reprints should be sent to Tim Brennen, Institute of Psychology, University of Oslo, Blindern, Boks 1094, 0317 OSLO, Norway. e-mail: tim.brennen@psy-kologi.uio.no

The author was supported by an ATIPE grant from the CNRS Région Rhône-Alpes during the preparation of the article. Thanks to Serge Brédart, Ragnhild Dybdahl, and two anonymous referees for their comments on earlier drafts.

rest of identity-specific information: access to a person's name from their face is dependent on prior access to semantic information (e.g. Bruce & Young, 1986).

The principal results and the more recent attempts to account for the elusiveness of people's names will be reviewed. Then the issue of *learning* new names will be tackled, because in the models proposed up to now the acquisition phase has been largely ignored. It will be argued that much of the difficulty one has with recalling people's names derives from the fact that new (i.e. previously unfamiliar) *people's* names are encountered much more frequently than new *common* names, which means that typically people's names are more likely to be underlearned than common names. More importantly, this leads to the need for a more precise specification of the phonology of a person's name. A consideration of the consequences of this will follow, leading to a more general hypothesis about name recall.

First, four studies will be considered, in order to illustrate the variety of paradigms showing that names of faces are hard to recall. Young, Hay, and Ellis (1985) carried out a cognitive diary study in order to investigate the sorts of errors that subjects make when identifying people in everyday situations. Their subjects were asked to note all instances where person identification did not occur faultlessly. Over an eight week period a wide range of phenomena were reported, for example failing to recognise a friend, or noticing a striking resemblance between a passer-by and a famous person, and, of course, instances where a face was recognised and identified but the person's name was temporarily unrecallable. The argument that names of faces are particularly difficult to recall was further strengthened by the fact that no cases of recalling a person's name in the *absence* of other semantic information about the person were reported (see also Hay, Young, & Ellis, 1991).

The sequential processing of the Bruce and Young model predicts that cues should be differentially useful according to the actual level of blockage. Hanley and Cowell (1988) tested this by presenting their subjects with faces, half of which were famous and half unfamiliar. The subjects had to try to name the famous faces, and were often able to do so. However, three types of errors also occurred; one where subjects failed to recognise a familiar face; another where they recognised a face as familiar but were unable to say where they knew it from; and the third type where a face was found familiar and correct semantic information was provided but the person's name was still unavailable. Each time one of these errors was produced, subjects were presented with one of three cues: a different view of the same person's face; detailed semantic information on the person; or information on the person's initials. From the Bruce and Young model, Hanley and Cowell predicted that: another photo should provoke more naming than the other two cues for the 'failure to recognise' type of error; semantic information should allow access to the name more for the 'familiarity only' errors; and initial information should be most useful for the tip-of-the-tongue state errors. Over all, the predictions were indeed supported, and the semantics/name sequence seems well-grounded.

Flude, Ellis, and Kay (1989) reported the case of an aphasic patient who had very little trouble recognising faces or indeed giving identity-specific information about them. However, of the many familiar faces shown to him, he was only able to name three. This case is not unique: many aphasic patients experience exactly the same sorts of difficulty, and similar case studies have been reported by Semenza and Zettin (1988; 1989) and Lucchelli and de Renzi (1992).

McWeeny, Young, Hay, and Ellis (1987) asked their subjects to learn to associate a surname and a profession to each of 16 familiar faces. They showed that when only one label could be recalled there was a much greater probability that it be the profession than the name; that is, subjects rarely recalled the name of a face without recalling its profession, but quite often recalled the profession without the name. An ingenious aspect of the experiment's design was that some of the labels, e.g. Baker, Porter, could be either a surname or a profession, and the main result held even for these ambiguous labels. Cohen (1990) replicated this result, naming it the Baker-baker paradox: the phonology 'baker' is more easily associated to a face when it represents that person's profession than when it represents their name.

The separation of names and semantics in the box-and-arrow models alluded to earlier thus provides a summary of these results: access to the name of a person seems to be dependent on prior access to the semantics of that person. However, such a functional separation does not *explain* names' disadvantages. Three recent papers have offered explanations of the difference between the recall of the name of a person and other identity information known about them, in terms of functional differences between the two types of information: one in terms of names' inherent lack of meaning (Cohen, 1990); an interactive activation model of the naming process (Burton & Bruce, 1992); and a model based on a previous model of language processing (Burke, Mackay, Worthley, & Wade, 1991; Mackay, 1982).

Cohen's claim is supported by experiments using a McWeeny-type paradigm. In one experiment, surnames and professions were to be associated to faces. One group of subjects learned surnames and professions that were potentially meaningful, e.g. Mr. Carpenter is a lawyer. Other subjects learned surnames that were nonwords and real professions, and the third group learned familiar surnames and nonword professions, such as "ryman" or "talmer". When both labels were familiar, names were recalled less frequently: a replication of McWeeny et al.'s (1987) effect. However, for the other groups, the nonword labels were at a disadvantage, meaning that "baker" was recalled more than "ryman", regardless of whether it was a profession or a name: a reversal, in one case, of the profession advantage. So, whichever label was 'meaningless' (i.e. was represented by a new phonology) was harder to learn, and it was concluded that in real life names (and nonwords) were harder to recall than professions because they are less interconnected to other stored knowledge.

However, one needs to consider what it means to 'learn a name'. In order to learn a name whose phonology was previously unfamiliar, two processes are necessary: Step 1, learning the phonology of the new name; and Step 2, associating the phonology to the person. Whereas, for names that were known to the subject prior to the current episode, only the second process need to be undertaken. So, to learn to associate the phonology "Yeltsin" to Boris Yeltsin's face, as many of us have done in recent years, requires the two processes for non-Russians; whereas, to associate the phonology "Major" to John Major's face, English-speakers require only the second step, because "Major" is an English word.

This two-step analysis of word learning leads one to expect a disadvantage for any group of words that were not pre-experimentally familiar, even if the task were a straightforward free recall task: it is easier to recall "Baker" than "ryman" *per se*. So, for subjects in some conditions of Cohen's experiments, it was not a case of associating a pre-experimentally familiar phonology to a face (Step 2 alone), but also of acquiring the phonology (Step 1). From this point of view it is not surprising that the name/semantic effect could be reversed. In sum, Cohen's (1990) results are probably due to underlearning, where the newly-encountered phonology suffers a disadvantage relative to the pre-experimentally familiar word. A consideration of the task demands involved in learning new names leads to an account of Cohen's (1990) results, obviating the need to propose an impoverished link-up to the semantic system.

Burton, Bruce, and Johnston (1990) proposed an interactive activation model of face identity processing. Using a Rumelhart and McClelland-type architecture, with excitatory connections between units at different levels, and inhibitory connections between units at the same level, they provided accounts of repetition priming and semantic priming. Burton and Bruce (1992) demonstrated that with this simple model, nodes in semantic memory that are connected to only one person have a lower asymptote than nodes that are shared by more than one person. Surnames, of course, tend to be extremely specific to a particular person, and the difficulty in recalling a name compared to recalling a person's profession emerges from the model. So this model successfully explains the difference in recall difficulty between the names of people and category information associated to them.

Burke et al. (1991) present a theory of the tip-of-the-tongue state, based on the earlier Node Structure Theory of language processing (e.g. Mackay, 1982). In it, the reason that recall of proper names is more difficult than recall of common names is similar to the reason proposed by Cohen (1990): "baker" when used as a common name is linked up directly to nodes in semantic memory, such as "sells cakes", "gets up early" etc.; however when "Baker" is used as a proper name it is not linked up *directly* to the semantic system, but via a proper noun phrase representing the person, e.g. "John Baker". This is consistent with Burke et al.'s reflection that one is very limited as to what information one can give about the name "Baker" itself. The inherent lack of meaning of proper names is the underlying cause of their propensity for causing TOTs.

These models do not *learn* new facts or names. A new entry can only be plugged in to the model, and the influence on the system's processing dynamics studied. A corollary of this is that these explanations tacitly assume that the names and the semantic information are *equally well-learned*. Of course, if names are simply less-learned than semantic facts the observation that they are more difficult to recall does not require extensive modelling, and would appear to be uninteresting. However it will now be argued that even if people's names are as well-learned as common names, learning must be considered in order to understand the difficulty with recalling people's names.

THE SET SIZE OF PLAUSIBLE PHONOLOGY (SSPP)

Over the past ten years many persons' names will have been encountered for the first time, including, for many, Gorbachev, Lineker, Quayl(e) and Depardieu. Over the same period, however, very few new names of professions will have been encountered; perhaps ombudsman and knowledge engineer. The nature of more traditional professions may have changed, but their names have stayed the same.

One direct consequence of this fact is that people's names *may* be less well-learned than the best-learned semantic facts associated to that same person, because the phonology associated to the name may have been less frequently encountered than the phonology of the common names describing facts about the person. This corresponds to the psychologically-uninteresting possibility mentioned earlier: all models would predict that an item to which one had dedicated much time, and with which one had had much learning opportunity, would be better recalled than an item that had had less exposure. The thing to note, however, is that the learning of new phonology is more frequently undertaken for people's names than for common names.

This fact leads on to the second thread of the argument. The observation that we encounter many more new people's names than new common names means that there is a wider range of phonologies that are *plausible* and *acceptable* for the former. According to the hypothesis being put forward here, the difference between recall of people's names and of their professions is due to these different ranges of phonologies plausible for each. An example illustrating the idea of the relatively extended universe of possibly phonology for people's names is found if one considers one's reaction to being told that someone's surname is an unfamiliar phonology, for instance, "dreaner". This would not be remarkable; however if one were told that the person was being paid for being a "dreaner", one is likely to think that one has not heard correctly. At the very least, one is going to be *surprised* at this name of profession. The reason for this is that our experience tells us that many more phonologies are *plausible* for people's names as compared to common names. The hypothesis put forward here claims that it is not the *actual* set size but the *potential* set size that is important, regardless of whether the actual number of people's names stored in the lexicon is lower or higher than the number of common names stored there. In other words, the size of the set of *plausible* phonologies for people's names is very much larger than the corresponding set size for common names, and indeed for other types of proper name.

The reason for this difference is that different domains of words have different 'new exemplar' rates. For instance, people's names are much more frequently new exemplars than are, say, names of professions. The difference in recall difficulty derives from this, because in a word domain with a high new exemplar rate a word will have to be specified more accurately in order to distinguish it from potential alternatives to the correct word. This, in turn, is because in a domain with a high new exemplar rate, neighbouring (perhaps unfamiliar) phonologies are credible alternative exemplars of that domain. This is not the case for word domains with low new exemplar rates.

One effect of the size of a word domain's plausible phonology set is on the utility of any partial phonology in specifying the correct phonology. Consider a second thought experiment. On the basis of partial phonology you are asked to guess the profession or the surname being thought of. If you are told that it begins with [b] you could reply "boxer" or "bus driver" for professions, and "Brown" or "Bush" for surnames: if the next phoneme is [ei], the responses might be "baker", "bailiff", and "baker", "Bayliss". Finally, if one is told that the first two phonemes are [bei], and the last one is [ʌ] then one might only be familiar with [beik ʌ] for professions and surnames. But one will be much more sure in one case than in the other; there is a minuscule chance of there being another name of profession beginning with [bei] and ending with [ʌ]. However, for surnames it is with much less assurance that one can confirm incomplete phonology as deriving from one particular target, because the universe of plausible names for people is much larger than the universe of plausible common names: the surname could *plausibly* be Baler, Bamer, Bater or Bazer.

What exactly is meant by 'new' or 'unfamiliar' phonologies? It is obviously not being claimed that people's names often contain new *phonemes* in a language. A more reasonable meaning would be that people's names can contain novel syllables, and any such examples would indeed be considered new phonologies. The principal category of new phonologies however would surely be the cases where names are novel combinations of familiar syllables, i.e. a string of phonemes that was not previously a familiar word. An example (for me) of such a novel phoneme string composed of familiar syllables that I came across recently was Intriligator, the surname of a co-author of a recent psychological article (Kosslyn & Intriligator, 1992). Here, when talking about new phonologies, both of these types of new words are included.

Is there any phonology that is *not* plausible for people's surnames, in any given language? There is the phonology that is not phonotactically legal in that language. But apart from that, is all phonology plausible? For instance, are *all* professions plausible names? Imagine one's reaction on being told that someone was called Mr Biotechnologist. It does not appear to be a plausible name for a person. However there are examples of professions as names, other than McWeeny et al.'s (1987) ambiguous labels. In the cognitive psychology literature alone, for instance, there is an A. Mechanic (e.g. Mechanic, 1964), and also the more cited L. Postman (e.g. Postman, 1964); as surnames are indeed often strange (see also the Intriligator example cited earlier), perhaps all legal phonology is indeed plausible for a person's name.

The issue is an empirical one, and Rubin, Stoltzfus, and Wall (1991) reported a study investigating whether word domains have characteristic surface forms. They showed that subjects do indeed rely on prototypical surface forms when generating new exemplars from a particular category, and when assigning new exemplars to given categories. For instance, there was much inter-subject agreement that radioactive chemical elements end in "ium" and that names of soap powders often consist of one meaningful word. There are perhaps certain regularities in the surface forms of people's names, and experimental study of these regularities would be an interesting domain for future research.

THE MECHANISM OF THE PLAUSIBLE PHONOLOGY HYPOTHESIS

It is hypothesised that the recall of words' phonology resembles the "Baker" thought experiment. On the basis of any partial phonology that is recalled, the phonology of a common name can be focused in on rapidly; however for people's names, the search for phonology has to be more diffuse.

It is well-established that access to the phonological lexicon can be a gradual process, as shown by partial knowledge of word targets that subjects can give when in TOTs (Brown & McNeill, 1966; Rubin, 1975). These studies provided evidence that knowledge of the initial letter of a word, the number of syllables it contains, and (in English) its stress pattern, can all be available before the full phonology.

Assuming that access to a word's phonology always initially occurs by such a gradual process, then at a certain point this partial information will be sufficient to uniquely specify a word in a user's lexicon. At this point, it is hypothesised here that another parameter influences the ongoing recall of words' phonology: access to the stored phonology is assumed to continue in the same way as *before* the partial phonology uniquely specified the word, but this process will be *accelerated* for words from domains with a low new exemplar rate. The missing elements of the word's phonology will be accessed more quickly because the system's behaviour is adapted to the fact that it rarely encounters new exemplars from certain domains, which allows it to select the remaining elements of a word's phonology from the lexical store with a high level of certainty.

The problem faced when recalling people's names is that this kind of accelerated fragment completion will be less sure of producing the desired target. Even if the partial phonology that has been recalled is consistent with only one name that is stored in a particular lexicon, the nature of the phonology of people's names is such that neighbouring, unfamiliar phonologies are also plausible candidates. For this reason, the accelerated completion process cannot be so relied on for people's names, and the standard unaccelerated lexical process has to be relied on, in order that the intended phonology will be sure to be produced.

To specify even further the way in which set size of plausible phonology might influence word recall, it is necessary to take a closer look at what other processes influence it. In many models of the semantic system and the output lexicon, a name can be recalled if sufficient semantic activation passes to the node or unit representing it. There may also be top-down processes influencing word recall, by which I mean the influence of the context on recall of the word. In laboratory situations it has been shown that seeing Oliver Hardy's face speeds up the naming of Stan Laurel's face (Brennen & Bruce, 1991), and that seeing a picture of an object speeds up the naming of a closely-associated object, (McCauley, Parmalee, Sperber, & Carr, 1980). Top-down processes are, however, not the focus of more discussion because it is assumed that they will operate equally for common and proper names.

However, the SSPP constitutes another type of top-down influence that can play a role in recalling a name. I shall draw a distinction here between top-down *processes* and top-down *constraints*. A top-down constraint is an element of the naming attempt that is independent of any particular attempt: it is invariant over *all* attempts to recall a particular name. We may, for instance, know that we are looking for a high familiarity word. That fact acts as a top-down constraint by providing important information that enables us to monitor the internal phonology accessed during the attempt to recall a name, and thus to articulate only words that satisfy the high familiarity criterion. Other top-down constraints on word recall may be, for instance, knowing that it is a foreign-sounding word, or knowing that the surname being searched for is also the name of a fruit. The SSPP is another top-down constraint.

The words for which the SSPP constraint will be useful in specifying the phonology will be those that come from domains with low new exemplar rates. For such items, the full phoneme string can be generated from a few phonemes of partial phonology, because these first-recalled phonemes will tend to uniquely specify a member of the target word domain. This, in concert with the knowledge that there are very few new exemplars in this domain, will allow the generation of the desired phonology with a high degree of certainty.

On the other hand, words that are very well-learned or words that come from domains with a high new exemplar rate will benefit little from this accelerated lexical access. The phonology of very well-learned items (regardless of word domain) will be specified with very little help from the SSPP top-down constraint, because the activation of the phonology by the standard lexical processes will already be rapid. For words from domains with high new exemplar rates, this top-down constraint is simply not much of a constraint: for people's names, as argued earlier, very many phonologies are plausible, and so extrapolating from some partial phonology to a particular phoneme string is less likely to result in the desired phonology being made available.

For this account to be correct, it is necessary that the *domain* of the word whose phonology is to be recalled be known *before* the phonology is specified. In fact, this is an assumption made by many current psycholinguistic models (see for instance Kempen & Huijbers, 1983). Thus, it is hypothesised that this knowledge influences subsequent phonological selection by allowing more or less completion of partial phonology according to whether the word's domain has a low or high acquisition rate.

In the cognitive psychology literature there is a class of effects called set size effects (for a review see Nelson, Schreiber, & McEvoy, 1992). Over a 15-year period, Nelson and colleagues have studied subjects' memory for previously-presented words. The majority of work has used a cued recall paradigm, and the principal result is that the number of associates that a word has in long-term memory influences both its efficiency as a cue and its probability of being recalled as a target. With many different experimental manipulations, a cue with a large number of associates will be less useful than a cue with a low number of associates, even controlling for pre-experimental cue-target strength. Similarly, under most conditions, a *target* with a large set of associates is less likely to be recalled than a target with a small set. Different types of set can be defined, e.g. the meaning set (containing the number of meaningfully related associates a word has); the rhyme set; the set of category instances. Manipulating the rhyme set of the cue and the meaning set of the target, it has been possible to show that the target set size and the cue set size effects are independent of each other.

The appropriate analogy between these set sizes and the SSPP is not clear. First, naming, as considered so far in this article, is not an episodic cued recall task. It is a semantic task. Second, in person naming, for instance, the cues for the recall of names are not only *related* to the target name, but uniquely specify it, e.g. a face, a semantic description of a person. So the cues typically used in Nelson et al.'s experiments are of a different nature from those used in naming. There is however a set of experiments that use a task closer to the naming task— a word fragment completion task, where the cues for recall of the previously-presented words are structurally derived from the target word itself (Nelson, Canas, Bajo, & Keelean, 1987).

As pointed out earlier, lexical access is widely believed to be a gradual process. During the recall attempt, some of the word's partial phonology will be accessed, and the task becomes one of (implicit) fragment completion, with the partial phonology acting as a cue for recall. It is at this point that the word domain's SSPP influences word recall. The experimental condition that most closely resembles this hypothesised operation of lexical access is one where the cues for recall of previously-presented words are fragments of the same word, with a small or a large number of possible completions. Nelson et al. (1987) found the standard cue set size effect with such word fragments, regardless of whether the instructions explicitly referred to the prior study phase or not: with the cue-target strength kept constant, cues with large lexical sets led to lower levels of recall than cues with small sets.

The set size of plausible phonology and the cue set size for word fragments appear to make the same predictions about recall—a smaller set leads to higher recall. They are similar too, in that they operate implicitly. The cue set size has been shown not to be sensitive to the number of meaning-related associates of the target, which would also be the prediction for the plausible phonology hypothesis. Furthermore, Nelson et al. (1992) review experiments showing that set size effects generally do not operate for recognition tasks, another similarity with the plausible phonology hypothesis (see Anomia section, following).

The most important difference between Nelson et al.'s set size effects and the one under consideration in this article is in the nature of the members of the sets. The members of the cue set are all real words: the set in the case of fragment completion contains all words consistent with a certain letter frame. The plausible phonology set for word domains with high new exemplar rates, on the other hand, includes phonologies that have never been encountered. The relationship between the set of plausible phonology and Nelson et al.'s sets could usefully be explored experimentally.

THE LEXICON AND PHONOLOGICAL SPECIFICATION

In models like Morton's (1979) it is assumed that each familiar word (and thus each name too) has an *input* representation that allows recognition of the word, and an *output* representation that must be accessed in order to produce the word. Each lexical entry (or logogen), be it input or output, is an independent unit that accumulates evidence for the word it represents.

However, it is the idea that logogens are independent of each other that has led cognitive psychologists to overlook the potential effect of the size of phonological universe of word domains on recall of words from those domains. Logogens gather evidence for the individual word each represents, and will fire if sufficient evidence can be accumulated for the word's presence (input) or its semantic specification (output). However, each logogen proceeds unaffected by the activation state of others. In output, this fails to take into consideration the need, in specifying a word, to distinguish between its phonology and all other possible (or plausible) phonologies. It implicitly assumes that the words forming a language are sampled randomly and evenly from the phonological space, which, even within the phonological constraints of a given language, is manifestly not the case; in English, for example, many words begin with the suffix "inter", and the presentation of any one of them will activate the representations of all of them. In contrast, only one begins with "giraf", and so the computational task of deciding which word was uttered will be completed more rapidly. The logogen account does not consider the effect of phonological neighbours.

A similar misgiving led Marslen-Wilson to propose his cohort model of spoken word recognition (e.g. Marslen-Wilson, 1987). In this model, the latency taken to recognise a spoken word is determined by the closeness of the recognition point of a word to the beginning of the word. The recognition point in turn largely depends on a word's uniqueness point. A word's uniqueness point is the hypothetical place in a word at which the phonemes uttered from the beginning of the word *uniquely specify* it in a particular language. There are words with their uniqueness point near the beginning of the word, e.g. "cigarette", as no other words in English begin [sig ∧]. Thus the uniqueness point of kettle is at the [∧]. Other words require many more phonemes in order to be uniquely specified. For instance, starting from the beginning of the word, "internment" is not uniquely specified until the [m] sound; one phoneme before, there will be other words, e.g. international, internal, which will be consistent with the phonemes uttered up to that point. Marslen-Wilson (1984) showed that words with early uniqueness points were recognised more quickly in an auditory task than words with late uniqueness points. This supports his model's prediction that in recognising spoken words the proximity of the phonological 'rivals' of candidate words determines the difficulty of recognition.

Marslen-Wilson's main point is that the conceptualisation of logogens as independent detectors blinds us to the nature of the task when making sense of spoken language. The potential candidates must be taken into account for recognising words, and the point of this paper is that the argument also applies to the *recall* of words. Furthermore, if, as previously argued, people's names have many more plausible phonologies than common names, then they will be more difficult to access, because the range of choices of output will be so much bigger.

The cohort model deals with *input* of (auditory) verbal material, and the key discrimination when recognising a word is between its phonology and the phonology of all other *words*. Only familiar phonology has to be taken into account in order to perform a recognition judgement. However, in naming, where phonology must be *generated*, and not merely recognised, the discrimination that the system must make is between a certain (familiar) phoneme string and all other phoneme strings, including unfamiliar ones.

The more general point is that identifying a particular entity depends on the response options that are open to the system. For instance, it applies to face recognition too, where it has been shown that a densely prosopagnosic patient was able to recognise and name all of a set of eight premorbidly familiar faces if told that they all came from the same semantic category (Sergent & Poncet, 1990). Prosopagnosic patients can derive basic visual information from the face, such as hair colour, gender, and age, and in concert with the constraining information provided by the experimenters, this patient could identify the faces. Presumably the possible response set would initially have been very large: a familiar face presented to a patient could be any one of hundreds of public faces. The information provided by the experimenter will have allowed the patient to use the little information derived from each face, in an interactive manner, to the point where identification was possible.

EXPLANATIONS OF EXPERIMENTAL NAMING RESULTS BY THE PLAUSIBLE PHONOLOGY HYPOTHESIS

The difference in SSPPs between the names of professions and the names of people accounts for the Baker-baker paradox (McWeeny et al., 1987). During the recall attempt, as partial phonology is accessed, the utility of the phonology in specifying the rest of the word's phonology will differ according to whether it is a surname or a profession that is being recalled. For surnames, the constraint of the SSPP will be very weak, and so before a name can be recalled all of its phonology must be specified. In contrast, for the name of a profession, a small amount of partial phonology can reliably specify a particular lexical entry. On occasions when the unaided lexical access is insufficient to specify all of a word's phonology, persons' names will not be recalled because they do not benefit from the SSPP constraint. The names of professions, in contrast, *can* be recalled on such occasions because the SSPP constraint will allow the specification of the word's phonology on the basis of the initially accessed partial phonology.

Cohen's (1990) first experiment can also be accounted for. In it, subjects had to associate a profession, a surname, and a possession to unfamiliar faces. When the possession was a real word, e.g. "boat", the surnames were recalled less often than the other two pieces of information. However, when the possession was a nonword, e.g. "blick", surnames and possessions were recalled less often than professions. Cohen's reasoning was that because names were not recalled better than nonwords, they are effectively processed as meaningless entities, as nonwords must be. The data are also consistent with the plausible phonology hypothesis, because the set size of plausible phonology will be enormous for nonwords, as it is for names of people: partial access to phonology will be of negligible utility in recalling a nonword, as in recalling the name of a person. If there are any phonological constraints on person's names (see previous paragraph), then one would expect that person's names would be better recalled than nonwords. It might require a paradigm more powerful than an association experiment in order to observe the effect.

However, the plausible phonology hypothesis does not, at first glance, provide a ready account of some experiments reported by Young, Ellis and Flude (1988), and Johnston and Bruce (1990). These experiments tested Bruce and Young's (1986) hypothesis of a separation of the representation of the name from the rest of information stored on a person. In Young et al.'s experiment, subjects performed a matching task on pairs of familiar faces. In one condition they had to decide whether the faces shared the same profession (politician or pop star) and in the other they had to decide whether the faces shared the same first name (David or Michael). Even for this small set of familiar faces, which were seen many times during the course of the experiment, the semantic decision was performed more rapidly than the name decision. Johnston and Bruce (1990) pushed this result further by showing that on a matching task, a name decision (Do both these faces have the same first name? James or John) was slower than a decision as to whether both were dead (or alive), or whether both were British or both American. This was taken as support for the separation of the name of a person from other information stored on them because, on presentation of a face, even a non-essential semantic property appeared to be more rapidly known than the name.

Because, for both the semantic and the name tasks, a binary decision was required, the response set size for the name task and the semantic task is equivalent. However, the response set (which is determined by the experimenter) is not the same set as the plausible phonology set, and the constraining potential of the SSPP would operate even when the actual response set is experimentally-fixed. If we assume that when recalling the word "dead" from a familiar face and when recalling the word "David" from a familiar face, the *pre*lexical stages are equivalent, then the plausible phonology hypothesis can explain the longer latencies for the latter task: when the key words come from a domain with a low new exemplar rate (e.g. the words "dead" and "alive"), their phonology will be accessed more quickly than when they come from a domain with a higher new exemplar rate (e.g. "David" or "John"), because the initially available partial phonology will allow specification of the word's phonology more quickly, via the influence of the SSPP constraint. A prediction made by this account is that the domain of first names has a higher new exemplar rate than the domain of professions.

The aphasic patients, whose cases were cited earlier (Flude et al., 1989; Lucchelli & de Renzi, 1992; Semenza & Zettin, 1988, 1989), are assumed to have a problem with the process of accessing phonology at the level of the output lexicon; that is, with unaided, standard lexical access. The SSPP constraint reduces the impact of this problem for word domains with low new exemplar rates. This constraint is particularly weak for people's names, which are therefore harder to name.

RECALL OF WORDS FROM DIFFERENT DOMAINS

The plausible phonology hypothesis claims the differences in recall difficulty of words from different domains is due to the size of the universe of plausible phonologies for words in any particular domain. Because the plausible phonological set size is determined by the frequency of encountering new words from a given domain of words, it is thus more general than an explanation of the recall difficulties with *people's* names. For word domains where many new exemplars are encountered, the universe of plausible phonologies will be much bigger. This hypothesis does not draw on philosophical differences between word domains; it depends only on real-word practical differences between word domains. What exactly is meant by a word domain? Linguists distinguish between certain word classes, but here finer distinctions, corresponding to functional categories, will be considered.

For instance, proper names can be divided into many subgroups, according to what the label actually refers to—thus we have the domain of words referring to people, another domain referring to commercial products, a domain referring to places, etc. But this classification is not fixed, of course. The prediction of the plausible phonology hypothesis is that if the 'new exemplar rate' of a subcategory of, say, people's names, becomes noticeably different from the rest of the category, the utility of partial phonology will change accordingly.

An important consequence of this is that domains of proper names should not pose equivalent recall problems. For instance, it might be expected that first names should pose fewer problems than surnames, because intuitively it seems that there are fewer new exemplars of first names, and thus the SSPP will be smaller for this domain. Similarly, the new names of towns are much less regularly encountered than the new names of people. Hence the prediction of this hypothesis is that the names of people should be more difficult to remember than names of towns, even for equal amounts of learning. As a general rule, the higher the frequency of encounter of new phonologies within any category of words, the harder the recall of words from that domain will be.

Cohen and Faulkner (1986) asked subjects to recall in detail an instance of a naturally occurring proper name block. It is interesting to note that 85% of the reported name blocks were for the names of people, with the remainder for all other types of proper name, e.g. place names, brand names, pop group names. Such diary studies are however susceptible to reporting biases. They may simply reflect the frequency of recall of words from different domains.

Unfortunately, there is no easy way to compare recall of names from different domains. Generating TOTs for words from different domains in the laboratory cannot be more than suggestive either, because in such studies the experimenters choose the materials, which may introduce sampling biases leading to different levels of difficulty into word domains of essentially equivalent difficulty. A solution is artificially to create name recall categories, with different rates of new exemplars, but where other factors such as recall frequency and learning encounters can be controlled.

The idea of response set size can also be extended to the recall of familiar numbers, e.g. telephone numbers. After the local code, the digits of a person's telephone number are in an arbitrary order, and one can not conclude anything about someone from it. If one manages to recall all but the final digit of someone's telephone number, the digits that one has remembered are useless in specifying the missing one. This is analogous to the "Baker" thought experiment described earlier, where knowing all the phonemes but one did not allow the missing one to be specified with assurance. Drawing an analogy between a digit in a telephone number and a phoneme in a person's surname, it can be seen that recalling a telephone number should be difficult for the same reasons as recalling someone's surname is difficult: the range of possible responses is enormous. The reasons for the large response set size are, nevertheless, different in the two cases.

For phonemes in people's surnames the set size is enormous because of the high rate of new exemplars. For digits in telephone numbers, on the other hand, the set size is enormous due to the transposability of the digits in telephone numbers, and not due to the high new exemplar rate. Thus, although there are only ten digits to choose from, normally the only illegal numbers are those starting with a zero, leaving 900,000 different possible permutations for six-digit telephone numbers. In this context, one of Lucchelli and de Renzi's (1992) observations is noteworthy: their patient, whose anomia was restricted to proper names, scored within normal limits on a retrograde memory questionnaire and had a digit span of 6, was unable to recall his own telephone number. The claim is that telephone numbers should be (at least) as difficult to remember as surnames.

ANOMIAS

Anomias provide a rich testing ground for the plausible phonology hypothesis. Combining an assumption that the phonological lexicon is accessed after the meaning of the stimulus is known and the plausible phonology hypothesis, the types of anomia reported in the literature can be explained. A brief description of the architecture of current models of visual cognition is useful here. Typically, there is a sequence of information processing modules that allows identification of visual stimuli. According to these models, perceptual processing precedes the activation of stored structural codes representing familiar stimuli. After recognition has been achieved at this level, the meaning of the stimulus can be accessed in the semantic system, which in turn allows access to the name of the stimulus. In such a model, comprehension difficulties derive from abnormalities of the semantic system. Furthermore, because access to the name of a stimulus is dependent on prior access to its meaning, the names of stimuli for which the semantic representations are damaged or inaccessible should also be unavailable. Thus, the demonstration of a patient able to name faces while unable to give correct information about them would falsify the class of models with this semantics/name sequence (e.g. Bruce & Young, 1986).

This type of architecture has corollary assumptions. For instance, the semantic system is assumed to be unitary, in that access is achieved to the same store regardless of the modality of access, or modality of information required. Furthermore, the semantic system is deemed to be organised categorically. The output lexicon, on the other hand, is supposed to be phonologically organised, not categorically organised.

Several cases of anomia will be discussed here, in order to show that cases that, at first sight, might seem to falsify the hypotheses presented here can, in fact, be explained simply. McKenna and Warrington (1978) reported a global aphasic patient whose linguistic abilities appeared to be restricted to naming countries. He could, however, match countries to appropriate objects, demonstrating access to semantic information about countries too. In all other tested domains, he could neither name stimuli, nor was he able to demonstrate evidence of semantic access. He scored zero on the Token test, implying very severe comprehension difficulties. This suggests an extremely disrupted semantic system, with sparing of the category of countries, and no phonological deficit. Naming performance was, in fact, deficient for all stimuli for which there was also a semantic deficit, in agreement with the assumption stated earlier.

This is also the case for the patient reported by Hart, Berndt, and Caramazza (1985). Here though, there was only one category affected, rather than only one preserved. The patient had a satisfactory level of comprehension and naming for all stimuli except fruits and vegetables. Importantly, though, he was also slow, uncertain and error-prone when categorising pictures of fruit and vegetables, implying a semantic deficit that would also cause the category-specific naming deficit.

The case of an agrammatic patient reported by McCarthy and Warrington (1985) shows excellent recall of people's names but very poor recall of action words, like "give", "sell". However, his *comprehension* of action words was also poor: for example, he was at chance in deciding which of two related verbs was appropriate for a picture, e.g. whether a hunter standing over an impaled lion was "killing" or "dying". This category-specific anomic patient had better recall of people's names than of action words. This may, at first sight, seem to contradict the plausible phonology hypothesis, because it predicts a deficit for people's names compared to other stimuli's domains. However, as his category-specific naming deficit was underpinned by a *comprehension* deficit for that stimulus domain, his deficit can be accounted for by a deficit at the semantic level.

In contrast, what we may call phonological anomias, such as the patient reported by Flude, Ellis, and Kay (1989), have no comprehension deficits and a generalised word production deficit that is not category-specific (see also Kay & Ellis, 1987). The plausible phonology hypothesis predicts that word domains will not all be affected equally, but rather that words from domains with high new exemplar rates should be worse recalled, because the SSPP constraint is less useful for these domains. Indeed, as expected according to the plausible phonology hypothesis, the naming problems of Flude et al.'s (1989) patient were most severe for people's names.

Furthermore, recent cases demonstrate that a naming deficit can be restricted to proper names (Lucchelli & de Renzi, 1992; Semenza & Zettin, 1988, 1989). A prediction that derives from the plausible phonology hypothesis is that *all* anomic patients who do not show comprehension deficits will have problems with proper names. Thus, the demonstration that a patient with no comprehension deficit showed spared naming of proper names relative to common names, would falsify the hypothesis. To my knowledge, no such report exists.

Some aphasic patients appear to have an overall normal level of comprehension and a naming deficit for a particular domain of common names, which provide potential rejections of the plausible phonology hypothesis, but have no test of recall of people's surnames (Farah & Wallace, 1992; Rapcsak, Kaszniak, & Rubens, 1989). The prediction is that such patients would have severe deficits in recalling people's names.

It is important to note that this prediction of the plausible phonology hypothesis concerns only the *recall* of the phonology of proper names; it does *not* concern recognition judgements to proper names, or access to semantic information from proper names. These types of *input* functions are functionally separate from, and operate on an entirely different basis to, recall (Valentine, Brédart, Lawson, & Ward, 1991)—whether one supposes that there are abstract recognition units for familiar words or whether one prefers an episodic account of recognition, the plausible phonology hypothesis would not operate at recognition because essentially the task is identical for all types of names: it is a matter of matching input phonology to memory traces. Furthermore, the distinction to be made at the recognition level is binary, between familiar and unfamiliar stimuli. So, unlike at the level of name recall, the response sets at the recognition level are identical for proper and common names, i.e. 'familiar' and 'unfamiliar'. There is thus no reason to suppose that recognising *proper* names or accessing semantic information from them should be more difficult than would be recognising, or accessing semantic information from, *common* names.

Indeed, Van Lancker and Klein (1990) reported four global aphasic patients with preserved ability to match the names of famous people to the correct face, while being unable to match names of common objects to the correct drawing. This shows the domain-specificity of *input* systems; but the case that would falsify the hypothesis would be one that was able to name faces, but *not* objects, in a confrontation naming task. In fact, Van Lancker and Klein's patients were unable to name *anything* in a confrontation naming task.

This differentiation between *recognition* and *recall* of proper names has not always been very clear in the neuropsychological literature. For instance, Warrington and McCarthy (1987) present a patient who was unable to match a spoken name to an array of six objects, but *was* able to match a spoken name to all other tested categories, including people's names. Semenza and Zettin's (1989) patient with a deficit for the recall of proper names led them to cite Warrington and McCarthy's (1987) case as evidence of a double dissociation with their own case. It was claimed that this meant that proper and common names are "separately represented or, at least, separately accessed in the intact brain" (Semenza & Zettin, 1989, p.678). However, the reverse dissociation to Semenza and Zettin's (1989) would be a patient who could recall people's names and other proper names, but could not recall common names. Warrington and McCarthy's (1987) patient had *extremely* limited verbal output, was unable to repeat simple sounds, to name common objects or to produce *any* propositional speech whatsoever, and so obviously does not constitute the reverse of Semenza and Zettin's (1988; 1989) dissociation. This confusion arises from failing to distinguish between the recognition and the recall of proper names.

The prediction that the plausible phonology hypothesis makes regarding neuropsychological case studies concerns the relative overall *naming* performance in different word domains. It predicts that words in domains with high new exemplar rates will be more difficult to recall than words from domains with low new exemplar rates. Thus, a patient showing globally superior recall of people's names compared to common names would falsify the hypothesis.

Note that this prediction is subtly different from that made by Bruce and Young's framework. In their model, name recall is dependent on prior access to the semantics of the face, and thus would be falsified by a patient (or indeed anyone) naming faces without having the semantics of the person available. Furthermore, in theory, a *single* trial where someone names a face without knowing who it is falsifies the framework. The plausible phonology hypothesis, in contrast, is *not* falsified by this single demonstration because it does not make predictions about single trials.

To sum up, as predicted by the plausible phonology hypothesis, people's names are systematically more difficult to recall than other word domains. In cases of anomia with intact comprehension where recall of people's names has been tested, the recall of people's names is always deficient.

OTHER PREDICTIONS OF THE PLAUSIBLE PHONOLOGY HYPOTHESIS

Besides the predictions about neuropsychological deficits and about different word domains outlined earlier, there are others that derive from the plausible phonology hypothesis too.

A puzzling aspect of Cohen and Faulkner's (1986) results was that there was an inverse frequency effect on naming blocks: the more frequent a name was judged to be, the more tip-of-the-tongue states were experienced. As pointed out by Brennen, Baguley, Bright, and Bruce (1990), the evidence for this inverse frequency effect comes from self-report diary studies, and so may be biased by certain factors. For instance, subjects may be more struck by a failure to recall a frequent name and so tend to over-report it; or it may be due to the fact that there may be fewer attempts to recall infrequent names. Thus, in absolute terms there may be fewer name blocks, but as a proportion of recall attempts it would still be possible for names of low familiarity to be at a disadvantage. The plausible phonology perspective predicts a frequency effect the other way round: names less frequently recalled should be more susceptible to TOTs than frequently recalled names. This is because the recall of a seldom-encountered person's name will rely heavily on top-down constraints, such as the SSPP, and that the vast SSPP for people's names will be unhelpful in specifying the name's phonology. This is not the only way of explaining a frequency effect, of course, but it offers a mechanism for it.

In fact, Brédart (1992) reported support for this prediction from a study where he compared naming difficulty for famous people, with their rate of appearance on television over a six month period. Naming success in his laboratory study was higher for the names of people who had been seen *less* frequently.

There are predictions concerning McWeeny et al.'s (1987) paradigm. First, if one asked subjects to evaluate the confidence in their responses, the plausible phonology hypothesis predicts that they will have less confidence in their recall of names compared to their recall of professions, even (1) when the response is correct, and (2) for ambiguous labels, e.g. Baker.

Second, it makes a prediction about children's performance of McWeeny et al.'s task. For adults, people's surnames are difficult to recall because the SSPP is vast, and this in turn is due to the fact that there is a high new exemplar rate for this domain. For children, many domains will have such high new exemplar rates, and so the prediction is that McWeeny et al.'s (1987) name/profession difference should be reduced and might even disappear at certain stages of development. This prediction is not made by Cohen's explanation of naming difficulty, and it is unclear whether Burton and Bruce's (1992) explanation would predict it either. It has previously been argued that all words learned at an early age will be stored in a complete form (e.g. Brown & Watson, 1987). This too would argue for a reduction in the size of McWeeny et al.'s effect for children.

Other predictions derived from the plausible phonology hypothesis concern a word fragment completion task. If the task was to complete a word fragment with a word from a particular domain, the prediction would be that the higher the new exemplar rate of a domain, the more different words would be proposed by subjects. Furthermore, words from high new exemplar rate domains should be completed with less *confidence*, even when the same fragment is presented and the same word is offered by the subject.

THE RELATIONSHIP BETWEEN THE PLAUSIBLE PHONOLOGY HYPOTHESIS AND OTHER EXPLANATIONS OF NAMING PHENOMENA

Previously, there have been explanations of proper names' difficulty in terms of item-related parameters, such as imageability, distinctiveness, and frequency. McWeeny et al.'s (1987) results demonstrated that these factors cannot explain all the difficulty that we have with proper names, because even when they are nullified by having the same items acting as professions and as surnames, the name disadvantage remains. The explanations offered by Burton and Bruce (1992) and by Burke et al. (1991), considered at the beginning of this article, also effectively locate the difficulty with proper names in properties of the items themselves. Burton and Bruce suggest that people's names are difficult to remember because they tend to be unique to a particular person. Whereas, in Burke et al.'s (1991) model the fundamental reason for proper names' difficulty is their lack of meaning.

It is possible that the plausible phonology hypothesis should be considered as one of several factors contributing to the particular difficulty with the recall of proper names. There is however the more radical possibility that the plausible phonology hypothesis replaces item-related explanations. An argument in favour of this is that the item-related dimensions will tend to be confounded with the dimension of new exemplar rate. For instance, consider the classic result that concrete words are better recalled than abstract words: typically this is taken as evidence for the importance of imagery in recall tasks. However, this might also be due to the fact that as adults we learn many more new abstract words than new concrete words. Thus, according to the plausible phonology hypothesis too, recalling abstract words should be more difficult than recalling concrete words.

The only other explanation of naming difficulty that is not related to properties of the items themselves is Brédart's (1992), where he proposes that proper names are more difficult to recall because normally they are the only label by which we can name the referent. In contrast, many objects have several labels that are appropriate. Exploiting the fact that there are *some* famous faces that are known by two different names (e.g. Harrison Ford & Indiana Jones), he showed that having multiple labels reduced naming problems. The plausible phonology hypothesis cannot replace *this* hypothesis.

Recently, Morrison, Ellis, and Quinlan (1992) have argued that the widespread belief that word frequency affects performance on object naming tasks is mistaken because this factor has no effect independent of other factors such as the age-of-acquisition. In emphasising the rôle of the stage of *acquisition* of words in determining difficulty of recall, their position is similar to the one taken here. They suggest that a parsimonious account of age-of-acquisition effects will require a more detailed specification of the phonological stage, of which the plausible phonology hypothesis is an example.

The explanatory status of the plausible phonology hypothesis is, of course, speculative at the moment. It is to be hoped that future studies will determine whether or not all naming phenomena can be explained by the problem of phonological specification.

CONCLUSION

This paper offers a simple explanation of some of the difficulty of recall of people's names. The explanation derives from observations about the rate of new acquisition of exemplars in different word domains in the real world, and has not been taken into consideration so far in the cognitive psychology literature on person naming. In fact, it is more general than just the name versus profession difference. Any word domain where there are very few new exemplars can benefit from the plausible phonological set size constraint, because access to partial phonology of a name can pick out one candidate phonology with a high level of assurance. People's names are often new words, a real world fact that will tend to make their recall problematic.

Manuscript accepted 23 June 1993

REFERENCES

Brédart, S. (this issue). Retrieval failures in face naming. *Memory*.

Brennen, T., Baguley, T., Bright, J., & Bruce, V. (1990). Resolving semantically-induced tip-of-the-tongue states for proper names. *Memory and Cognition, 18*, 339–347.

Brennen, T. & Bruce, V. (1991). Context effects in the recognition of familiar faces. *Psychological Research, 53*, 286–304.

Brown, G.D.A. & Watson, F.L. (1987). First in, first out: Word learning age and spoken word frequency as predictors of word familiarity and word naming latency. *Memory and Cognition, 15*, 208–216.

Brown, R. & McNeill, D. (1966). The "tip-of-the-tongue" phenomenon. *Journal of Verbal Learning and Verbal Behavior, 5*, 325–337.

Bruce, V. & Young, A.W. (1986). Understanding face recognition. *British Journal of Psychology, 77*, 305–327.

Burke, D., Mackay, D., Worthley, J. & Wade, E. (1991). On the Tip of the Tongue: What causes word finding failure in young and older adults? *Journal of Memory and Language, 30*, 542–579.

Burton, A.M. & Bruce, V. (1992). I recognize your face but I can't remember your name: A simple explanation? *British Journal of Psychology, 83*, 45–60.

Burton, A.M., Bruce, V., & Johnston, R. (1990). Understanding face recognition with an interactive activation model. *British Journal of Psychology, 81*, 361–380.

Cohen, G. (1990). Why is it difficult to put names to faces? *British Journal of Psychology, 81*, 287–297.

Cohen, G., & Faulkner, D. (1986). Memory for proper names: age differences in retrieval. *British Journal of Developmental Psychology, 4*, 187–197.

Farah, M.J., & Wallace, M.A. (1992). Semantically-bounded anomia: implications for the neural implementation of naming. *Neuropsychologia, 30*, 609–621.

Flude, B., Ellis, A.W., & Kay, J. (1989). Face processing and name retrieval in an anomic aphasic: Names are stored separately from semantic information about people. *Brain and Cognition, 11*, 60–72.

Hanley, J.R., & Cowell, E. (1988). The effects of different types of retrieval cues on the recall of names of famous faces. *Memory and Cognition, 16*, 545–555.

Hart, J., Berndt, R., & Caramazza, A. (1985). Category-specific naming deficit following cerebral infarction. *Nature, 316*, 439–440.

Hay, D.C., Young, A.W., & Ellis, A.W. (1991). Routes through the face recognition system. *Quarterly Journal of Experimental Psychology, 43A*, 761–791.

Johnston, R., & Bruce, V. (1990). Lost properties? Retrieval differences between name codes and semantic codes for familiar people. *Psychological Research, 82*, 62–67.

Kay, J., & Ellis, A.W. (1987). A cognitive neuropsychological case study of anomia—implications for psychological models of word retrieval. *Brain, 110*, 613–629.

Kempen, G., & Huijbers, P. (1983). The lexicalisation process in sentence production and naming: Indirect election of words. *Cognition, 14*, 185–209.

Kosslyn, S.M., & Intriligator, J.M. (1992). Is cognitive neuropsychology plausible? The perils of sitting on a one-legged stool. *Journal of Cognitive Neuroscience, 4*, 96–106.

Lucchelli, F., & de Renzi, E. (1992). Proper name anomia. *Cortex, 28*, 221–230.

Mackay, D.G. (1982). The problems of flexibility, fluency, and speed–accuracy trade-off in skilled behavior. *Psychological Review, 89*, 483–506.

Marslen-Wilson, W.D. (1984). Function and process in spoken word recognition. In H. Bouma & D.G. Bouwhuis (Eds.), *Attention and performance X: Control of language processes*. Hillsdale, NJ: Lawrence Erlbaum Associates Inc.

Marslen-Wilson, W.D. (1987). Functional parallelism in spoken-word recognition. *Cognition, 25*, 71–102.

McCarthy, R.A., & Warrington, E.K. (1985). Category specificity in an agrammatic patient: the relative impairment of verb retrieval and comprehension. *Neuropsychologia, 23*, 709–727.

McCauley, C., Parmalee, C.M., Sperber, R.D., & Carr, T.H. (1980). Early extraction of meaning from pictures and its relation to conscious identification. *Journal of Experimental Psychology: Human Perception and Performance, 6*, 265–276.

McKenna, P., & Warrington, E.K. (1978). Category-specific naming preservation: a single case study. *Journal of Neurology, Neurosurgery and Psychiatry, 41*, 571–574.

McWeeny, K., Young, A.W., Hay, D., & Ellis, A.W. (1987). Putting names to faces. *British Journal of Psychology, 78*, 143–149.

Mechanic, A. (1964). The responses involved in the rote learning of verbal materials. *Journal of Verbal Learning and Verbal Behavior, 3*, 30–36.

Morrison, C.M., Ellis, A.W., & Quinlan, P.T. (1992). Age of acquisition, not word frequency, affects object naming, not object recognition. *Memory and Cognition, 20*, 705–714.

Morton, J. (1979). Facilitation in word recognition: experiments causing a change in the logogen model. In P.A. Kolers, M. Wolstrad, & H. Bouma (Eds.), *Processing of visible language*, pp. 259–268. New York: Plenum Press.

Nelson, D.L., Canas, J., Bajo, M.T., & Keelean, P. (1987). Comparing word fragment completion and cued recall with letter cues. *Journal of Experimental Psychology: Learning, Memory and Cognition, 13*, 542–552.

Nelson, D.L., Schreiber, T.A., & McEvoy, C.L. (1992). Processing implicit and explicit representations. *Psychological Review*, *99*, 322–348.

Postman, L. (1964). Short-term memory and incidental learning. In A.W. Melton (Ed.), *Categories of human learning*. New York: Academic Press.

Rapcsak, S.Z., Kaszniak, A.W., & Rubens, A.B. (1989). Anomia for facial expressions: evidence for a category-specific visual–verbal disconnection syndrome. *Neuropsychologia*, *27*, 1031–1041.

Rubin, D.C. (1975). Within word structure in the tip-of-the-tongue phenomenon. *Journal of Verbal Learning and Verbal Behavior*, *14*, 392–397.

Rubin, D.C., Stoltzfus, E.R., & Wall, K.L. (1991). The abstraction of form in semantic categories. *Memory and Cognition*, *19*, 1–17.

Semenza, C., & Zettin, M. (1988). Generating proper names: A case of selective inability. *Cognitive Neuropsychology*, *5*, 711–721.

Semenza, C., & Zettin, M. (1989). Evidence from aphasia for the role of proper names as pure referring expressions. *Nature*, *342*, 678–679.

Sergent, J., & Poncet, M. (1990). From covert to overt recognition of faces in a prosopagnosic patient. *Brain*, *113*, 989–1004.

Valentine, T.R., Brédart, S., Lawson, R., Ward, G. (1991). What's in a name? Access to information from people's names. *European Journal of Cognitive Psychology*, *3*, 147–176.

Van Lancker, D., & Klein, K. (1990). Preserved recognition of familiar personal names in global aphasia. *Brain and Language*, *39*, 511–529.

Warrington, E.K., & McCarthy, R.A. (1987). Categories of knowledge: further fractionation and an attempted integration. *Brain*, *110*, 1273–1296.

Young, A.W., Ellis, A.W., & Flude, B. (1988). Accessing stored information about familiar people. *Psychological Research*, *50*, 111–115.

Young, A.W., Hay, D., & Ellis, A.W. (1985). The faces that launched a thousand slips: Everyday difficulties and errors in recognising people. *British Journal of Psychology*, *76*, 495–523.

MEMORY, 1993, *1* (4), 433–455

Proper Names and How They Are Learned

Marie La Palme Reyes and John Macnamara
McGill University, Montreal, Canada

Gonzalo E. Reyes and Houman Zolfaghari
Université de Montréal, Canada

Proper names function in our conceptual lives as means for denoting individuals in kinds. Kinds are denoted by common names, more precisely count nouns, and so there are important interrelations between proper names and common nouns. All of this shows up in the way we interpret proper names and employ them in everyday inferences. For example, an airline may count three passengers in relation to a single person Jane, if Jane takes three trips with the airline. Each of the three passengers is Jane, but there is only one Jane. To handle such operations we propose a theory of proper names as part of the theory of kinds. This enables us to specify certain resources (some of them unlearned) that are necessary for the learning of proper names and also a theory of how they are learned. We review the experimental literature on the learning of proper names from the standpoint of the theory. We do not extend the theory to cover recognition or recall.

INTRODUCTION

Take a proper name (PN), 'Jane' for example, and ask yourself who or what its reference is. It appears to pick out the bearer of the proper name, whereas common nouns, or more precisely count nouns (i.e. nouns that allow counting), such as 'woman', 'person', 'wife', and 'passenger', appear to denote kinds to which the bearer may or may not belong. Indeed we would not be surprised to learn that Jane is in all of these kinds: a woman, a person, a wife, and a passenger. However, these are rather different things; she may be a passenger just for a few hours, whereas she is a person all her life. To make matters worse, if Jane travels twice this year with Canadian Airways, the company will count

Requests for reprints should be sent to John Macnamara, Department of Psychology, McGill University, 1205 Docteur Penfield Ave., Montreal, Quebec, Canada, H3A 1B1.

Work on this paper was funded in part by a post-doctoral fellowship awarded by the Social Sciences and Humanities Research Council of Canada to Marie La Palme Reyes, and by grants from the National Science and Engineering Research Council of Canada to John Macnamara and Gonzalo E. Reyes. Houman Zolfaghari was supported in part by the grant of Gonzalo E. Reyes. The authors gratefully acknowledge this support.

two passengers in relation to her; but in the scenario there is only one Jane, not two. For all that, each of these passengers is Jane. So what is the relation among these various kinds and how does the PN relate to them?

Notice that we say without hesitation both: "This passenger is Jane" and "Jane is this passenger". In the first the PN is in predicate position, whereas in the second it is in subject position. Does this make any difference to how the name is interpreted? Notice further that someone might introduce her to you with the words "This passenger is Jane". You will not, however, assume that Jane did not exist before the trip began or that Jane will cease to exist when the trip is over.

PNs also play a role in reasoning. The following syllogism is unexceptionable as a line of reasoning, although the name 'Jane' changes grammatical role and although it is associated once with the count noun 'passenger' and once with the count noun 'mother':

> This passenger is Jane
> Jane is a mother
>
> This passenger is a mother.

How does the PN function to carry the inference?

To rush impatiently past these issues, protesting that everyone knows what a PN is, is to court certain disaster in one's psychological theorising about PNs. One simply must sort out the intuitions with care and persistence, because any psychological theory of the learning, recall, recognition or processing of PNs presupposes an adequate account of what they are. We begin therefore with a theory of PNs. After (1) this introduction, we lay the foundations of the theory of PNs in the form of (2) a set of three basic theses. These theses, we hold, express obvious and basic facts about the manner in which we interpret PNs; thus guiding us to a correct understanding of what PNs are. Foundational in our whole approach is that PNs denote individuals in kinds (like DOG or PERSON) which individuate the bearer of a PN and trace the bearer's identity through change. We therefore in (3) sketch the logic of kinds to the extent that is required. This work permits us to study (4) the cognitive resources that are logically necessary for the learning of a PN. By means of two criteria we distinguish those resources that are learned from those that are unlearned. With these resources we are able to specify the form of the learning of a PN. In (5) we survey, from the standpoint we have reached, the scant experimental literature on the learning of PNs. As the experimental work to date does not address PNs in the fullness that our analysis reveals, we also outline some new experimental work that the theory suggests.

Our paper is introductory particularly in its presentation of the logic of PNs and kinds. Further details about the logic of kinds will be found in La Palme Reyes, Macnamara, and Reyes (1993), and about the learning of proper names in

Macnamara and Reyes (1993). A fuller analysis of the experimental literature from the perspective of the logic of kinds is to be found in Hall (1993).

2. THREE BASIC THESES

2.1 PNs Refer Rigidly

This thesis, inspired in part by Kripke (1972/1982), means that a PN refers to a unique bearer indifferently across all the actual and counterfactual situations, past, present, and future of which the bearer is a constituent. For example, a biographer of Nixon would use the single PN 'Nixon' to refer to the boy who grew up in California, the young politician, and the president who was forced from office. If the biographer is unsure whether Nixon used fraudulent means to win his first election he may consider the possibility that he did and the possibility that he did not. As both cannot be true, the biographer must consider counterfactual as well as factual situations, referring throughout to the bearer involved as Nixon.

PNs should be contrasted with descriptions, such as 'The President of the United States', or pronouns, such as 'you', whose reference varies with occasion of use. It is a rule of the language that you must determine who is being addressed by the user of 'you' in order to assign it a reference. Now, the name 'Nixon' does not have a unique bearer; there being many persons who share that name. It follows that the reference of 'Nixon' will also depend on speaker and context. However, PNs are different from indexicals in that the reference of PNs does not vary as systematically with occasion of use; so there is a weak sense in which their reference is rigid. It is in this weak sense that we intend thesis 2.1.

The fact that a PN may have several bearers is a complication that we ignore in the sequel, not because it is unimportant but because it does not affect any of the claims we wish to make. A more complete theory that accounts for the multiplicity of bearers of a PN will have to incorporate the theory we present here. In passing, it is not part of thesis 2.1 that an individual has only one name. The multiplicity of names for a single individual is another matter altogether, though it can be handled within the theory we present.

2.2 The Reference of a PN is a Unique Individual in a Kind

This assertion, which characterises our whole approach, rests on the observation that to specify the reference of a PN like 'Jane', to individuate her and trace her identity through time and situations, a kind is needed. A few words to bring this out.

One might imagine at first that the job of specifying the bearer of a PN and tracing its identity might be performed by a demonstrative ('this') or a pronoun ('he' or 'she'). Demonstratives are often used to teach PNs, as in '*This* is Jane'. Can it be that demonstratives on their own individuate the bearer of the PN? The answer is clearly no. As Wittgenstein has pointed out, demonstratives are woefully vague. Suppose you see an elephant at the zoo pacing up and down and someone says "Look at this", to what does 'this' refer? It could refer to the elephant, but it could also refer to its trunk, or the texture of its skin or to its way of walking. To make the reference precise a common noun is needed. It follows that if, after the introduction "This is Jane", the name 'Jane' does not inherit the vagueness of the bare demonstrative, then some unspoken factor has been specifying the reference of the demonstrative. We suggest PERSON as a psychologically central kind, although we have more to say about the issue. Similar remarks apply to pronouns. If, on their own, demonstratives and pronouns fail to specify the bearer of a PN, then neither do they trace the bearer's identity on their own.

We now consider some alternative approaches to the tracing of identity, less for the purpose of reviewing the literature than of bringing out the role of identity and its relevance.

In keeping with reductionist tendencies in modern psychology one might feel that it might be possible to trace identity through the cells, molecules, or atoms of a person's body. One can be as scientific as one wants. Note, however, that the suggestion makes an appeal to a kind to handle identity: CELL, MOLECULE, etc. As such it supports the thesis. Nevertheless none of these proposals will do the job.

The bunch of molecules that constituted Nixon's body when he was president was not the same as that which constituted his body when he first entered politics. Even more dramatically, the bunch of molecules that constituted his body when he first became President, weighing as it no doubt did some 170 lbs, was never born; though Nixon was born. It follows that Nixon is not identical with a bunch of molecules. Neither can we trace his identity through the kind MAN on its own. When he was born he was a baby and not a man.

Leibniz has a quite different solution to the problem of individuation and identity which really does contradict our thesis. As his solution is taken for granted by classical logicians, and is consequently built into the theories of PNs available to psychologists, we will consider it briefly. Leibniz would have us individuate and trace identity by a set of predicates (e.g. to be male, to be 45 years old, to have been born in Brazil, etc.). Several modern philosophers have followed his lead. The solution is tantamount to the claim that individuation is to be done through predicables (adjectives, verbs, prepositional phrases, etc.) rather than through count nouns. But do adjectives, for example, individuate? Take 'white'. If you are asked to count whatever is white in some particular room and you notice a white shirt, should you count the white shirt as something white; or should you count the sleeves and pockets separately on the grounds that they are sewn on; or should you count each thread separately; or each fibre of each thread? You do not know how to begin let alone end, as Geach (e.g. 1957) has frequently insisted. The reason is that 'white' gives you no indication what to count as one white. Of course there is no trouble deciding what to count as one white shirt, but that is because the adjective 'white' has the support of the kind SHIRT. Matters do not become any better if instead of a single adjective one takes a combination of predicables. The union or intersection of fogs is still a fog.

This being so, why has Leibniz's point of view been so persuasive? The reason seems to be that he makes the tacit and apparently plausible hypothesis that count nouns have the same logical role as adjectives, verbs, and prepositional phrases. Thus he places membership in the kind SHIRT on the same logical footing as possession of the property white. Standard formalisations of first-order logic have followed him in this. From our realistic point of view, which starts with the relation of reference, all this makes sense only if we allow a universal kind named by some such word as 'thing' or 'object'. Granted such a kind one can have such predicates as 'to be a shirt' or 'to be white' on the same logical footing. This is tantamount to the claim that there are bare particulars. One trouble with allowing such a kind, as we have seen, is that it is inaccessible. We do not know how to individuate one *thing* from another *thing*. In other words the unconstrained count noun 'thing' does not perform for us any of the duties that we expect a count noun to perform. In this connection see Gibbard (1975).

At bottom the individuation of a property depends on the logically prior individuation of one or more individuals that possess it. This is fatal for the program we are analysing, admittedly from our point of view, because there is no secure access to bare particulars that might individuate the properties in the desired way. We admit that things might well look different if we analysed them from Leibniz's nominalist position (see Mates, 1986) or from the antirealist positions of some contemporary semanticists. This is not, however, to concede that either nominalism or idealism is coherent.

2.3 A PN Denotes its Reference Only in the Context of a Sentence

It is important to appreciate that a PN lives twice over: (1) as a linguistic entity, that is, as a member of a certain grammatical category of words; (2) as a logical entity, that is as a word denoting a particular individual. To distinguish the two, logicians speak of *mention* and *use*. When speaking about a PN (or any expression) as a linguistic entity, logicians say the PN is mentioned; when the PN is employed to denote its reference they say it is used. In writing we mark the difference by means of quotation marks to indicate mention. Thus we can say that 'Nixon' has two syllables, whereas Nixon, the person, is not made of syllables at all. In speech we do not mark this difference, so the sound associated with a PN (any word, for that matter) is ambiguous between use and mention. To decide between them we must appeal to context, but that means, at the very least, a sentence. This is one motivation for the thesis.

If we lay aside the use/mention distinction and imagine, as we are inviting readers to do, that there is only one person called 'Richard Nixon', it might seem that a PN does not need a linguistic context to refer to its bearer. But one can say such things as "Don't try to do a Richard Nixon on me", where the phonological string surfaces as a count noun. Or one might say "That's very much a Richard Nixon move", where it surfaces as an adjective. What it is on any particular occasion depends on the sentence in which it occurs. Where the name is used in isolation and still denotes its reference, a surrounding sentence is understood. For instance if asked "Who was the US president who was impeached?" you may respond "Richard Nixon". Here the understood sentence is "The US president who was impeached was Richard Nixon". The thesis is justified logically, even in the absence of a surface sentence.

To look ahead for a moment. The way these theses function in the theory is that the first supplies a rule that guides the learner in taking an expression to be a PN. The second (the need for a kind) supplies a logical reason for claiming that the learning of a PN presupposes the availability of a suitable kind to perform the task of individuating and handling the identity of the bearer. This in turn means that the theory of learning must make provision for a suitable common noun to invoke the kind. Needless to say, the common noun in question need not be a word in the learner's mother tongue—but more about this in a minute. The third thesis (sentence as context) implies the necessity on the learner's part of a sentence to determine the reference of the expression that is to be learned.

3. PNS AND THE LOGIC OF KINDS

Thesis 2.2 requires that each use of a PN be typed by a common noun. To express the typing we employ the notation that we illustrate by: (Jane:person), (Richard Nixon:person), (Atlantic:ocean). This is a marked departure from classical logic, which places all uses of common nouns on a par with the use of predicables (adjectives, verbs, prepositional phrases). For example, classical logic regiments "Some man is tall" as:

There is an x such that x is a man and x is tall.

Apart from the fact that this does serious violence to grammar by attempting to set nouns and predicables on a single logical footing, it asks us to interpret a variable 'x' that is untyped by any kind. This we cannot do, for the same reason that we cannot interpret an untyped PN. In the logic of kinds that sentence is regimented as:

There is an (x: man) such that (x: man) is tall.

We conceive of kinds as sets together with a relation. For example the kind PERSON is conceived as the set P comprising all the persons who ever were, are, and will be, together with the relation E_p, which assigns to each person all the situations of which he or she is a constituent. We think of E_p as the domain of existence of persons. We express the structure of the kind PERSON as (P, E_p). We take the notion of situation as intuitively given, and do not attempt to develop a theory of situations as do Barwise and Perry (1983).

Implicit in this is the position that in their logical function common nouns are modally constant, which means that they pick out the same kind regardless of the occasion on which they are used. The modal constancy of common nouns is on a par with the rigid reference of PNs (thesis 2.1). It is because of modal constancy that PNs continue to pick out the same person even after death. Modal constancy ensures that the person is in the set denoted by 'person' and is thus available as the reference of the PN. For example, the modal constancy of 'person' guarantees the possibility of using 'Plato' to refer to Plato today long after Plato's death. This in turn implies that PERSON is an abstract entity producing no effects in time and space and unaffected by causes that operate in time and space. Common nouns and PNs differ radically in their references, for although Richard Nixon is a flesh-and-blood being who operates in space and time, the kind PERSON to which he belongs is not. More dramatically, one can see Richard Nixon; one cannot see PERSON. This is surely of importance for theories of how the two sorts of words are learned and understood, for it requires the learner to posit an abstract and imperceptible kind in order to learn a PN for a perceptible individual.

We began by drawing attention to the fact that the PN 'Jane' may be employed in association with several common nouns, 'woman', 'wife', 'person', and 'passenger'. What are the relations among these kinds? The answer of classical logic, assumed unquestioningly in the psychological literature, is that there are set-theoretic relations of inclusion and intersection among them. This is certainly wrong. Take PASSENGER and PERSON. Every passenger is a person, so one might be tempted to conclude that PASSENGER is included in PERSON. If that were true each passenger would have to be identical with just one person, and each person who was a passenger would have to be identical with just one passenger. For the set-theoretic relation of inclusion is one-one as far as it goes. We saw, however, that two or more passengers may be counted in association with Jane. It follows immediately that PASSENGER is not included in PERSON.

There is nothing logically wrong with this way of counting passengers. We do the same with customers in a shop, patients in a hospital, majors in a university. The last of these is particularly instructive, because a single person may simultaneously major in mathematics and philosophy, and be counted by the university as two majors. Time, then, does not distinguish between the two majors, as it does between the two passengers associated with Jane. But we can reach the same conclusion without appeal to such ways of counting.

Suppose, as the literature claims, that GIRL and WOMAN are both included in PERSON. Let g be the girl that Jane was and w the woman she later became.

Now g is a person and so is w; in fact they are the same person. Let us call that person p. It now follows, on the view we are exploring, that g = p and w = p and by transitivity of identity we cannot escape the conclusion that g = w. But this is nonsense, because a girl is not a woman and a woman is not a girl. One cannot say either that a girl is the same girl as a woman, or that the girl is the same woman as a woman. One might attempt to evade this catastrophic result by identifying the girl with p over a certain range of time t_1 and the woman with p over another range of time t_2. This would suggest saying g = (p, t_1) and w = (p, t_2). But this fails to explain the relation between (p, t_1) and (p, t_2), which is the problem we began with. Class inclusion will not help. Instead you will need something like the theory we now propose in place of class inclusion. Needless to say, the user of a PN for a person must be able to interpret the PN correctly in relation to the different phases of the person's life.

We need another approach to the relations in question. In the logic of kinds there are underlying maps among kinds instead of inclusions. For example there is an underlying map u from GIRL to PERSON in the sense of map (function) familiar since primary school. Being a map u associates a unique p in PERSON with each g in GIRL. There is one further constraint on underlying maps: for a map u from kind K to kind L it is required that $E_K(k) \leqslant E_L(l)$. That is, it is required that the domain of existence of a k in K be included in the domain of existence of the l in L with which u associates k. To return to our example, the map u: GIRL ⟶ PERSON does not make g = p for any p; rather, u(g) = p for some p in PERSON. Likewise there is a map u': WOMAN ⟶ PERSON, such that u'(w) = p. Now we can say that u(g) = u'(w); they are in fact the same person.

Although the move from inclusions to maps is essential it is not enough. We said that Jane is a woman, Jane is a wife, Jane is passenger #1, and Jane is passenger #2. What are we to make of all these identifications? How are we to construe them without logical shipwreck? Consider a system of kinds with underlying relations among them. We can illustrate the idea with the examples before us:

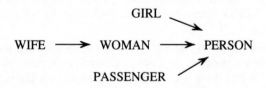

By which kinds can a PN be typed?

We assumed earlier that if the PN is 'Jane' it can be typed by 'person'— (Jane: person). We accept the proposal that PERSON, being a basic-level kind in the sense of Rosch (1977), is a psychologically privileged kind. But a person is an animal, so it makes sense to ask if 'Jane' can also be typed by ANIMAL. The answer is no. Constructions in the category-theoretic theory of kinds constrain a PN to refer to an individual in just one kind. We are assuming that the kind will normally be a basic-level kind; that it is part of what one means in attributing psychologically privileged status to basic-level kinds, that they type PNs. So what do we mean when we say that a certain animal, or a certain mother, is Jane? We cannot mean that Jane is identical with the animal in question, or with the mother.

The first thing to notice is the form of the sentence we are considering: "A certain animal is Jane", or "A certain mother is Jane." Here 'Jane' is in predicate position. Indeed the predicate as a whole is 'is Jane'. At the outset we warned that the logic of a word in predicate position is different from that of the same word in subject position. We now make this precise by saying that at the syntactic level 'is Jane' is a predicable, which at the semantic level is interpreted into a predicate of the kind that features in subject position. This leads to the conclusion that in the first of our sentences 'is Jane' denotes a predicate of ANIMAL and in the second a predicate of MOTHER. By a predicate in this context we mean a subset: a subset of animals in one sentence, namely the set containing that animal that is connected by a chain of underlying maps with Jane the person; a subset of mothers in the other sentence, namely the set containing that mother that is connected by a chain of underlying maps with Jane the person. Notice that the chain of maps may be no more than the identity relation, as in "This person is Jane,"; or it may be a single map as in "This mother is Jane"; or it may be quite complicated and indirect. We note in passing that our theory is in keeping with Jackendoff's (1987) guideline to make interpretation rules reflect syntax as far as possible.

We now are in a position to explain how there can be three passengers, each of which is Jane, and yet there is only one Jane. Nothing prevents several passengers from sharing a predicate—such as being elderly, or being sick. And nothing prevents three passengers from sharing the predicate of being Jane. Just as from the fact that three passengers are sick it does not follow that there are three sicks. Neither from the fact that three passengers are Jane does it follow that there are three Janes. From such a fact nothing follows about the number of Janes. Predicables do not individuate.

To bring home the main point, compare "Jane is a passenger" with "A passenger is Jane." The standard approaches cannot distinguish between the two: they regiment the two sentences as: Some bare particular has the property of being a passenger and of being Jane. This raises the following problem. If three bare particulars have the property of being passengers and also of being Jane, then there are three Janes. Three bare particulars, each with the property of being Jane, can only mean three Janes. Failure to distinguish between the interpretation of subjects and predicables leaves no means to prevent this unfortunate entailment. Whereas in the logic of kinds, "Jane is a passenger" is regimented as, The person Jane has the property of being a passenger; "A passenger is Jane'' is regimented as, Some passenger has the property of being Jane. There is a logically substantial difference between the two.

This is all important when we consider the syllogism we noted, which we repeat

> This passenger is Jane;
> Jane is a mother.
>
> This passenger is a mother.

One logical problem that needs careful handling is that in the first premiss 'is Jane' is a predicate typed by PASSENGER, whereas 'Jane' in the second premiss is (implicitly) typed by PERSON. What is the logical connection between these two expressions, and how is the validity of the syllogism guaranteed? Just to indicate what can go wrong with change of typing even when there is an underlying relation, consider the following pseudosyllogism:

> This is a heavy infant;
> All infants are persons.
>
> This is a heavy person.

Although every infant is a person, a heavy infant is not a heavy person. Just to be sure about this: one would regard a 40lb toddler as heavy, but to be a heavy person one needs to weigh something like 200lbs. We say of predicables like 'heavy' that they fail to *keep phase* as they move over the underlying maps. We say of predicables like 'male', which are semantically well behaved, that they *keep phase* as they move along underlying maps. Obviously what is needed is that 'is a mother' should keep phase as it moves along the underlying relation (or complex of relations) from PASSENGER to PERSON.

The first premiss states that a certain passenger has the property of being Jane; the second, that the person Jane has the property of being a mother; the conclusion is that the passenger in question has the property of being a mother. What guarantees the appropriate connection between 'is Jane' as a property of a passenger and the person Jane? In response we propose that 'is Jane', applied here to the kind PASSENGER, be regimented in such a manner as to recognise the intuitively compelling fact that 'to be Jane' is true of a particular passenger if and only if the underlying relation associates Jane the person with that passenger. This means that each passenger who is Jane is sent by the underlying relation to the person who is Jane. Since we wish our presentation to be informal and introductory we will not give the definition in its fully general form. In our remarks on syllogisms, too, we have kept the standard interpretation of natural-language expressions in mind. This is the most relevant interpretation psychologically. If we were presenting a logical study of the syllogism, we would have to bear in mind all possible interpretations of those expressions (see La Palme Reyes, Macnamara, & Reyes, in press).

Now we come back to our syllogism. La Palme Reyes et al. (in press) show that predicables derived from common nouns keep phase. It follows that 'is a mother' keeps phase as it transfers from the kind PERSON (involved in the interpretation of 'Jane') in the second premiss to PASSENGER in the conclusion. This handles one source of logical difficulty. The theory of La Palme Reyes et al. (in press), applied to this syllogism, brings out that any situation satisfying the truth condition of "this passenger is Jane" has Jane as a constitutent in addition to the passenger in question; or they say, Jane is coincident in that situation with the passenger. This is because in that situation both the passenger and the associated person are constituents—the person, of course, being Jane. Since 'to be a mother' keeps phase, it follows from Jane's being a mother that the passenger that is coincident with her is also a mother. This is the desired conclusion.

Notice how nimbly our minds pick their way through the networks of underlying relations that we discover among kinds. We have a very firm grasp of which predicables keep phase over which underlying relations. Sometimes pragmatic factors indicate which kind is relevant for the typing of a PN. For example, if told "Jane is tall", we may take it as claiming that Jane is a tall person. More probably we will take it as claiming that the woman associated with Jane by the underlying relation is tall. The important point is that the logic of PNs makes provision for such shifts of typing, even though which shift should be made in a particular context may be a matter of knowledge about what people's interests are likely to be. Pragmatics here presupposes logic.

4. COGNITIVE RESOURCES FOR LEARNING A PN

Of course young children do not start out with elaborate systems of kinds. Their first PNs seem to be associated with just basic-level kinds—see Macnamara (1986, ch. 4). Soon, however, they begin to situate basic-level kinds in systems that comprise higher-order and lower-order kinds. For simplicity we confine attention just to the relation between PNs and basic-level kinds.

4.1 Unlearned Logical Resources

We begin by proving a theorem relevant to learning: There are unlearned logical resources. The proof is straightforward granted thesis 2.3 in slightly extended form: a word denotes its reference only in the context of a sentence. Now consider the first word that a child learns. The child needs the other words that form the sentence context for the word to be learned. By hypothesis these other words have not been learned. It follows that to learn a word one must have the use of unlearned words. The general argument is made by Fodor (1975).

Granted that there are unlearned logical resources, how can we tell which they are? We offer two criteria: (1) they are primitives (that is, undefined) in our conceptual system; (2) their interpretation lacks characteristic perceptual features. Any word that satisfies both conditions we take to be an unlearned logical resource. A few words in explanation follow.

If a word is a primitive it is undefined, and hence one road to its acquisition is blocked. If the reference lacks a characteristic appearance, the second road to learning is blocked. As guidelines to primitive status we propose that the resource is a linguistic universal available to everyone, regardless of education, and that children manifest command of the resource very early and without explicit instruction. We take "dog" to be a primitive of our conceptual system; certainly no one knows how to define the word. But even if it is primitive there is no need to take it as unlearned, because it can be learned on the basis of perceptual characteristics.

Some of the unlearned logical resources to which we will draw attention are symbols that can be combined with other symbols to form sentences. It is necessary, then, to situate these symbols in a language. As children learn all the symbols of their mother tongue, English for example, the unlearned symbols are not part of English. Indeed these other symbols are needed for the learning of English. There is an ancient tradition that goes back through Leibniz, William of Ockham, St. Thomas Aquinas, and St. Augustine to Aristotle's claim in the *De Anima* that there has to be a sense that is common to the external senses, such as vision, audition and smell. Aristotle's sense that is common is a sense in which the external senses can communicate—so that we can, for example, relate what we hear to what we see. In medieval psychology this emerged as a language of the mind or language of thought (LT). In recent times Fodor (1975) has resurrected the notion for reasons similar, but not identical to, those offered here. Fodor does not go into the detail that we do.

4.2 Representation of Learning

For liveliness of presentation let us imagine a little boy, 15 months of age, whose father brings home a new puppy. The boy is fascinated by the puppy and somehow picks up that the puppy's name is 'Freddie'. Let us see what is involved.

The boy sees the puppy and hears the word 'Freddie'. His task is to discover that 'Freddie' refers to the puppy. At the point of learning, of course, he cannot use the word 'Freddie' on its own to refer to the puppy because that is precisely what he must learn. Because it is the simplest (see Macnamara, 1986, p. 57), let us assume that the child uses the demonstrative 'this', or rather its counterpart in the language of thought (LT). Therefore it seems natural, as a first try, to represent his state of knowledge by:

(4.1)   This is Freddie.

The demonstrative 'this', however, is vague. Something must steer the child from taking it as representing part of the carpet as well as the dog, or as representing just the left front paw or the visible exterior. The child must end up using 'this' to designate the entire dog including the invisible interior but excluding the collar he may be wearing. In short, the interpretation of 'this' in the situation should be a member of some kind that individuates the dog and traces its identity in the appropriate manner. DOG and ANIMAL are suitable candidates, but we take it that DOG is the operative one because it is a basic-level kind.

There is another difficulty with our representation as stated: 'This' may belong either to LT or to English. A similar ambiguity appears in formal systems of logic, say in the formal system of arithmetic. To solve it, we distinguish between the numerals '0', '1', '2', '3' … which are symbols of the language of arithmetic and '0', '1', '2', '3' … which are the (ordinary) symbols for natural numbers in the English language. Thus the sequence of symbols $2 + 3 = 5$ is a sentence of the language of arithmetic which is true because $2 + 3 = 5$, i.e. because the operation of addition applied to the couple (2,3) gives the number 5. Notice that we have allowed ourselves an abuse of notation: we have used '+' for both the symbol of the language of arithmetic and English. Similarly for '='. We hope that this does not create confusion.

We will use a similar distinction and indicate that a word belongs in LT by placing it in italics, e.g. '*this*'. Recall that the language of our representation is a mixed one containing expressions such as 'Freddie' (which belongs to English) and '*this*' (which belongs to LT). Recall too that we type a term by placing a colon followed by a common noun: e.g. (*this*:*dog*) and (Freddie:*dog*), which are read "*this* in the kind DOG" and "Freddie in the kind DOG" respectively. We accordingly represent the child's state of knowledge at the node representing the acquisition of 'Freddie' as:

(4.2)(i)   (Freddie:*dog*) = (*this*:*dog*)

Associated with (4.2)(i) is the rule for interpreting it which we will give shortly. This rule is not part of the representation of the child's knowledge; it is rather our representation of how the child must interpret the sentence expressing his knowledge. The rules of interpretation, then, are expressed in ordinary English. Our general claim is that the child forms sentences that fix the meaning of the words to be learned and that he interprets them in conformity with the rules of interpretation, and that he judges the interpreted sentences to be true or false. We will come back to this.

Surprisingly, we have so far represented only half of the child's knowledge. The word he learns is not only an English word but it is a particular kind of English word, a PN. He needs to know this if he is to use it as an English PN. The rules of English syntax are all stated over the grammatical categories of

English, of which PN is one. Although the child may not be aware of this at the moment he picks up the word, he needs this information at the point where he begins to use the word creatively in English sentences—in other words, before very long.

But now there is an added difficulty. It is Freddie's name that is a PN, not Freddie. In order to represent this the child must be able to distinguish between a name for the puppy and a name for the puppy's name; he must be able to distinguish mention from use. Recall that in English writing we do this by means of quotation marks: Freddie for the puppy and 'Freddie' for the puppy's name. By thesis 2.2 the use of 'Freddie' must be typed by an appropriate kind to individuate the name and trace its identity across various phonological realisations. We suggest the kind WORD. This all leads to (4.2)(ii) as a representation of the child's linguistic knowledge when he learns that 'Freddie' is a PN:

(4.2)(ii)   *PN* ('Freddie':*word*).

There is evidence that infants are sensitive to the distinction between words and non-linguistic sounds by the age of nine months—Waxman & Balaban (in preparation) and Markow & Waxman (in preparation). They seem to appreciate that words are about the world in ways that non-linguistic sounds are not. Moreover, phonology does not distinguish among grammatical categories but it does recognise word boundaries (although it remains problematic what to treat as a word—see Sciullo & Williams, 1987). With Jackendoff (1987, ch. 14) we believe that phonology, not syntax, describes the perceptual presentation of words. This leads us to treat WORD as a basic-level perceptual type and therefore employ it in the representation of word learning.

We remark that the sorted demonstrative as well as the equality symbol '=', the underlined symbol *PN* and the underlined count nouns are examples of primitive symbols in LT.

But is all this enough? If the child is to use the word 'Freddie' correctly, he needs to realise that 'Freddie' is a word that designates a unique member in a particular kind, namely Freddie in the kind DOG, and that it does so regardless of the situations in which the word is used. In particular, he needs to realise that 'Freddie' does not refer to the kind DOG or to just any individual in that kind. The child has clearly not learned the use of the PN 'Freddie' if he calls every dog that he meets in the street "Freddie".

Here is where thesis 2.1 comes into play: PNs refer rigidly. This suggests the following psychological rule at least for young children:

Rule for classifying a word as a PN: assign a word to the syntactic category PN if it is a rigid designator of a member in a basic-level kind.

Although it might seem odd attributing syntactic knowledge to so young a boy as we have in mind, there is no avoiding the attribution if he manages to use the word correctly. It is not part of our thesis that children must learn the syntactic category of a PN at the moment they learn its reference. Nevertheless, it is interesting that Bloom's (1990) study of several young children's language suggests that their early combinations of words recognise PNs as a distinct category. Our rule for classifying a word as a PN is guided by semantics. It may be, then, that children classify a word as a PN very early.

With that we can give the rules for interpreting (4.2)(i & ii), using U to signal a situation:

(4.2)′
(i)   The sentence "(Freddie:*dog*) = (*this*:*dog*)" is true at the situation U if and only if the term '(*this*:*dog*)' is interpretable at U and 'Freddie' is the name of the dog that is assigned to it as interpretation.
(ii) the term '(*this*:*dog*)' is interpretable at U if at U there is a unique dog at the focus of attention.
(iii) Assign the truth value *true* to "*PN* ('Freddie': *word*)" if at U 'Freddie' is taken as rigidly referring to the perceptual entity to which it is applied.

Before we go on, let us be clear about what (4.2) and (4.2)′ are supposed to represent. The child must recognise that 'Freddie' is a PN, that Freddie is a dog and not a cat, say, and he must be able to determine which dog it is. We represent these intentional abilities by (i). He must be able to use the proper name in question in LT, not only mention it. Notice that the fixing of the reference of 'Freddie' depends on a situation, namely the situation in which the dog in question appears and, moreover, is the only dog designated by the demonstrative '(*this*:*dog*)'. Nevertheless, if the child is successful in learning the name, he will use it independent of situations, because the rule of interpretation for (4.2)(ii) states that the name refers rigidly. In sum, what we are representing is the intentional ability of the child to go from perception to conceptualisation. In conceptualisation the learner must specify a kind (the interpretation of '*dog*') and also a particular member of this kind denoted by '(*this*:*dog*)'. Similarly, the child must perceive a token of the word 'Freddie' for which in conceptualisation he must specify a kind. We have suggested that the kind is WORD.

Once again, let us emphasise that our representation is not meant to imply that the child has the English words 'word' or 'proper name' to express (4.2). What we do claim is that (4.2)′ captures an essential element of his competence: that it specifies how he interprets 'Freddie' and classifies the word syntactically.

The process of learning a PN is the process of forming sentences that express the content of (4.2)(i) and (ii); interpreting these sentences in accord with rules (4.2)′(i)–(iii); *judging* that the sentences so interpreted are true; and storing this information in memory. A word about judgement. It is distinct from interpretation. People can fully understand the sentence 'The world will end at midnight tonight' without believing it, without judging it to be true. If they perform actions that depend on the truth of the sentence, such as giving away property and turning to prayer, they must have judged it to be true. As the child will perform such actions as calling the dog 'Freddie' and looking for the dog when told 'Show me Freddie', the child will have to have judged the relevant sentences to be true. Judgement is of a whole different order, but it is logically implicated in the type of learning we are discussing.

We are not claiming that young children learn each PN told them at the first shot. On the other hand, we observe that there does not seem to be any such thing as part of a PN, unless by that you mean something like one of its syllables. Reference seems to be all or nothing. Which is not the same as saying that the learning of a PN is single-trial learning. Normally, one will not say that a PN has been learned until it has been committed to long-term memory and is available for use. Committing the PN to memory may take several trials.

There is skill in pronouncing a PN, which is particularly apparent when the learner is a child. Nevertheless, the type of learning that we have been considering is not a skill; it is propositional learning. In the jargon, it is learning-that, not learning-how. No amount of practice at pronouncing a PN, even in contexts that are somehow constrained to be appropriate, yields the sort of syntactic and semantic knowledge that we have in mind. From a logical point of view and also from a psychological one, mistakes are possible on the child's part. Particularly at an early age, the child might mistake the proper name 'Freddie' for, say, the count noun 'dog'. Member and kind are in dialectal relation. The child is never confronted with an individual that he recognises as such without his recognising that it belongs to a kind that specifies what to count as an individual. So what he needs to decide somehow is whether to assign the new word to the individual dog or the kind DOG. We will see that children make hardly any mistakes in doing so, but that is another matter. The decision is of fundamental importance in the learning of grammar. From the purely logical and syntactic standpoints, the feat of making the correct decisions seems well nigh impossible.

A word about the language LT. Although certain of its expressions such as 'This' are primitives of L, others are English words ('Freddie'). As a consequence, some of the sentences are linguistically mixed. There is nothing to be disturbed about in this. Any sentence such as:

(4.3) The German word '*Gabel*' means the same as the English word 'fork'.

that gives the meaning of an expression of one language in another language must be mixed. It cannot be that '*Gabel*' in (4.3) is a loan word in English, because the sentence claims it is German.

We might also observe that our account presupposes that the bearer of the name is present at the situations in which the PN is learned, as indicated by the demonstrative '(*this:dog*)' in (4.2) and (4.2)'. If the name bearer is absent, some substitute for the indexical must be found. Similarly, if the bearer of the PN is fictitious, a demonstrative is out of the question. Here there is the added complication that the relevant kind is one whose members are fictional entities. We will not go into the matter, being content to observe that the logic of reference in fictional texts is worked out in La Palme Reyes (1993).

4.3 Specifying the Unlearned Logical Resources

In section 3 we proved that there are unlearned logical resources and we laid down two criteria that decide if a logical resource is unlearned: the resource is a primitive and it is not associated with a distinctive perceptual characteristic(s). To help decide if a resource is primitive we suggested two criteria: the resource is lexically expressed in all or almost all languages; the resource is available to children, as evidenced by their actions and words, when they are very young. We did not however single out any logical resources for unlearned status.

If we apply our criteria to the sentences that represent the learner's knowledge at the point of learning a PN we find as *primitive*

(i)   equality, '='
(ii)   membership, ':'
(iii)   predication, *PN* ('–':*word*)
(iv)   use/mention, quotation marks
(v)   '*word*'
(vi)   '*dog*'
(vii)   indexical, '(*this:basic* K)'
(viii) *PN*

Every language possesses lexicalised means for expressing identity, membership in a kind and for predicating, and clearly infants grapple with those relations long before they speak. For example, they show their appreciation of identity by refusing to go to anyone except their own mothers. They reveal their grasp of membership in kinds by treating cookies differently from plates. They reveal their grasp of predication by, for example, the way they treat some objects as their own. Admittedly dogs' behaviour is superficially not very different from that of infants in these matters and one does not attribute to dogs the logical powers that we here attribute to infants. But as Quine (1960) has taught us with his gavagai example, children's intentional states are inevitably a matter for reasonable but non demonstrative assessment. Admittedly, we anthropomorphise when assessing infants' intentional states but not (usually) when assessing those of dogs. After all an infant is an *anthropos*, whereas a dog is not.

All languages possess means for distinguishing use from mention. Mention, for instance, can be marked by such metalinguistic expressions as 'word' and 'name' or their counterparts. When children begin to speak they are confronted by lightning switches from use to mention and back again. A child introduced to its uncle with the words 'This is your Uncle Norman'' (use) may suddenly be asked to say 'Uncle Norman' (mention) and in the next breath to shake hands with Uncle Norman (use). Even small children never seem to be confused by the switch, which suggests that they have an easy command of logical resources that play the same logical role as the addition and removal of quotes. We therefore treat quotes as a psychological primitive.

Right from the beginning of language learning, children need to treat words differently from other sounds, because words have special status in revealing the intentional states of speakers and because they relate in special ways to the non linguistic world. This leads us to assign primitive status to 'word'. We do the same for 'dog' which is clearly undefined in our conceptual lives, seeing that no one at all knows how to define it. We see it as the counterpart in the language of thought of the perceptual type associated with dogs.

There is also the indexical 'this'. We take it to be an indexical that functions in conjunction with perceptual attention. It designates the perceptual figure that perception has carved out at the moment of its use. The perceptual figures to which it is applied are not assigned a common kind by the perceptual system. It follows that in itself 'this' is untyped, though as our representations of learning indicate, the first step in the interpretation of the perceptual experience will usually be to assign a kind to the object giving rise to the perceptual figure to which 'this' is applied. The universal applicability of 'this' to perceptual figures and to individuals in perceptible kinds bears out the claim that in the first instance the indexical is untyped. It would, for example, be a serious mistake to read the indexical in the learning of a PN as typed by, say, VISUAL GESTALT, because the claim made in (4.2) is that the sort of this is 'dog'. But DOG does not include any visual gestalts as members. Demonstratives, as Perry (1979) and Putnam (1975) have shown, play an essential and ineliminable role in cognition. 'This' cannot be defined, and all natural languages have indexicals. It follows that we should take 'this' as a psychological primitive.

There is finally the predicable PN. We do not define it. We imagine that children are guided in their learning of proper names by a psychological procedure that invokes PN when they construe their parents' words in a certain manner—in fact as applying a word as a rigid designator to an individual in a kind, in accordance with the rule we specified. Notice, however, that this procedure (if we do not miscall it) is different from the procedures of computer science in that both its input and its output is intentional:

Construal of word ──→ Procedure ──→ PN is evoked

The main attraction to call this operation a procedure, in addition to the fact that it produces an effect when certain conditions are satisfied, is that it seems to do its work automatically and unconsciously.

The second criterion for unlearned status (*no perceptually distinctive characteristic*) yields the following list:

(i)   equality, '='
(ii)   membership, ':'
(iii)   predication, *PN*('-':*word*)
(iv)   use/mention, quotation marks
(v)   '*word*'
(vi)   ...
(vii)   indexical, '(*this:basic* K)'
(viii) *PN*

The equality of an individual with itself, though signalled by such perceptual phenomena as recognition, is really not perceivable at all, being a relation, in particular a relation between an individual and itself. Membership in a kind, though perceptually cued, is a relation to an abstract object and therefore not perceptual. Predication signals membership in a subkind; in our case the membership of a word in the subkind PROPER NAME. The distinction between use and mention is signalled perceptually in written language by the presence or absence of quotes or by italics; in spoken language it is not signalled at all. As words can assume any physical form that is licensed by the phonology/phonetics of the language, words as a class of objects are not associated with a distinctive perceptual characteristic. Obviously the references of '*this*' do not share a common perceptual characteristic. Neither do PNs. They are not, for instance, the only monosyllables in the language, neither are they reliably pronounced in a distinctive tone of voice.

Together, because they must be jointly applied, the two criteria for unlearned status yield:

(i)   equality, '='
(ii)   membership, ':'
(iii)   predication, "*PN*('-':*word*)"
(iv)   use/mention, quotation marks
(v)   '*word*'
(vi)   ...
(vii)   indexical, '(*this:basic K*)'
(viii) *PN*

5. EXPERIMENTAL LITERATURE

The theory of name learning specifies that a suitable common noun is a logical prerequisite to the learning. It follows that if children lack any common noun with which to individuate and handle the identity of a dog, say, then they cannot know a PN for it. The common noun, however, need not be in the mother tongue; it can be a symbol in any language available to the learners; a language of one of the perceptual systems, for example, or in LT. There is a growing literature to the effect that infants as young as nine months have access to basic-level typing in visual perception—see, for example, Roberts and Horowitz (1986). This, if confirmed, would indicate that they already have access to some kinds well before they utter their first word.

Aware of all this, Hall (1991) taught 2-year-olds nonsense words for two sorts of object: one sort whose kind was familiar to children (a cat) and another of an unfamiliar kind (a strange monster). The word was taught in a frame that could accommodate a PN or an adjective—"This is Zav". On testing, the children were far more likely to take the word to be a PN than an adjective if the object was of a familiar kind; if it was not, there was a marked tendency to ignore grammar and take the word as a common noun. It was as though the children were principally concerned with assigning the unfamiliar creature to a kind, and took the word to be a name for the kind. This is very much in keeping with predictions.

Katz, Baker and Macnamara (1974) taught some 2-year-olds a nonsense word for a doll and others a nonsense word for a block. The word was taught in a PN frame (This is Zav) or in a common noun frame (This is a Zav). There was a marked tendency to take the word as a PN provided (a) it was applied to a doll and not a block; (b) it was taught in a PN syntactic frame. This finding obtained even for 1½-year-old girls. Further details are given in Macnamara (1982, ch. 2). The finding was replicated, with interesting additions by Gelman and Taylor (1984), who showed that if children did not take the nonsense word to be a PN, they tended to take it as a count noun.

Perhaps even more convincing are the diary data presented in Macnamara (1982, ch. 2) for his son Kieran. Kieran never gave evidence of having confused a PN with any other category of word. When he was introduced to a person he took the word he then learned as a PN for that person. When given a common noun, he never hesitated to apply it to other members of the kind. He never seemed to fumble, even at the earliest stages of language learning. Jill and Peter de Villiers report similar findings for their son Nicholas. No doubt this is not an exceptionless rule. Nevertheless children do seem to have a firm bias against taking words applied to most objects as PNs, confining PNs initially to persons, household pets, dolls, and stuffed animals.

People sometimes ask whether 'Dada' or 'Daddy' is not an exception. Note, however, that 'Dada' is not a PN but a 'function word'. Each child has a dada and children early learn that the child next door also has a dada. They also hear stories in which there is a dada bear.

Incidentally, the syntactic frame for teaching a PN (This is Zav) would also serve for teaching a mass noun. There are several studies, more recently those by McPherson (1991) and Soja, Carey, and Spelke (1991), showing that young children are highly sensitive to the mass-like quality of stuffs to which mass nouns are typically applied. There seems to be no tendency for young children to be misled by syntactic ambiguity and to impose a PN reading on a mass noun.

Basic-level kinds have an affinity with perceptual gestalts. The affinity is best conveyed by means of examples. The perceptual system carves out a whole dog from the background as a perceptual whole, rather than just the dog's tail or the dog together with part of the carpet. Because of the psychologically privileged position of basic-level kinds in our conceptual systems and in the systems of kinds associated with PNs, one would predict that it would be difficult to teach a young child a PN for anything that is perceptually distinct from a member of a basic-level kind: for a dog's tail or for a dog together with part of its environment for example. The prediction is borne out in the experimental results reported by Shipley, Kuhn, and Madden (1983).

These are the only relevant findings that we have come across. Several hitherto untried lines of research suggest themselves to test the psychological cogency of the theory.

The only studies of children learning PNs that we have found relate to English. It would be interesting to have contrastive studies of PN learning in languages with different phrase-structure rules such as Japanese, which has no determiners, and German, which permits determiners to combine with PNs in ways that are not allowed in English.

There have been several studies of children's fumbling attempts to relate basic-level common nouns ('dog') to higher-order nouns ('animal') and lower order ones ('terrier'). We know of none in which children's grasp of how PNs relate to such systems is studied. For example, if young children are taught explicitly that a certain *puppy* is called 'Spot' do they automatically extend the name to cover the adult life of the dog in question?

PNs in natural languages are not restricted to a phase of a person's life. For example, kings and popes are given new names when they take office: Elizabeth II of England was given the name 'Elizabeth II' on taking office. Nevertheless it is quite in order to say that Elizabeth II was born before the Second World War, although she was not called Elizabeth II until long after the war. It would be interesting to see whether young children have any difficulty in so extending PNs—or, to put it differently, in attaching new names in the appropriate manner to the kinds in the relevant system of kinds. It would also be of interest to study children's abilities to count several passengers in relation to the bearer of a PN, say 'Jane'. It would be important to do exploratory work to see what kinds, like passenger, are familiar to children.

6. CONCLUSION

We have focused throughout on PNs while paying some attention to count nouns and predicables. A fuller treatment would deal also with PNs in conjunction with mass nouns like 'water'. We have PNs for lakes, seas, and oceans. But then 'lake', 'sea', and 'ocean' are count nouns. A lake, for example, is not identical with the body of water it contains, for that body is continually changing, though the lake remains the same lake. It seems that we never give PNs to masses conceptualised precisely as masses. Some problems we have not dealt with arise, particularly in fiction. One such is how to trace the identity of Robin the Brave (PN) who in the fairytale is turned into a frog by a wicked witch and back into a prince by the kiss of a princess. Such a metamorphosis may violate the laws of biology but not those of logic. Even quite young children can follow the story of the Frog Prince. On the functioning of PNs in fiction see La Palme Reyes (1993). We mention these additional aspects of the logic of PNs to emphasise our opening remark that our paper is introductory, but also to give the reader some inkling of how rich the study of PNs is in implications for cognitive psychology and hence for the theory of memory.

Manuscript received 7 January 1993
Manuscript accepted 7 May 1993

REFERENCES

Aristotle. (1941). *Metaphysics*. (Translation W.D. Ross). In R. McKeon (Ed.), *Basic works of Aristotle*. New York: Random House.

Aristotle. (1941). *Physics*. In R. McKeon (Ed.), *Basic works of Aristotle*. New York: Random House.

Barwise, J., & Perry, J. (1983). *Situations and attitudes*. Bradford: MIT Press.

Bloom, P. (1990). *Semantic structure and language development*. Unpublished PhD thesis, Department of Brain and Cognitive Sciences, M.I.T.

Fodor, J.A. (1975). *Language of thought*. New York: Crowell.

Geach, P.T. (1957). *Mental acts*. London: Routledge & Kegan Paul.

Gelman, S., & Taylor, M. (1984). How 2-year-old children interpret proper and common names for unfamiliar objects. *Child Development, 55*, 1535–1540.

Gibbard, A. (1975). Contingent identity. *Journal of Philosophical Logic, 4*, 187–221.

Hall, D.G. (1991). Acquiring proper names for familiar and unfamiliar animate objects: Two-year olds' word-learning biases. *Child Development, 62*, 1142–1154.

Hall, D.G. (1993). How children learn common nouns and proper names. In J. Macnamara & G.E. Reyes (Eds.), *The logical foundations of cognition*, (pp. 212–240). Oxford University Press.

Jackendoff, R. (1987). *Consciousness and the computational mind*. Bradford: MIT Press.

Katz, N., Baker, E., & Macnamara, J. (1974). What's in a name? A study of how children learn common & proper names. *Child Development, 45*, 469–473.

Kripke, S. (1972/1982). *Naming and necessity* (first published in a collection in 1972; appeared as a book in 1982). Oxford: Basil Blackwell.

La Palme Reyes, M. (1993). Referential structure of fictional texts. In J. Macnamara & G.E. Reyes (Eds.), *The logical foundations of cognition*, (pp. 309–323). Oxford University Press.

La Palme Reyes, M., Macnamara, J., & Reyes, G.E. (1993). Reference, kinds and predicables. In J. Macnamara & G.E. Reyes (Eds.), *The logical foundations of cognition*, (pp. 90–143). Oxford University Press.

La Palme Reyes, M., Macnamara, J. & Reyes, G.E. (in press). Grammatical role and functoriality in syllogisms. *Notre Dame Journal of Formal Logic*.

Macanamara, J. (1972). The cognitive basis of language learning in children. *Psychological Review, 79*, 1–13.

Macnamara, J. (1982). *Names for things: A study of human learning.* Bradford: MIT Press.

Macnamara, J. (1986). *A border dispute: The place of logic in psychology.* Bradford: MIT Press.

Macnamara, J., & Reyes, G.E. (1993). Foundational issues in the learning of proper names, count nouns and mass nouns. In J. Macnamara & G.E. Reyes (Eds.), *The logical foundations of cognition,* (pp. 144–176). Oxford University Press.

Markow, D.B., & Waxman, S.B. (in preparation). *The influence of labels on 12-month-olds' object category formation.* Dept. of Psychology, Harvard University.

Mates, B. (1986). *The philosophy of Leibniz.* New York: Oxford University Press.

McPherson, L.M.P. (1991). A *little* goes a long way: Evidence for a perceptual basis of learning for the noun categories COUNT and MASS. *Journal of Child Language, 18,* 315–338.

Perry, J. (1979). The problem of the essential indexical. *Nous, 13,* 3–21.

Putnam, H. (1975). The meaning of "meaning". In K. Gunderson (Ed.), *Language, mind and knowledge. Minnesota studies in the philosophy of science.* Minneapolis: University of Minnesota Press.

Quine, W.V. (1960). *Word and Object,* New York: Wiley.

Roberts, K., & Horowitz, F.D. (1986). Basic level categorization in seven- and nine-month-old infants. *Journal of Child Language, 13,* 191–208.

Rosch, E.H. (1977). Human categorization. In N. Warren (Ed.), *Advances in cross-cultural psychology.* London: Academic Press.

Sciullo, A.M. Di, & Williams, E. (1987). *On the definition of a word.* Cambridge, MA: MIT Press.

Shipley, E.F., Kuhn, I.F., & Madden, E.C. (1983). Mother's use of superordinate category terms. *Journal of Child Language, 10,* 571–588.

Soja, N.N., Carey, S., & Spelke, E.S. (1991). Ontological categories guide young children's inductions of word meaning: Object terms and substance terms. *Cognition, 38,* 179–211.

Waxman, S.R., & Balaban, M.T. (in preparation). *The influence of words vs tones on 9-month-old infants' object categorization.* Dept. of Psychology, Harvard University.

MEMORY, 1993, *1* (4), 457–480

Naming Faces and Naming Names: Exploring an Interactive Activation Model of Person Recognition

A. Mike Burton and Vicki Bruce
University of Stirling, Scotland

In this paper we present an interactive activation and competition (IAC) model of name recognition. This is an extension of a previous account of name retrieval (Burton & Bruce, 1992) and is based on a functional model due to Valentine, Bredart, Lawson, and Ward (1991). Several empirical effects of name recognition are simulated: (1) names that are known are read faster than names that are unknown; (2) common names are read faster than rare names; and (3) rare names are recognised as familiar faster than common names. The simulations demonstrate that these complex effects can arise as a natural consequence of the architecture of the IAC model. Finally, we explore a modification of the Valentine et al. functional model, and conclude that the model as originally proposed is best able to account for the available data.

INTRODUCTION

There is now a considerable body of evidence to support the view that the retrieval of proper names is in some way different from the retrieval of other personal information. For example, it has reliably been shown, in experiments where task demands are carefully controlled, that when subjects are shown a face, the person's name is retrieved more slowly than information about that person's occupation or nationality (Johnston & Bruce, 1990; Young, Ellis & Flude, 1988). It is also harder to learn names than other personal information about new faces, even when the words to be learned are the same (i.e. ''Mr Baker'' is harder to learn than ''a baker'', McWeeny, Young, Hay, & Ellis, 1987). Furthermore, retrieval of some personal information is possible without retrieval of a name, but the converse has never been demonstrated unequivocally. In neither a naturalistic 'diary' study (Young, Hay, & Ellis,

Requests for reprints should be sent to A. Mike Burton, Department of Psychology, University of Stirling, Stirling FK9 4LA, Scotland.

This research was supported by a grant from the ESRC to the authors (R000 23 2898). Some of the work in this paper was presented to a symposium of the 1992 meeting of the European Society for Cognitive Psychology. We would like to thank Tim Valentine and Serge Bredart (the convenors), and Tim Brennen for useful discussion of the work.

1985), nor a large-scale laboratory study (Hay, Young, & Ellis, 1991), was a single error observed of the type where subjects correctly recall a name but no other personal information about the person. Further converging evidence for a distinction between retrieval of names and retrieval of other personal information is found in the neuropsychological literature. Flude, Ellis, and Kay (1989) describe a patient who is able to recognise familiar faces, and access information about the people whose faces are shown (e.g. their nationality or occupation), but appears to have no access to their names. To our knowledge, no patient showing the converse pattern has been given tests appropriate to rule out other interpretations (e.g. see Bruce & Young, 1986, for a discussion of one such patient).

These results have influenced a number of theoretical accounts of face and person recognition (e.g. Bruce & Young, 1986; Ellis, Young, & Hay, 1987; Ellis, 1986; Hay & Young, 1982). These broadly similar theoretical treatments all include a hierarchically organised architecture: first a seen person may be recognised as familiar, then personal information is retrieved, and finally a name may be retrieved. Each of these accounts posits a store for names that is functionally separate from the store for other personal information, and which can only be accessed after personal information. Although this suggestion is consistent with the empirical data, it is itself problematic. First, it is clear that we do not have to retrieve *everything* known about a person before retrieving their name. It is possible to recognise Dustin Hoffman, and recall his name, but be temporarily unable to remember all the films in which he has starred (as noted by Bruce & Young, 1986). This suggests that a simple linear process by which *all* personal information is accessed before a name is inadequate. Second, the idea of a separate store for names is evolutionarily uncompelling. It is only in relatively recent times that European names have come to lose their semantic associations. So, in English, people are called Smith or Cooper precisely because their ancestors were blacksmiths or barrel-coopers.

Two more recent accounts of the data on name retrieval avoid the necessity for the problematic separate store for names. Cohen (1990a; b) has proposed than names are harder to remember than other personal information because they are typically meaningless. Meaningless words are more difficult to retrieve than meaningful ones, and Cohen proposes that this is a consequence of semantic embeddedness—meaningful information will be more highly connected to other representations, and so receive supporting activation from them. Support for this position comes from Cohen (1990a, Experiment 2) in which subjects were taught a set of people each with a surname and an occupation. When the surname is meaningful and the occupation meaningless (e.g. Mr Baker is a ryman), the normal recall advantage for occupations over names is reversed. This suggests the possibility that names are not stored separately from other information. Rather, it is a property that names tend to share which sets them apart from other information in tests of recall.

We have recently proposed an alternative account of name retrieval (Burton & Bruce, 1992) couched within the terms of an existing interactive activation and competition (IAC) model of face recognition (Bruce, Burton, & Craw, 1992; Burton, Bruce, & Johnson, 1990). The essence of this account is that names are hard to retrieve not because they are meaningless, but because they are typically *unique*. So, although we know many teachers, many Americans, and many politicians, we typically know only one Margaret Thatcher.

In this paper we offer an extension of the IAC account of name retrieval. Following a brief summary of the IAC model, we will describe an extension that allows analysis of name *production* and *reading* mechanisms. So, whereas our previous model considered only name retrieval from face input, in the model presented here we will simulate effects of reading people's names, and also of producing names. We will use this extended model to offer an account of further published empirical data on name recognition and production.

THE IAC MODEL OF PERSON RECOGNITION

Figure 1 shows the core of the IAC model. As with all IAC architectures (e.g. Grossberg, 1978; McClelland, 1981) the model comprises a set of simple processing units which can take on activation levels between fixed minimum and maximum values. The units are organised into pools such that all units within a pool are connected to each other with inhibitory links (not shown in the figure). There are also excitatory links between particular units which allow activation to pass between pools—these are the links shown in Fig. 1. Models such as this are used to monitor activation in highly connected systems. Particular units (e.g. FRUs) may be given activation by an experimenter, and this activation will be passed through the system over a number of processing cycles (each unit being updated on each cycle). There is a global decay function, which drives all units to a universal resting level of activation. Constant input, coupled with this decay, causes the network to stabilise over a number of cycles. McClelland and Rumelhart (1988) provide software for exploring the properties of such systems, and also discuss details of the available functions for passing activation between units. (See Appendix for details used in the simulation to be presented here.)

In the model presented here all links are bi-directional, and have equal strength in each direction. Furthermore, all excitatory links have equal strength, and all inhibitory links have equal strength. This homogeneity of connection-strength is not psychologically plausible; we would expect some connections (for example those most commonly used) to be stronger than others (indeed in other work we explicitly develop an account of weight change as a mechanism for learning and priming—*cf.* Burton, 1992). Nevertheless, the homogeneity does allow one to explore the *global architecture* of the model. Results demonstrated here are therefore a consequence of the architecture, rather than

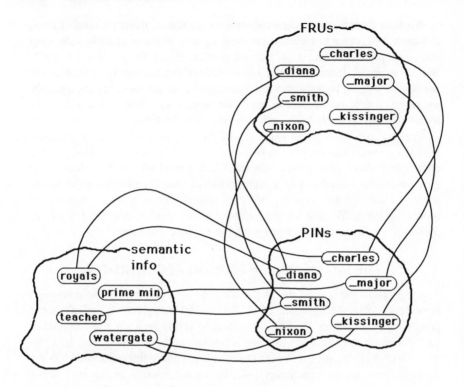

FIG. 1. Central architecture of the Interactive Activation Model.

manipulations of convenient local parameters. See Burton et al. (1990) for a
more detailed discussion of this aspect of the model.

Following Bruce and Young (1986) we propose pools of units corresponding
to face recognition units (FRUs), person identity nodes (PINs) and semantic
information units (SIUs). FRUs are units that code a particular face. So, for each
known face there is a single unit which becomes active on presentation of any
(recognisable) view of that face. These units are connected to corresponding
PINs. This is the level of classification of the person, rather than the face. PINs
are multimodal units, and take input not only from faces (as shown in Fig. 1) but
also from heard or read names, voices, and so forth. We have proposed that
activation at a PIN signals familiarity. A threshold activity-level is set for the
pool, and familiarity is signalled if any PIN crosses this threshold. Activation at
PINs also leads to activation in connected SIUs: having recognised (say) Prince
Charles as familiar, units corresponding to British, royal, and so on also become
active. Retrieval of information is simulated using a constant threshold on the
SIU pool. Activation in any SIU that rises above the threshold corresponds to
retrieval of information coded by that SIU.

Using this model we have proposed very simple accounts of priming and distinctiveness effects in normal face recognition (Burton et al. 1990). We have also used it to propose a model of covert recognition in prosopagnosia (Burton et al., 1991). Figure 2 shows an extension of the model in which we offer the account of name retrieval (from Burton & Bruce, 1992), and it is this aspect of the model that is the concern of the present paper.

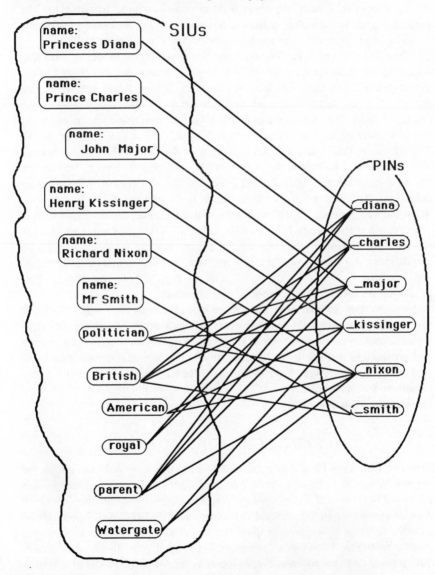

FIG. 2. Connection of names and other semantics to PINs.

In this account we propose units in the semantic information pool that specifically code the person's name. Just as there are units coding occupation (e.g. "politician") and nationality, (e.g. "British"), so there are also units that code, for example, "Name is Margaret Thatcher". Note that this is quite different from an account in which names are stored separately from other information. As these 'name' units are in the pool with SIUs, they are interconnected in exactly the same way as other semantic information. The present suggestion (detailed in Burton & Bruce, 1992) avoids the problematic 'separate store' hypothesis of models such as Bruce and Young (1986).

When this account is implemented, the behaviour of the model is consistent with data on name retrieval. If an FRU is given activation, this passes to the appropriate PIN. In turn, activation is passed to all the SIUs connected to that person. If other factors are held constant (in particular, the weight of all excitatory links) it is *always* the case that SIUs that are unique rise more slowly and to a lower asymptotic activation than SIUs that are shared by other people. The reason for this lies in the bidirectionality of the links. When a face is seen, and it is that of a politician, the politician SIU will become active. This in turn passes a small amount of activation *back* into the PIN pool to PINs of other politicians. This activation then feeds back again into the SIUs. In this way, SIUs that are common in the population will gain some (small) support from other people sharing them. It follows, then, that SIUs that are unique will tend to receive less activation than shared SIUs (see Burton & Bruce, 1992, for simulations). Moreover, on this account, any 'unique' semantic information known about a person should be difficult to retrieve, not just names. This prediction is currently being tested in our laboratory.

Note that this account does not require that all names are unique. Rather it depends on them being less common in the population than other information. In typical experiments on name retrieval, the comparison has been between names and occupations, nationality or 'dead-or-alive'. The semantic categories used in such experiments are very large. So, it is the relative rarity of the names that is important for our explanation of this effect; it does not rely on an absolute requirement for uniqueness.

AN EXTENSION OF THE IAC MODEL

It is clear from Figs 1 and 2 that the IAC model to date does not have a route for the *production*, as opposed to the *retrieval* of names or other information about people. There are, of course, many possible output systems that could be recruited following initial retrieval via activation at the SIU level. One might be shown a face and be required to speak the person's name, to write it, or even to press a particular button in a laboratory experiment (e.g. Johnston & Bruce, 1990). None of these different output routes is shown in the model as it stands. We shall see that there are several established findings on the production of familiar names. A model, extended to include outputs, should provide an account of these findings.

There is another obvious way in which the original model is incomplete, because it shows no route by which input names can access person information, or be read. Although we know that it is typically hard to retrieve names from faces, we also know that it is not correspondingly hard to *read* names, and any extension of the IAC model must account for this. Moreover, although reading a known name should cause activation in the person recognition system, the process must also be able to proceed without such access—otherwise it would be impossible to read unfamiliar names.

It is therefore not sufficient merely to make the trivial addition of a 'name input' route to the original (Fig. 1) model. This simple extension alone would suggest that it should be as hard to retrieve (i.e. read) a name from a name input as it is to retrieve a name from a face input, which is clearly wrong, and would provide no route for reading unfamiliar names.

There is a further reason that the existing model cannot trivially be extended to incorporate a name input mechanism. The original proposal for an account of name retrieval relied on SIUs coding *whole* names, i.e. usually a forename and a surname. We hypothesised that the SIU coding a person's name will typically represent the name by which we know that person. So, we have may SIUs representing "Name: Margaret Thatcher", "Name: Margaret Mead" and "Name: Margaret", where the final example might be someone who is so well known to us that we do not typically use her surname. This requirement is crucial to the success of the IAC account of name retrieval, as the account rests on relative rarity of names. Most people know only one Margaret Thatcher, but several people called Margaret, and possibly several people called Thatcher.

Despite the proposal that SIUs *code* whole names, it is clearly the case that forenames and surnames can be *read* separately. Indeed, this is a necessary requirement of European naming conventions, as novel names are often created by combination of familiar component parts. Any model of name recognition or name processing must allow the separation of name components. It is not possible to imagine a system that could read the words "Richard Nixon", but could not read the word "Richard".

In the model to be developed here, we show how all these requirements for input, and output routes, can be met by an extension of the IAC model. First, however, we review the empirical findings that an extended IAC model should account for, and consider a previous theoretical account of these findings, which forms the basis for our IAC extension.

Name Processing

There are a number of findings in the person recognition literature that should inform the extension of our account. We will first consider experiments on reading names aloud. Young, McWeeny, Ellis, and Hay (1986) showed that known names can be read out loud faster than unknown names. So, subjects are faster to read the names "Jack Nicholson" and "Dean Martin" than they are to read "Jack Martin" and "Dean Nicholson". This result is difficult to explain if name reading involves only a process of simple word-by-word reading. The person recognition system appears to be interacting with the word production mechanism.

Valentine, Bredart, Lawson, and Ward (1991, Experiment 2) have shown that the population frequency of names also has an effect on naming latency. Common names are read faster than rare names. Subjects were shown initial–surname pairs and asked to say the surnames out loud. Some of the initial–surname pairs corresponded to known people (e.g. M. Jackson, M. Jagger) whereas others were of people unknown to subjects (e.g. G. Webster, R. Waycot). In this experiment subjects were faster to pronounce the more common names (e.g. " Jackson" and "Webster") than the rare names (e.g. "Jagger" and "Waycot"). The advantage exists both for known and unknown initial–surname pairs.

Valentine et al. (1991, Experiment 3) have also shown that the effect of name frequency *reverses* when the task is changed to a name familiarity judgement. When using a forced-choice familiar/unfamiliar decision, using button presses on a tachistoscope, subjects are *faster* to recognise (as familiar) the names of people with rare surnames than to recognise (as familiar) the names of people with common surnames.

In order to account for these findings, Valentine et al. (1991) proposed a functional model of face, name, and word recognition, reproduced here as Fig. 3. This model is an extension of the Bruce and Young (1986) model of face recognition. Following early structural coding, Valentine et al. propose a stage of 'word recognition units' (WRUs). The notion is that there is one unit for each known word, and this becomes active as a result of input from any recognisable instantiation of that word (i.e. it is not tied to visual features of the stimulus such as size or font). Those words that are not names pass activation to a pool of units called 'word specific semantics'. However, those that are names pass activation to a new set of units 'name recognition units' (NRUs). These units are intended to be analogous to FRUs, i.e. there is one name recognition unit for each familiar person (whose name is known), and this can feed activation directly into the PINs. However, unlike FRUs, they have a direct link to lexical output codes: processes that allow assembly of phonological or other responses. Note that NRUs code whole names. So, the proposal is that there will be an NRU "John Wayne", which will receive input from WRUs "John" and "Wayne", and will feed activation to the PIN representing the person John Wayne.

In the following, we will present an IAC implementation of the Valentine et al. function model. However, there are two places where we found it necessary

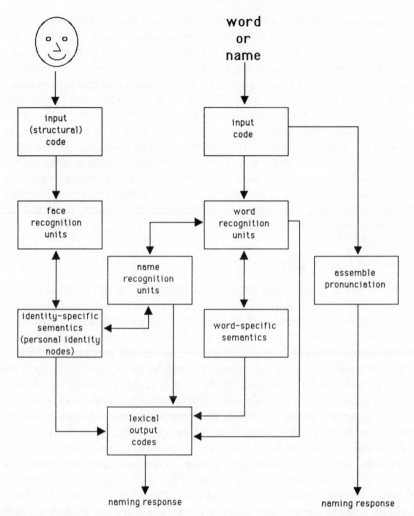

FIG. 3. Valentine et al.'s (1991) functional model of face, name, and word recognition. (Used with permission.)

to make alterations to this model. First, Valentine et al. do not separate PINs from a pool of SIUs coding semantic information. This is consistent with the Bruce and Young (1986) model of face recognition, but not with the IAC model (Burton et al., 1990). This means that there have to be separate semantic stores for information about people (taken to be part of the PIN system) and words (labelled 'word-specific semantics' in Fig. 3). The result of this is that there is no mechanism in this functional account to answer questions such as "Give me a list of teachers". From input of the word teacher, the appropriate semantics are accessed, and this leads to assembly of lexical output codes. However, as shown in Fig. 3, there is no route from the 'word specific semantics' back into the person recognition system. Second, the Valentine et al. model proposes several separate mechanisms for accessing lexical output codes. These can be accessed from PINs, NRUs, WSSs, and through a grapheme to phoneme conversion routine shown on the extreme right of Fig. 3. In the account we will propose, the number of different access routes to this information is reduced.

Despite some small amendments, the following model is intended to be in the spirit of Valentine et al. (1991). The authors stated that it was intended purely as a functional proposal, and not tied to any particular implementation. In the development we propose, we have made only those changes that are necessary in order to make the model consistent with our IAC model. This should therefore be seen as an exercise in developing the Valentine et al. model, rather than an attempt to propose an alternative to it.

Implementation and Simulations

The structure of the extended IAC model is shown in Fig. 4. The pools of units showing FRUs, PINs, and SIUs are exactly the same as in the original proposal for name retrieval (Figs. 1 and 2). We have now added a pool of units representing lexical output codes. Access to these units from the person recognition system comes immediately from the SIUs. We have also added a pool of units (NRUs), which give activation to the PINs. These are intended to correspond exactly to the NRUs proposed by Valentine et al. Finally, there is a pool of units labelled WRUs, which represent word recognition units. The intention is that this pool includes a unit for all known words. Those units that represent a name are connected to the NRUs. So, there is a link between WRU "John" and NRU "John Wayne". This NRU is also connected to WRU "Wayne". Those WRUs that do not code names bypass the person recognition system, and instead are connected directly to SIUs—units coding their semantics. Finally, there are direct links between all WRUs and corresponding lexical output units. These links correspond to direct links proposed in many models (Ellis & Young, 1988; Warren & Morton, 1982) and are also present in the Valentine et al. functional model. It is important to note that the introduction of NRUs (by Valentine et al., and in this simulation) does not correspond to the 'separate store for names' hypothesis described earlier. The NRUs correspond to input-level analysis of names, and are not implicated in the *retrieval* of names from faces.

In order to remain consistent with the Valentine et al. proposal, all the links in this model are bidirectional, with the exception of links directly connecting WRUs to lexical output units. Note that this architecture automatically provides an advantage over the original (see Fig. 3). This architecture allows access to the personal information from words that are not names. So, if the WRU representing "teacher" is activated, activation will pass to the "teacher"

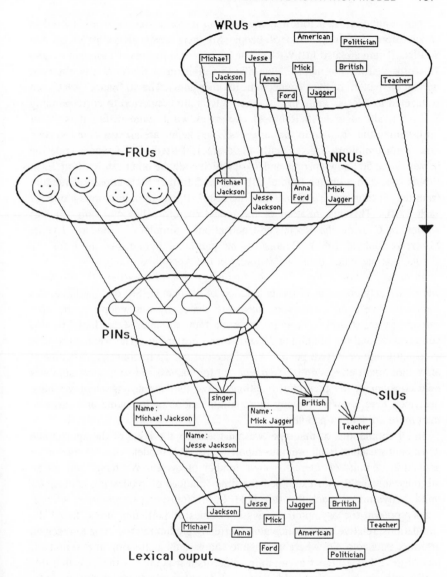

FIG. 4. An extension of the IAC Model

SIU, and then back (through the bidirectional links) to any PINs that code persons who are also linked to the "teacher" SIU. So, semantic cuing is possible in this model, though of course it will not give access to the person recognition system in such a direct way as would the input of a name.

The simulations that follow come from an implementation of this model in which information is coded for 50 people. So, there are 50 FRUs, 50 NRUs, and 50 PINs. There are also 110 WRUs. These code 30 surnames, 10 forenames, and 70 words that are not names. Note that this division of the WRUs is observed only in the pattern of their connections to other pools. The 40 'name' WRUs are connected to NRUs, while the 70 other WRUs are connected to corresponding SIUs. So, although the WRU pool comprises words with different types of information, they remain in the same pool, and hence are all connected to each other with inhibitory links. Finally there are 120 SIUs, 50 of which code the names of the 50 known people and 70 of which code the other information. Each PIN is linked to a unique 'name' SIU and to 5 further SIUs chosen at random from the 70 'non-name' SIUs. There are also 110 lexical output units—one for each WRU. This instantiation of the model therefore has 490 units. It was written in C using the Rochester Connectionist Simulator (Goddard, Lynne, Mintz, & Bukys, 1989). Details of the particular parameters used for the simulations presented here can be found in the Appendix.

In order to capture the effects of frequency described earlier, the surnames were variously common in the population of 50 people. So, one surname was shared by five people, two surnames were shared by four people each, three surnames were shared by three people each, four surnames were shared by two people each, and the remaining 20 surnames were unique. The forenames were all equally common: five people shared each of the 10 forenames. Valentine et al. do not report effects on the frequency of forenames, and so this variable was held constant in the present simulations. Note that the arrangement we have described here allows for many more combinations of forename and surname than there are known people.

In all simulations of this type, we must address the issue of the appropriate dependent variable. In all previous reports of the IAC model, we have shown the activation of units of interest over a number of cycles. We have then set an arbitrary threshold, and examined the time (number of processing cycles) for units' activation to reach this threshold. In the following simulations, we will simply present the asymptotic activation values of particular units. In all the simulations, relative asymptotic values perfectly predict relative time to reach an arbitrary threshold. So, where we wish to compare the activation of two units, if one of them has a higher asymptotic value, then it is always the case that this unit would reach any threshold the fastest. In other words, there are no cross-over interactions in these data between cycles (time) and unit activations. Given this fact, we have chosen to present only asymptotic values for unit activations. This makes the data more easily readable, as the important point can be illustrated with a single number rather than a graph.

Simulation I: Effects of Familiarity on Reading Names Aloud

The first empirical finding that we will simulate with this model comes from Young et al. (1986), who found an advantage (in latency) for reading known ("Jack Nicholson") compared with unknown ("Jack Martin") names. This can be simulated in the model by simultaneously activating two units from the WRU pool: one forename and one surname. We may then examine the activation at the lexical output units corresponding to these words. In the following demonstration we contrast the behaviour of the model when the two WRUs correspond to a known person (e.g. "Jack Nicholson") with the situation in which they do not (e.g. "Jack Martin").

In this simulation, activation of units in the lexical output pool is measured, with the assumption that higher levels of activation should correspond to faster outputs in the behavioural data we aim to simulate. Table 1 shows the asymptotic values of the lexical output units after the model has been presented with various combinations of names. So, the first line of Table 1 shows the activation of two lexical output units after two WRUs have simultaneously been given full activation. For this demonstration, we chose two equally common forenames (F1 and F2), and two equally common surnames (S1 and S2). The model in fact 'knows' people corresponding to combinations F1,S1 and F2,S2. That is, there are NRUs representing F1S1 and F2S2, and PINs for these two people. However, there are no NRUs or PINs representing people called F1S2 and F2S1.

Table 1 shows that the model behaves exactly as predicted from the results of the Young et al. study.[1] The data presented are examples from particular units in the model. However, the effect is robust: while all other things are equal (i.e. the frequency of the names), it is always the case that output units corresponding to *known* combinations of names gain more activation than output units corresponding to *unknown* combinations of names. As noted earlier, the

TABLE 1
Asymptotic Activation of Lexical Output Units

		Forename	*Surname*
Known Combination	F1 S1 (e.g. "Dean Martin")	336	336
	F2 S2 (e.g. "Jack Nicholson")	330	330
Unknown Combination	F1 S2 (e.g. "Dean Nicholson")	289	287
	F2 S1 (e.g. "Jack Martin")	289	287

---

[1] Note that the model contains no random element. As weights do not change, the model produces exactly the same behaviour every time it is tested. It is therefore not appropriate to use inferential statistics on data such as these. Instead, we simply note that known combinations of names always produce higher activation in lexical units than unknown combinations of names.

asymptotic values given here could have been presented as time-to-threshold values. So, for any given threshold value, both components of a name reach threshold faster when this combination is known.

This effect can be explained as follows. The bulk of the activation in the output units arises as a result of activation passed directly from WRUs. However, both words in these experiments are names, and so will pass activation to the NRUs. For those combinations for which there is an NRU (e.g. Jack and Nicholson) one NRU will come to dominate the activation in that pool (it will be competing with other "Jacks" and other "Nicholsons", but because of within-pool inhibition, it will win the contest and become highly active). This will then activate the Jack Nicholson PIN, and then all the SIUs connected to this PIN. One of these SIUs codes "Name: Jack Nicholson" and this will pass activation to both output units for Jack and Nicholson. So, for a known combination, these units gain some advantage from activation within the person recognition system.

In contrast to this, when the combination is unknown ("Jack Martin"), no NRU will come to dominate (although several will become slightly active, none will win the contest). There will therefore be no subsequent advantage for the output units from the person recognition system.

Although this explanation is complex, it arises through a very simple architecture. The behaviour displayed shows how complex behaviour can emerge from such simple interactions. This result would have been difficult to predict with any certainty from a 'box model' of the system. Implementation allows us to examine the performance that actually arises from a particular proposed architecture.

Simulation 2: Effects of Frequency on Reading Names Aloud

We now consider the findings of Valentine et al. (1991, Experiment 2) concerning the effects of population name frequency. These researchers report a speed advantage for reading surnames that are common in the population. In order to simulate these effects, we can again activate two names in the WRUs: a forename and a surname. Furthermore, we can choose more or less common surnames. Table 2 shows the asymptotic values of lexical output units corresponding to surnames (as in the Valentine et al. experiment). In this simulation, a common surname (shared by five people in this case) was paired with forenames to produce either a known or an unknown combination. The same forenames were also paired

TABLE 2
Asymptotic Activation of Lexical Output Units for Surnames

	Known Combination	Unknown Combination
Common surname	328	288
Rare surname	317	275

with a rare surname (unique in this case) to form either a known or an unknown combination. (Recall that all forenames are equally common.)

Once again, the simulation behaves as predicted: the lexical output units corresponding to common surnames gain more activation than the equivalent units for rare names (or, equivalently, common surnames reach a given threshold faster than rare surnames). We propose that this extra activation provides an account of Valentine et al.'s results. Although we have illustrated this effect with only one example, it is in fact robust. So, all other things being equal, it is always the case that lexical output units for common surnames will gain more activation (or reach some threshold faster) than lexical output units for rare surnames. Furthermore, this effect holds whether the 'read' combination of forename and surname corresponds to a known person or not.

The reason for the effect, in terms of the IAC model is as follows. When a common surname is read (as in Michael Jackson), some activation is passed to all NRUs sharing this surname; not only Michael Jackson, but also Jesse Jackson, Millie Jackson, Stonewall Jackson, etc. This has an effect on the eventual activation of the lexical output units through two distinct routes. First the PINs corresponding to all these people will gain *some* activation (though of course the "Michael Jackson" PIN gains most). Activation in these PINs leads to all SIUs of the form "Name: FORENAME Jackson". Further, all these SIUs pass activation to *the same* lexical output unit "Jackson". So, the fact that there are other Jacksons known by the person recognition system leads to extra support at the lexical output unit "Jackson". The second route that affects lexical output depends on activation being passed back from NRUs to WRUs. As links between NRUs and WRUs are bi-directional, all the different "forename–Jackson" NRUs will pass activation back to the "Jackson" WRU. There are uni-directional links from WRUs to lexical output units, and the "Jackson" lexical output unit will therefore benefit from the increased activation in the "Jackson" WRU.

To summarise this effect: reading the name "Michael Jackson" will cause several NRUs to gain some activation. This has the effect of passing activation (1) through the semantic system (via PINs and SIUs) so that several SIUs of the form "Name: FORENAME Jackson" converge on the "Jackson" output unit; and (2) back to the "Jackson" WRU, which in turn is directly linked to the "Jackson" lexical output unit. We will see in the next section that this commonality is not always advantageous for the system, but depends on the task required of the system.

Simulation 3: Effects of Surname Frequency on a Familiarity Judgement

Finally, we turn to the Valentine et al. (1991, Experiment 3) finding that common surnames are recognised *as familiar* more slowly than rarer surnames.

In order to simulate this finding, the same procedure as in Simulation 2 was repeated. So, forename–surname pairs were fed into the system (i.e. activated in the WRU pool). However, in this case, we examine the activation at the *PIN* level—the pool of units in which we assume familiarity decisions to be made (*cf.* Burton et al., 1990; 1991). As the effects we are trying to simulate here are based on time to make a *positive* familiarity judgement, all forename–surname pairs were known by the model.

Table 3 shows the asymptotic activation of PINs following simultaneous activation of a forename and a surname. We have presented data from the most common surname (A) and five unique surnames (V to Z). The same five forenames were paired with the common surname or with a unique surname, so that the model is familiar with each pair chosen (forenames are equally common).

Once again, we see the effects are as predicted: in general, people with common surnames gain slightly less activation *at the PIN level* than those with rare surnames. In four out of five cases shown in Table 3, the forename–surname combination is recognised as familiar more slowly for common surnames (while the forename remains the same across comparisons). To understand why this happens it is necessary to follow the activation through the system as in Simulation 2. When a common surname is read (as in "Michael Jackson") all NRUs with this surname gain some activation. This leads to competition at this level. Furthermore, all corresponding PINs are activated to some extent, and again there is competition within this pool. This competition leads to a reduced (or slower acceleration of) activation in the PIN pool. This would not occur if there was only one NRU and only one PIN with this surname. In this case, the target (correct) PIN would rise without competition from other units. This is the basis of the advantage for rare names in familiarity judgements. Note that this contrasts with Simulation 2. In the case of articulation, all competing units are feeding *to the same* lexical output units, and so there is an advantage in sharing.

TABLE 3
Asymptotic Activation of PINs

Common Surname				Rare Surnames		
Forename	*Surname*			*Forename*	*Surname*	
a	A	529		a	V	533
b	A	474		b	W	553
c	A	481		c	X	525
d	A	572		d	Y	534
e	A	493		e	Z	504

In the familiarity case, the sharing units are competing rather than pooling together. Once again, we have complex behaviour emerging from a very simple architecture.

One might ask why the effects of competition and pooling do not cancel each other out. In other words, why does the competition at the PINs not eliminate the effect of convergence at lexical output units, as described in Simulation 2? To answer this, recall that the facilitation of common names at output (Simulation 2) is the result of two routes: one through the semantic system, and one through the direct links between WRUs and output units. So, even if competition in the semantic system were entirely to eliminate the facilitative effects of converging SIU to output unit links, there would remain the second, direct, route, which would give the effects reported in Simulation 2. Note that this route is entirely independent of the semantic system, and so will not affect the result of Simulation 3.

In contrast to Simulations 1 and 2, which give consistent effects, Simulation 3 is not so robust. In the demonstration just provided, four out of five PINs with rare surnames take on higher activations than PINs with common surnames. As shown in Table 3, it is possible to find examples within the simulation for which the predicted effect does not exist. Although the advantage of familiarity decision for rarer names is usually observed, it is not universal. This is because of the complex pattern of connections between pools. It is possible to find two people who have very different patterns of interconnection to SIUs. Recall that connection of PINs to SIUs was performed at random such that each PIN is linked to six SIUs. As a result of this, it is possible for one PIN to be linked to very common SIUs (e.g. British, teacher, colleague, etc) and another to be linked to much rarer SIUs (e.g. New Zealander, frog-diver, polo-player). In general, PINs coded with common SIUs gain a slight advantage, and on occasion this effect outweighs the effects of rare or common surnames described here. For this reason, Simulation 3 is not robust over large differences in connectivity between PINs and SIUs. Note that the empirical results we are simulating here (Valentine et al., 1991) employed a strong manipulation of the independent variable (frequency of surname), analogous to our selected demonstration. Under these conditions, the effect shown by our model is consistent.

Exploring the IAC Model: Are NRUs Necessary?

In the simulations reported here we have sought simply to implement the functional model proposed by Valentine et al. (1991), in which both word recognition units and name recognition units mediate person recognition from names. However, the introduction of a special 'stage' of name recognition units might be seen as inconsistent with other aspects of the model. Compared to face recognition, this proposal requires that information from words must pass through an extra stage in order to access the person recognition system.[2] Is this stage necessary to produce the effects demonstrated? It is possible to construct a model in which the WRUs feed directly into the PIN level. (Recall that in our model familiarity decisions are taken at PIN level—the elimination of NRUs does not therefore destroy name recognition.) Here we report the results of the same three simulations using this version of the model, without NRUs.

The architecture of the model constructed for these simulations is shown in Fig. 5. The model is exactly like that shown in Fig. 4, with the exception that the NRUs have been eliminated. In the original, WRUs corresponding to "Jack" and "Nicholson" are both linked to an NRU coding "Jack Nicholson", and this NRU is connected to a PIN coding the person Jack Nicholson. In this variation the two WRUs are both linked directly to the appropriate PIN.

Tables 4, 5, and 6 show relevant output activation in the revised model, and correspond to Tables 1, 2, and 3 respectively. In each case, the same input units were activated in exactly the same fashion as in Simulations 1, 2, and 3.

An interesting pattern of results emerges from these simulations. Of course, the absolute levels of activation are not the same in the two versions of the model. However, it is the relative activation values that interest us here. The output advantage for known names is consistent across both simulations (Tables

TABLE 4

Asymptotic Activation of Lexical Output Units in the Model Without Name Recognition Units

		Forename	*Surname*
Known Combination	F1 S1 (e.g. "Dean Martin")	326	322
	F2 S2 (e.g. "Jack Nicholson")	321	318
Unknown Combination	F1 S2 (e.g. "Dean Nicholson")	296	286
	F2 S1 (e.g. "Jack Martin")	292	286

TABLE 5

Asymptotic Activation of Lexical Output Units for Surnames in the Model Without Name Recognition Units

	Known Combination	*Unknown Combination*
Common surname	312	295
Rare surname	319	276

---

[2] Note that this is just one possible interpretation. An alternative view would be that NRUs are analogous to FRUs, and that WRUs are analogous to the 'feature units' that feed FRUs in the original IAC model—*cf* Burton et al. (1990).

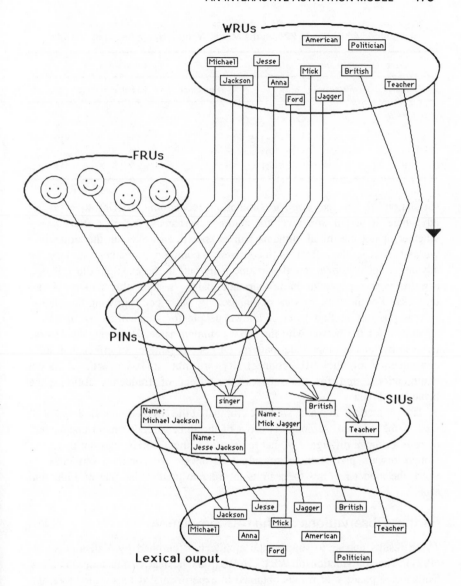

FIG. 5. The IAC model without Name Recognition Units

1 and 4: simulation 1). Furthermore, the recognition (familiarity decision) advantage for low-frequency surnames is also consistent across simulations (Tables 3 and 6: Simulation 3). However there is inconsistency between simulations in the effect of frequency on name output (Tables 2 and 5:

TABLE 3
Asymptotic Activation of PINs in the Model Without Name Recognition Units

Common Surname			Rare Surnames		
Forename	Surname		Forename	Surname	
a	A	430	a	V	554
b	A	502	b	W	568
c	A	482	c	X	537
d	A	303	d	Y	561
e	A	481	e	Z	525

simulation 2). In the original simulation (containing NRUs) there is an advantage at output unit level for common surnames, and this effect exists whether or not the initial–surname pair is known. However, in the simulation without NRUs, the effect is inconsistent: common surnames produce an advantage for unknown initial–surname pairs but, in the example illustrated, a *disadvantage* for known initial–surname pairs. In fact, this pattern is not universal. For the same reasons of connectivity described following Simulation 3, it is possible to find pairs of known people for which there is an output advantage for the person with the more common name. However, the reverse trend is by far the more usual pattern. Of course, patterns of effect that are a consequence of PIN–SIU connectivity are not at issue with unknown combinations, and for these cases, the effect of frequency follows the behavioural data.

The simulations in which we have eliminated the NRUs do not fit the data so well as the original. Although two out of the three effects remain unchanged, there is a crucial difference in that the model without NRUs does not make the straightforward prediction of an output advantage for common surnames. In short, the model requires these units in order to predict the data of Valentine et al.

Further Observations on the IAC Simulation

These results appear to support the architecture outlined by Valentine et al. (1991). The introduction of WRUs, NRUs, and lexical output units naturally leads to the patterns of results obtained in experimental data. Furthermore, the slight modifications we have had to make to Valentine et al.'s functional model, provide extra abilities missing in the original. So, it is possible by this account to activate the WRU corresponding to "teacher". This will cause several PINs (those who are teachers) to become active. By analogy then, it is possible in this model to retrieve people from semantic cues.

It is also possible in this model to retrieve information from partial cues. In this sense, it follows the original conception of the IAC architecture for cognitive modelling put forward by McClelland (1981). If one activates a common surname "Smith", several PINs, corresponding to all known Smiths, will become slightly active. On the other hand, if one knows only one person called Einstein, that person's PIN will become highly active.

Recent empirical observations by Valentine (this issue) are also consistent with this model. Valentine et al. have observed repetition priming between lexical decision and name familiarity when the same word can be either a name or a noun. So, for example, subjects may be asked to make a name familiarity decision to the name "Kenneth Baker" (at the time of writing, a famous English politician) and a lexical decision to the word "baker". Valentine et al. find repetition priming in this task.

Our account of repetition priming in face recognition rests on change to connection strengths. We have argued (Bruce et al., 1992; Burton et al., 1990) that repetition priming occurs due to Hebbian update of links within the model. When a familiar face is seen, the appropriate FRU becomes active. Following this, the appropriate PIN becomes active. A Hebbian weight change is applied throughout the model, such that when linked units are simultaneously active, the strength of the link between them is increased. When the same face is subsequently presented, the stronger link between FRU and PIN allows the PIN to gain more activation (and faster) than previously.

In the model presented in this paper, there were no ambiguous words. So, there were no WRUs that linked both to an NRU and directly to an SIU. However, it is simple to consider this possibility: many WRUs have multiple outputs (as in the case with common surnames) and so it is not unreasonable to assume that a single WRU ("baker", say) could have a link to an SIU and to a NRU. If such a WRU were activated, through reading the word, both the SIU and the NRU would become active. If the Hebbian update were to apply indiscriminately across the network (and we have argued elsewhere that it must—Burton, 1992), the result would be a strengthening of *both* connections to SIU and WRU, regardless of the task. We would therefore expect to observe repetition priming onto the word "baker" from a name familiarity decision to "Kenneth Baker" and *vice versa*, consistent with Valentine et al.'s data. In future work, we will explore with simulations the consequences of including words that can act as common nouns and also as names. For now it seems that the architecture presented here is at least consistent with the observed name–noun repetition priming.[3]

---

[3] Note that the Hebbian update will also allow investigation of a different type of frequency effect to that described here. It should be possible using this technique to examine effects of the number of times one has seen a particular name, in addition to those effects described in this paper.

DISCUSSION

We have shown here that the IAC model of person recognition may be extended in a plausible way to account for a number of findings in the literature on name processing. Using Valentine et al.'s (1991) functional model of face, name, and word recognition, we have simulated effects of familiarity and frequency. We have made some minor changes to the original proposal, but the most significant aspects of it remain. Furthermore, we showed that an alternative architecture (without NRUs) did not produce results that match data from experimental studies.

The implementation presented here, in addition to offering an account of name processing, retains the original features that make names hard to *retrieve* from presentation of a face. So, within the same model, we can demonstrate the phenomena whereby names are hard to retrieve from face input, but are not hard to read *per se*. Interestingly, the reasons we have offered for an output advantage of known over unknown and common over uncommon names are similar to those we offered for the difficulty of name retrieval from faces (Burton & Bruce, 1992). In each case, the relative advantage or disadvantage is a consequence of connectivity within the model. This connectivity has not been designed deliberately to achieve the various effects we have simulated: each of the links in Fig. 4 can be justified on theoretical as well as empirical grounds. However, it is a consequence of this connectivity that certain effects hold. It is extremely difficult to discover these consequences from a static (unimplemented) model. Nevertheless, simulations such as those in this paper reveal them quite straightforwardly.

How does IAC compare with other models of name retrieval and processing? We have already shown in a number of studies (Burton et al. 1990; 1991) that IAC can accommodate findings that were difficult for earlier, sequential stage models of person identification, such as that of Bruce and Young (1986). Despite the fundamental difference in the account of name retrieval, we regard IAC as a natural development of these earlier models. In contrast, Cohen's (1990a) account of name-retrieval in terms of 'meaningfulness' is, superficially, a competing theoretical position. However, we have argued elsewhere (Burton & Bruce, 1992) that the IAC account and the 'meaningfulness' account are not necessarily contradictory. Highly-embedded concepts that are semantically rich will tend to be common in a population. Conversely, 'unique' attributes are almost by definition meaningless. It remains to be seen whether 'uniqueness' or 'meaningfulness' will prove the more powerful theoretical concept, and this must rest on the ability of one or other to offer new predictions that are supported empirically.

Manuscript received 3 December 1992
Manuscript accepted 23 March 1993

REFERENCES

Bruce, V., Burton, A.M., & Craw, I. (1992). Modelling face recognition. *Philosophical Transactions of the Royal Society, 335*, 121–128.

Bruce, V., & Young, A.W. (1986). Understanding face recognition. *British Journal of Psychology, 77*, 305–327.

Burton, A.M. (1992, June). *Learning in an IAC model of face recognition: how to live without distributed representations.* Paper presented to the Experimental Psychology Society, York.

Burton, A.M., & Bruce, V. (1992). I recognize your face but I can't remember your name: A simple explanation? *British Journal of Psychology, 83*, 45–60.

Burton, A.M., Bruce, V., & Johnston, R.A. (1990). Understanding face recognition with an interactive activation model. *British Journal of Psychology, 81*, 361–380.

Burton, A.M., Young, A.W., Bruce, V., Johnston, R.A., & Ellis, A.W. (1991). Understanding covert recognition. *Cognition, 39*, 129–166.

Cohen, G. (1990a). Why is it difficult to put names to faces? *British Journal of Psychology, 81*, 287–298.

Cohen, G. (1990b). Recognition and retrieval of proper names: Age differences in the fan effect. *European Journal of Cognitive Psychology, 2*, 193–204.

Ellis, A.W., & Young, A.W. (1988). *Human Cognitive Neuropsychology.* London: Lawrence Erlbaum Associates Ltd.

Ellis, A.W., Young, A.W., & Hay, D.C. (1987). Modelling the recognition of faces and words. In P.E. Morris (Ed.), *Modelling cognition.* London: Wiley.

Ellis, H.D. (1986). Processes underlying face recognition. In R. Bruyer (Ed.) *The neuropsychology of face perception and facial expression.* Hillsdale, NJ: Lawrence Erlbaum Associates Inc.

Flude, B.M., Ellis, A.W., & Kay, J. (1989). Face processing and name retrieval in an anomic aphasic: Names are stored separately from semantic information about familiar people. *Brain and Cognition, 11*, 60–72.

Goddard, N.H., Lynne, K.J. Mintz, T., & Bukys, L. (1989). *Rochester connectionist simulator.* Technical Report 233 (Revised), Department of Computer science, University of Rochester, New York.

Grossberg, S. (1978). A theory of visual coding, memory and development. In E.L.J. Leeuwenberg & H.F.J.M. Buffart (Eds.) *Formal theories of visual perception.* New York: Wiley.

Hay, D.C., & Young, A.W. (1982). The human face. In A.W. Ellis (Ed.), *Normality and pathology in cognitive functions.* London: Academic Press.

Hay, D.C., Young, A.W., & Ellis, A.W. (1991). Routes through the face recognition system. *Quarterly Journal of Experimental Psychology, 43A*, 761–791.

Johnston, R.A., & Bruce, V. (1990). Lost properties? Retrieval differences between name codes and semantic codes for familiar people. *Psychological Research, 52*, 62–67.

McClelland, J.L. (1981). Retrieving general and specific information from stored knowledge of specifics. *Proceedings of the Third Annual Meeting of the Cognitive Science Society*, 170–172.

McClelland, J.L., & Rumelhart, D.E. (1988). *Explorations in parallel distributed processing.* Cambridge, MA: Bradford Books.

McWeeny, K.H., Young, A.W., Hay, D.C., & Ellis, A.W. (1987). Putting names to faces. *British Journal of Psychology, 78*, 143–149.

Valentine, T., Bredart, S., Lawson, R., & Ward, G. (1991). What's in a name? Access to information from people's names. *European Journal of Cognitive Psychology, 3*, 147–176.

Valentine, T., Moore, V., Flude, B.M., Young, A., & Ellis, A.W. (this issue). Repetition priming and proper name processing. *Memory.*

Warren, C., & Morton, J. (1982). The effects of priming on picture recognition. *British Journal of Psychology, 73*, 117–129.

Young, A.W., Ellis, A.W., & Flude, B.M. (1988). Accessing stored information about familiar people. *Psychological Research*, *50*, 111–115.

Young, A.W., Hay, D.C., & Ellis, A.W. (1985). The faces that launched a thousand slips: Everyday difficulties and errors in recognising people. *British Journal of Psychology*, *76*, 495–523.

Young, A.W., McWeeny, K.H., Ellis, A.W., & Hay, D.C. (1986). Naming and categorising faces and written names. *Quarterly Journal of Experimental Psychology*, *38A*, 297–318.

APPENDIX

The simulation reported here was run using the Rochester Connectionist Simulator. The update function was the standard IAC update (see McClelland & Rumelhart, 1988, p.13 for equations). The global parameters were set as follows:

Maximum activation	1.0
Minimum activation	−0.2
Resting activation	−0.1
Decay rate	0.1
Alpha (strength of excitatory input)	0.1
Gamma (strength of inhibitory input)	0.1
Estr (strength of external input)	0.4

All excitatory connections had weight 1.0, and all inhibitory connections had weight −0.8.

Subject Index